THE ROCKY MOUNTAINS OF CANADA

NORTH

AMERICAN ALPINE CLUB
ALPINE CLUB OF CANADA
CLIMBER'S GUIDE

THE
ROCKY MOUNTAINS
OF
CANADA
NORTH

ROBERT KRUSZYNA

WITH

WILLIAM L. PUTNAM

THE AMERICAN ALPINE CLUB
NEW YORK
THE ALPINE CLUB OF CANADA
BANFF

First Edition 1921
Second Edition 1930
Third Edition 1940
Fourth Edition 1943
Fifth Edition 1966
Sixth Edition 1974
Seventh Edition 1985

© The American Alpine Club, Inc. 1966, 1974, 1985

ISBN 0-930410-19-X
LIBRARY OF CONGRESS CATALOG NUMBER 84-72248
Manufactured in the United States of America

Published by

The American Alpine Club, Inc.   The Alpine Club of Canada
113 E 90th Street   P.O. Box 1026
New York, New York 10128   Banff, Alberta T0L 0C0

To all the trusting friends
who have been willing
to tie onto the other
end of our rope.

CONTENTS

*As the mountains near Banff have no glaciers and are not even ten thousand
feet high, the place is of little importance as a climbing centre.*

C. Klucker

INTRODUCTION

This seventh edition of *The Rocky Mountains of Canada North* is a somewhat less substantial revision than its immediate predecessor of 1974, in which both format and emphasis were greatly altered. It does represent, however, an ongoing effort to keep the information up to date, to correct errors, to eliminate anachronisms and to provide a guidebook useful to climbers of the 1980's. Much has changed since Howard Palmer and J. Monroe Thorington prepared, in 1921, the initial edition of what was the first alpine climber's guide in North America. We remain, nevertheless, mindful of the need to maintain a measure of continuity and have thus endeavored to produce a book consistent in spirit with the earlier editions of Thorington and Palmer.

This book is the companion volume to *Rocky Mountains of Canada South* (1979) and is part of the series which includes guides to the *Interior Ranges of British Columbia*.

The purpose of this guidebook is to enable the user to locate the peak or route he wishes to climb, to determine the most expeditious approach to that climb, and to have an idea of the salient features of the route, its difficulties, and the time normally required for the climb. We try not to provide so much detail that all sense of adventure is lost, for in such adventure lies the challenge and reward of mountaineering. Nor is it our intent to promote alpinism, but we wish to emphasize the responsibility laid on us all to care for these precious regions.

We have attempted also to give some feeling for the history of climbing in these mountains, enough at least that users of this book will be as respectful as we of those who have gone before, for it is upon their achievements that our enjoyable days amongst the peaks rest.

In preparing this revision, we have been fortunate in securing the help of many people, some who assisted in the research and editing, others who answered letters or sent in entries, and a few who abused us for past failures. We acknowledge with gratitude the contributions of: Glen Boles, Jean Kaddy, Hans Gmoser, Harriet Kruszyna, Arthur Maki, Dane Waterman and Helmut Microys. We are also indebted to Ed Cooper, Glen Boles and Tony Daffern for permission to print their photographs, and to Pierre Bastianelli who so ably converted one editor's color transparencies into black-and-white prints.

Here we continue our effort to move away from the guidebook as an historical record while still giving due credit. Thus we try to describe routes in terms of how one would go about making a given climb today, rather than merely condensing the account of the first ascent party. To the same end, we have continued to eliminate obsolete or hard-to-find references appearing in previous editions. More detail has been provided in some descriptions of popular and/or interesting routes; and, occasionally, we make a subjective appraisal of a climb's worth. And we have made a diligent effort to give "equal time" to modern, highly technical climbs. Finally, we have attempted to downplay the scholarly tone, to switch to the active voice from the passive, and to make reading the book more interesting even though the material hardly lends itself to "literary" treatment.

USE OF THE BOOK

The mountain groups described in this guide are organized into seventeen chapters, primarily on the basis of geographic proximity, but also by access. The basic arrangement is from south to north, with due allowance for the width of the area covered and other logical requirements. In any case, peaks which are adjacent on the ground appear with equal contiguity in the text.

The introduction to each chapter presents a brief discussion of the geography and topography of the specific area (watersheds, valleys, glaciers, etc.). We also include a resumé of the area's climbing history and observations on the character of the peaks and their climbing interest. Finally, the introductions contain information about access and approaches. We have provided a number of photographs, which give a further idea of the nature of the mountains and in some cases are useful to identify routes.

Supplied in the introduction to each group are the code numbers of the large-scale (1:50,000) topographical maps that cover the peaks described and which are available from the Map Distribution Office, 615 Booth Street, Ottawa, Ontario K1A OE9. We suggest that the small price of these maps makes them an item no well-equipped party should overlook. The most reliable sources of information on current road and trail conditions in most of these regions are the Warden Services of Banff and Jasper National Parks and the office of the Alpine Club of Canada in Banff. A hikers' manual, *The Canadian Rockies Trail Guide,* which is available at many locations in these mountains, offers more detailed trail information than is included here.

With each peak entry we list its elevation, locational data, and references regarding early attempts, etc. Then we describe the route of first ascent, with an evaluation (NCCS) of its difficulty, when one can be obtained. The description also includes the time normally required to make the climb, descent information, and pertinent references. We then describe other routes on the mountain in geographic order going clockwise around the peak (except where specified otherwise), with the same evaluations, references, etc. Generally the times given are those reported by the first ascent party, but when a more up-to-date figure is available (as when one of the editors has recently climbed the route), that will be given instead. Guides are denoted by italics; thus, *E. Fuez Jr.*

Space limitations preclude lengthy and elaborate route descriptions, particularly of the complicated, highly technical routes of recent years. We do provide, however, sufficient information to put the climber on the proper line and to apprise him of the problems and difficulties he will encounter, as well as acquainting him with crucial points along the way. On the matter of using hardware, we have tried to convey useful information without passing judgment, although we personally feel that the practices of the first ascent party determine an upper limit. We avoid statements like "this move can be done free," while including such as "protection often used." In any case, if a route is given a rating, as are most modern ones, one can gain a general notion of what may be required in the way of hardware.

Elevations and distances are given in metric units. However, since most of the pertinent maps have not yet been reprinted in a metric version (and indeed those used in preparing this book still utilize mile scales), a discussion of the conversion may be helpful to the user. We employ the internationally accepted definition: 2.54 cm = 1 inch. This translates into 0.3048m = 1 foot and 1.61 km = 1 mile. As in previous editions, when a surveyed elevation is not given, we take half the difference of the contour interval from the highest contour shown to the next. For example, with the usual interval of 100 feet, a peak whose highest contour is 10,200 feet would be estimated as 10,250 feet. Multiplying by 0.3048 yields 3124m, which we round *down* to the nearest 10m, in this case, 3120m. If an exact surveyed elevation is given, we simply convert and round to the nearest meter. Thus, Mount Columbia, at 12,294 feet, is 3747m high. For elevations other than those of peaks, we use the highest contour shown (the 50 feet is *not* added), convert, and round down to the nearest 10m. For those not possessing a basic mathematical facility, we include an abbreviated metric conversion table.

TABLE OF METRIC–ENGLISH CONVERSIONS

Meters	Feet	Feet	Meters
2400	7884	8000	2438
2500	8202	8250	2515
2600	8530	8500	2591
2700	8858	8750	2667
2800	9187	9000	2743
2900	9515	9250	2819
3000	9843	9500	2896
3100	10171	9750	2972
3200	10499	10000	3048
3300	10827	10250	3124
3400	11155	10500	3200
3500	11483	10750	3277
3600	11811	11000	3353
3700	12139	11250	3429
3800	12467	11500	3505
		11750	3581
		12000	3658

While we cannot make a broad statement, based on elevation or some other appropriate criterion, about what peaks are included in this book, we have endeavored to incorporate all those which have some mountaineering interest. Conversely, many insignificant lumps which took up space in earlier editions have been omitted. Even though the editors have sought all relevant information, it is possible that certain ascents may have escaped their attention. Thus, lack of mention in these pages does *not* constitute positive proof that an ascent has never been made. Those names shown in **boldface** type have been officially adopted by the Canadian Permanent Committee on Geographic Names. Names in *(italic)* with parentheses are alternate or former applications.

We caution the user that we assume a climbing party to be adequately equipped, in good condition, and blessed with sound judgment and fair weather. If you are unfamiliar with this region, we particularly urge you to read the full introduction before setting out.

GEOGRAPHY AND TOPOGRAPHY

This volume is one of a pair and encompasses the alpine territory northward from the line of the North Saskatchewan River, Howse Pass, and Blaeberry River. Peaks to the south of that line will be found in the companion volume published in 1979.

A major part of the area described in this guide lies within national and provincial parks. The first portion of the book covers the northern part of Banff National Park, and the immediately adjacent Jasper National Park contains a major share of the peaks herein described. Within British Columbia, to the west of the Continental Divide, two further parks include other peaks that concern us: Hamber Provincial Park in the area around Fortress Lake, and Moutn Robson Provincial Park, west of Yellowhead Pass. Far to the north, east of Fort Nelson on the Alaska Highway, lies an extensive area of glaciated summits, which, while detached from the main chain, are nonetheless geographically and geologically part of the Rockies.

It is important that persons unfamiliar with these mountains understand the nature of the bedrock and peculiarities of topography. Fundamentally, this is an area of severely glaciated sedimentary rock, much of it flat lying, although folded and thrust-faulted to the northeast. Certain formations, particularly within Cambrian and Devonian, offer excellent rock by local standards. However, those who are familiar with the nature of bedrock in such areas as Yosemite, the Dolomites, Laurentians, Chamonix or Shawangunks will need a serious readjustment of climbing practices and standards when on severe faces in the Rockies.

The principal glaciation in the Canadian Rocky Mountains occurs on or near the Continental Divide and lies in the area covered by this volume. While substantial glaciers do exist in other areas, both along the Divide peaks and in certain of the Maligne Ranges, there is nothing else comparable to the extent of the Columbia Icefield and its adjacent névé regions. In general, snowline is to be found at an altitude of 2400 to 2700m, depending on the exposure. This, of course, means that only on the more protected reaches of the higher peaks will there be found permanent snow. The glaciers extend to a lower limit of approximately 1500m and, without exception, show considerable recession within the last fifty years.

Users of this book should note that snowfall is not constant from year to year and that the problems of many routes are dependent on snow depth and cover. The descriptions in the text assume average snow levels as best the editors can determine; with greater or lesser amounts of snow, the routes may vary immensely in difficulty.

The main drainage is complex. The apex of Continental drainage is on the Columbia Icefield from which areas to the southeast and east drain through the North Saskatchewan and its Brazeau tributary to Hudson Bay and the Atlantic. Drainage to the northeast and north is via the Athabasca and its various tributaries to the Mackenzie River and Arctic Ocean. West drainage is to the Columbia via various tributaries (Bush, Wood,

Canoe) to the vicinity of the Ramparts whence all west drainage is to the Fraser. East drainage in the northernmost areas is through the Peace River system.

The Frontal Ranges, both north and south of the Brazeau River, form a distinct and separate climbing area in which snow or ice has been of lesser mountaineering importance. For the most part, the climbing has been on limestone or dolomite, only some of which is durable.

Most of the climbs in these frontal ranges are of two fundamentally different types. Most of the peaks were initially climbed from their generally gentle southwest slopes, which are largely conformable to the dip of the strata and littered with talus and broken rock. When approached from the northeast, however, these same peaks generally present spectacular cliffs. Approaches to most of the peaks of the frontal groups are relatively easy over trails maintained by the various park and forest authorities. However, even where trails are nonexistent, because of the substantially drier nature of these mountain areas, travel is relatively easy and the forests are substantially less luxuriant, although timberline remains at essentially the same level as in the areas to the west.

HISTORY AND REFERENCES

The early white travellers were associated with the Northwest Company—geographers, explorers, and fur traders: David Thompson opened the Athabasca Pass in 1811 (bibliography: CAJ **16**-194). David Douglas' ascent of Mount Brown, under winter conditions in 1827, attracted later mountaineers–explorers, although they failed to substantiate the great elevations attributed to peaks of the area. Accurate knowledge was advanced by the Palliser Expedition (1857–60) sent out by the British government to search for railroad routes. Dr. James Hector established the basic nomenclature retained by modern maps. The northeast frontal ranges were traversed from north to south in 1859 by the hunting party of James Carnegie, Earl of Southesk, whose route (uncertainly described in his *Sas-katchewan and the Rocky Mountains*, Edmonston and Douglas, Edinburgh, 1875) can now be identified.

Further historical information, where appropriate, is given in the introductions to individual groups or under specific peaks.

We have eliminated many older references, which, because of glacial recession or changes in approach, are no longer relevant, as well as some in hard-to-locate or obscure journals and books. The scholar who wishes to consult such references is referred to the 1966 edition of this guidebook which may be found in some of the libraries noted below.

Below we list a partial bibliography of the most useful and interesting books on the region. Most of them can be found in libraries in large cities or in those of various organizations such as The American Alpine Club, The Alpine Club of Canada, The Appalachian Mountain Club and the Sierra Club.

Coleman, Arthur Philemon. *The Canadian Rockies: New and Old Trails*. Henry Frowde, Toronto, 1911. An absorbing tale of a number of trips on foot and horseback over several years from both sides of the range.

Fraser, Esther. *The Canadian Rockies; Early Travels and Exploration*. M. G. Hurtig, Edmonton, 1969. A capsule summary of many of the early explorers and mountaineers and their principal exploits. Contains an excellent bibliography of historical material.

Kain, Conrad. *Where the Clouds Can Go*. Third Edition. The American Alpine Club, New York, 1979. An excellent autobiography of Canada's most famous guide.

Outram, James. *In the Heart of the Canadian Rockies*. Macmillan, London, 1905. To some extent, this overlaps and interlocks with Stutfield. It covers climbs made in the area generally south from Sunwapta Pass.

Schäffer, Mary T. S. *Old Indian Trails*. G. P. Putnam's Sons,

New York, 1911. Two women on an early horse-packing trip to many of the valleys of interest in this guide.

Smythe, Frank S. *Climbs in the Canadian Rockies.* Hodder & Stoughton, London, 1950. An account by the famous British climber of his seasons in Canada.

Stutfield, Hugh E. M. and J. Norman Collie. *Climbs and Exploration in the Canadian Rockies.* Longmans Green and Co., London, 1903. The basic book dealing with the Northern Rockies.

Thorington, J. Monroe. *The Glittering Mountains of Canada.* John W. Lea, Philadelphia, 1925. Largely an account of the author's first trips in this area but also containing much historic data of interest to scholarly mountaineers.

Wilcox, Walter D. *The Rockies of Canada.* G. P. Putnam's Sons, New York and London, 1900. This pertains largely to the southern part of the range.

Other references quoted are abbreviated as follows:

ABC: Alberta/British Columbia Boundary Survey Report;

AAJ: The American Alpine Journal, The American Alpine Club, New York;

AJ: The Alpine Journal, The Alpine Club, London;

App: Appalachia, The Appalachian Mountain Club, Boston;

CAJ: Canadian Alpine Journal, The Alpine Club of Canada, Banff;

Harvard: Harvard Mountaineering, The Harvard Mountaineering Club, Cambridge.

CLIMBING CONSIDERATIONS

The Canadian Rockies offer alpine climbing in a wilderness environment largely unspoiled by man—so far, anyway. There are significant differences, however, between climbing in these ranges and, say, the Alps or the Tetons. The key word is "wilderness"; indeed, it is not unusual to be out for a week or more without meeting another party. These mountains have not been extensively climbed, so many of the routes have not been repeated, leaving much scope for pioneering at all levels of difficulty.

In the Rockies the quality of the rock is often poor, although this has been greatly exaggerated. Certainly the rock here is no match for that in granitic areas; it is similar to that in a comparable sedimentary area, the Bernese Alps. However, because of the huge number of ascents over the years, the routes in the Bernese Alps have been cleared of much of their debris. On easy-angled slopes, in gullies and couloirs, the rock in the Rockies is usually of variable quality, while on the steeper ridges and faces it may be reasonably firm.

The reader should be aware that a great many of the routes in the Rockies involve little more than a strenuous uphill walk. Thus, if his objective is to climb a large number of high-quality and/or highly technical routes in a short period, then the Rockies are not for him. On the other hand, unlike the Alps, Tetons, or other "civilized" climbing areas, one does not need to wait in line to make a climb in the Rockies. Moreover, the very remoteness increases the risks and thereby enchances the satisfactions of having to rely on one's own resources. To experience these mountains to the full, one should enjoy the feeling of this remote and lonely country as much as the actual climbing. It is a question of becoming a part of the mountains rather than storming them.

In spite of the fact that much of the climbing here is relatively straightforward, it is also true that these mountains offer some of the finest alpine challenges in North America: face and ridge climbs that demand skill on rock and ice and sound mountaineering judgment. The problems facing the alpinist on these climbs are similar to those in other areas, although some additional factors are worth considering. The nature of the rock occasionally makes it impossible to establish sound belays. As a consequence one sometimes has to climb essentially unbelayed, and often at a fairly high standard. Some alpinists aver that the rope is a useless hazard on certain routes described here.

The weather also plays a part; while not generally as severe as the summer weather in the Mont Blanc region, it is more problematical than the considerate Teton weather. It is not uncommon for the nighttime temperature to remain high during the latter part of July and the first part of August, and, as a consequence, the freezing level may be around 3600m. This lack of freezing can make glacier travel unpleasant, and in addition will not solidify loose snow and rock, making certain climbs exposed to rock and icefall potentially hazardous. In connection with considerations of the freezing level, it should be emphasized that European guides and climbers have always made the most of whatever cold conditions exist by starting climbs that involve any degree of snow and ice at, or before, first light. Lacking the precedent of a host of guides crashing about in mountain huts and getting away by lantern light, North Americans commonly begin alpine climbs at a time when their European counterparts would typically be approaching the summit. Early starts, say 2 A.M., give one the best chance of good snow conditions, cool glacier travel before the heat of the day, a lot more time to play with, and, not least, the glory of the alpine sunrise.

The usual climbing season in the Canadian Rockies is from early July to early September, when there is usually a substantial snowfall. May is generally too stormy, and although the weather is often settled in June there are large masses of unconsolidated snow poised on ridges and faces. September and October generally have spells of clear, settled weather, and, though the days are short, snow and ice conditions can be superb; the freezing level has descended.

Winter climbing has been practiced for many years in the Rockies, although it is usually ski mountaineering as opposed to technical ascents. There are a number of points to consider in regard to winter climbing. First the weather is cold—far more severe than in the Alps, where winter climbing is now a regular thing. Though the cold itself is not the main deterrent, it leads to conditions that make winter mountaineering in the Rockies a serious business; unconsolidated powder snow and and depth hoar. Unlike the Alps, where, even in winter, freeze and thaw patterns occur, thus setting up the snow, this rarely happens in the Rockies. As a result there is considerable av- alanche danger. The 1972 accident on Mount Edith Cavell, when three highly qualified climbers were swept away, is a potent reminder of this danger. Winter climbing in the Rockies should only be undertaken by the most expert, and even then the price may be too high.

For those with a yen to get out into the Rockies in winter, ski touring and ski mountaineering are becoming increasingly popular. There is much potential for discovery, and the recent tour by C. Locke and companions from the Columbia Icefields to Lake Louise is just one example of what can be done at this time of year. (For a brief discussion of ski mountaineering, see the section on the Columbia Icefields in the "Apex of America" chapter.)

TRAVEL, ACCOMMODATIONS, AND SERVICES

It is a regrettable fact that a car makes a climbing vacation in the Canadian mountains a lot simpler. Public transportation, while adequate from town to town, does not reach into outlying areas. It is usually possible, however, to disembark from the Banff–Jasper bus at the Columbia Icefields (or other location of one's choosing on the highway) by making an arrangement with the bus driver. Hitchhiking, the climber's standby, is prob- lematical because the competition for rides from hordes of young people is keen, and the cars and trailers are mostly crammed to overflowing and driven by stern-visaged "holiday

makers." For those not coming into the area by car, good access
is provided by air to Calgary or Edmonton, and by rail or bus
to Banff, Jasper, and Golden.

In the mountains themselves, access is almost entirely on
foot, as there are few, if any, legally driveable access roads,
and the pack train, classic symbol of the Canadian mountains,
has disappeared. The coming of roads, in particular the Banff–
Jasper highway—A. O. Wheeler's "wonder trail"—has enabled
more people to see this stretch of country, and the roads have
opened up the back country to more persons than before.
However, it is not all to the good, and today organizations such
as The Alpine Club of Canada are fighting to preserve the
integrity of the remaining wild country in these mountain areas.
Helicopters are also used today to ferry climbers and their gear
into the more remote areas, although it must be noted that
helicopters are not permitted inside the National Parks, save
on official Park Service business. At the present time, helicopters are permitted into areas such as Hamber Provincial Park,
but the day may well come when they will be excluded from
the Provincial Parks. Helicopters may be chartered in Calgary,
Edmonton, Golden, Revelstoke and other locations.

Most climbers stay at the improved roadside campgrounds
in these ranges, operated by the National or Provincial Parks,
for which there is a fee, or camp in the back country. Registration is required for any camping in the National Parks beyond the roadside campgrounds (see below). For those with
less austere tastes Jasper offers the usual motels, though these
are generally booked up in the high season. Jasper also has
the best stores within a reasonable distance, and one may obtain
some climbing gear there. For those looking for a climbing
partner, the latest gossip or whatever, two places should be
mentioned: the Columbia Icefields campground, about the only
true climbers' meeting place in the Northern Rockies (apart
from the bar in the Athabasca Hotel in Jasper) and the ACC
clubhouse in Canmore, east of Banff, which has showers and

a well-equipped kitchen—a good place to go when the weather clamps down. On the other hand, it is a long way from the peaks and is often jammed with family groups.

The alpine huts in the range are described in the applicable chapter introductions. To use the Wates–Gibson Hut (Guardian) in the Ramparts or the Lawrence Grassi Hut in the Clemenceau Group, it is necessary to reserve space through the office of The Alpine Club of Canada in Banff. The Sidney Vallance Hut (Fryatt Group) and Centennial Hut (Colin Range) are designated campsites of Jasper National Park; reservation at Park Headquarters is required (see below). Unlike European huts, these huts are usually equipped only with cooking utensils, stove, and mattresses; it is necessary to bring food, fuel, and a sleeping bag.

Climbing guides are available in Jasper as well as in Banff, to the south. They may be contacted through the Association of Canadian Mountain Guides, 132 Banff Avenue, Banff, Alberta T0l 0C0, or through The Alpine Club of Canada in Banff.

REGISTRATION

Registration for the climbs in the National Parks, formerly mandatory, has been put on a voluntary basis. However, camping, in terms of both sites and numbers, is now severely restricted in an attempt to control environmental damage. Thus, a camping permit is now required for any overnight trip in the National Parks. The mountaineer will discover that many convenient campsites are now forbidden; indeed, no camping whatever is allowed in certain areas of interest to the climber. He will also find that he has been lumped with the backpackers, with whom he must compete, under a quota system, for a camping permit. Furthermore, the climber must obtain his permit in person, during regular business hours (usually 8 A.M. – 5 P.M. daily during the summer season), at Park Information Centers or Warden Offices, where he may also register out for climbing. He should always register in again after completing his climb to avoid the dispatching of a rescue party. The camping permit system was first implemented in 1977, after a year or two of experimental use. It is still undergoing refinement, so the climber is advised to obtain current information in advance of his trip by writing to the appropriate Park Superintendent: Banff National Park, P.O. Box 900, Banff, Alberta T0L 0C0; Jasper National Park, Jasper, Alberta T0E 1E0.

RATINGS

It is with considerable trepidation that the editors approach the thorny problem of rating routes, partly because of the intrinsic difficulty of making valid comparisons between different kinds of difficulty (e. g. rock versus ice) and between different mountain areas, and partly because classifying climbs is often perverted into categorizing climbers. Moreover, a multiplicity of classification systems, of varying degrees of usefulness, vie for our attention and add to the confusion. Regrettably, each new system that has come into use has not totally superseded older ones, often resulting in climbers' employing parts of various systems, without meaning to do so. Nevertheless, since providing some basis for evaluating the difficulty of a given route has long been a traditional function of a guidebook, the editors, with misgivings, have adopted a rating system and applied it to a number of routes described here, particularly the more recent and/or more technical ones. Indeed, if the feedback we have received gives any indication, our readers expect—nay, demand—that we do so.

Despite its proponents' claims of universality and certain pressures to conform, we have rejected the UIAA system primarily because it rates individual rock pitch difficulty alone. In the mountains of Western Canada, one is more often concerned with the magnitude of the enterprise as a whole, than with the marginal differences in technical difficulty. Thus, we employ a slightly modified version of the NCCS system, which has the merit of providing a measure of overall difficulty in addition to classifying individual pitch difficulty. Moreover, it seems to be the system most familiar to active North American mountaineers.

The NCCS classifies routes according to overall difficulty into six grades: Roman numerals I through VI. The grade takes into consideration a variety of unequal factors, including: the elevation of the peak and the uplift of the route; the length of the climb in terms of both distance and time; the difficulty of the hardest pitch; the average difficulty; how sustained the difficulties are; how strenuous the climbing is; how difficult it is to retreat; whether alternative, easier, descent routes exist; the impact of sudden bad weather and how likely it is to occur in a given range, etc. The NCCS grade is intended to give a relative measure of the "magnitude of the undertaking" or the "degree of commitment" in climbing a particular route, but it is evident that many of these factors resist objective assessment. Thus the grades are quite crude. Moreover, while it is reasonably simple to compare climbs on similar kinds of peaks (e. g. the Tetons, Mont Blanc massif, Interior Ranges), it is questionable whether valid comparisons can be made at all between dissimilar kinds, for example, the above groups against, say, Yosemite and the Dolomites—or the latter against the huge snow/ice mountains found in Switzerland or in the Canadian Rockies. In an attempt to improve correlation from range to range, and thus serve the diverse backgrounds of different climbers, the editors have utilized extensively their personal climbing experience in constructing the table comparing routes in terms of overall difficulty. We believe this to be legitimate since the grades are arbitrary in any case (i.e. a given grade is defined in terms of a specific climb) and because it supplies internal consistency.

COMPARISONS OF OVERALL DIFFICULTY

(Normal route is meant unless otherwise specified)

NCCS GRADE	TETONS	MONT BLANC MASSIF	INTERIOR RANGES	CANADIAN ROCKIES
I	Symmetry Spire (NW Ledges)	Aig du Tour Aig du Plan	Crescent Spire Avalanche Peak Eastpost Spire Rogers Peak	Mt. Rundle Mt. President Mt. Temple Mt. Athabasca
II	Mt. Owen (Koven) Grand Teton (Exum)	Aig des Pelerins Aig du Moine	Pigeon Spire Uto Peak Mt. Tupper	Yamnuska (Grillmair) Mt. Victoria Mt. Hungabee Mt. Louis
III	Symmetry Spire (Jensen) Grand Teton (E Ridge)	Dent du Requin Aig de Peigne Aig du Geant (w/o cables)	Mt. Swanzy (N Ridge) Bugaboo Spire Mt. Sir Donald (NW Ridge)	Mt. Assiniboine Wiwaxy Peak (Grassi Ridge) Mt. Biddle (N Ridge)
IV	Grand Teton (N Ridge)	Aig du Grepon (Mummery–Ravenel Traverse) Aig du Plan (Ryan Ridge)	Snowpatch Spire Bugaboo Spire (NE Ridge)	Mt. Robson Mt. Brussels Mt. Alberta
V		Petit Dru (N Face) Aig Noire de Peuterey (S Ridge)	Bugaboo Spire (E Face) South Howser (W Buttress)	Mt. Columbia (N Ridge) Mt. Alberta (N Ridge)
VI		Petit Dru (Bonatti Pillar) Grandes Jorasses (Walker Spur)	Snowpatch Spire (E face Beckey) N Howser (W Face)	North Twin (N Face)

UCCS GRADE	SWITZERLAND	EASTERN ALPS	YOSEMITE	NEW ENGLAND
I		2nd Sella Tower		Joe English Hill (any route)
II	Schonbielhorn Allalinhorn	Planspitze (N Face) Fleischbank (N Ridge) 1st Sella Tower (S Face)	Monday Morning Slab (W side) Lower Cathedral Spire	White Horse Ledge Mt. Washington (Pinnacle) Cannon Mountain (Whitney-Gilman) Cannon Mountain (VMC)
III	Zinal Rothorn Portjengrat (Traverse) Matterhorn	Cima Piccola Predigstuhl (N Corner)	Washington Column (Direct) Higher Cathedral Spire	
IV	Matterhorn (Zmutt) Zinal Rothorn (N Ridge) Mischabel (Traverse)	Cima Grande (N Corner) Cima della Madonna (Schleierkante)	Yosemite Point Buttress	
V		Cima Grande (N Face)	Lost Arrow Chimney	
VI	Eiger (N Face)		El Capitan (Salathe Wall)	

Much less troublesome is the problem of comparing the difficulty of individual rock-climbing pitches. Indeed, general agreement has been reached, even when comparing pitches on different kinds of rock or in different ranges. Again, we have adopted the NCCS approach, which divides pitch difficulty into eleven (at present) classes, denoted F1 through F11 (F for free). We prefer this system to others because the subdivisions are rather less hairsplitting. A table of correlations between commonly used systems is given below. Based on this table, we have also prepared a table comparing, according to pitch difficulty, some familiar routes in various ranges. If a route requires the use of direct aid, the level of difficulty of such aid is denoted by the symbols A1 through (at present) A5.

Although the NCCS, like any system, is designed to impart standardized information concisely, that very virtue can mislead. We therefore urge the user to consult our comparative table of climbs and to read the complete route description before he decides a climb is within his powers.

CORRELATION OF COMMON SYSTEMS FOR RATING INDIVIDUAL PITCH DIFFICULTY

NCCS	Decimal	UIAA	Adjective	British
F1	1	I	Easy	Easy
F2	2 & 3	II		Moderate
F3	4	III −	Moderate	Moderately difficult
	5.0	III		
F4	5.1	III +	Moderately difficult	Very difficult
	5.2	IV-		
F5	5.3	IV	Difficult	Severe
	5.4	IV +		
	5.5	V −		

NCCS	Decimal	UIAA	Adjective	British
F6	5.6	V	Very difficult	Very severe
F7	5.7	V +		
F8	5.8	VI −		Hard
F9	5.9	VI	Extremely difficult	
F10	5.10	VI +		

COMPARISON OF INDIVIDUAL PITCH DIFFICULTY
(Unless otherwise noted, most difficult pitch on route is meant)

NCCS Class	Range	Peak	Route
F3	Tetons	Grand Teton	Owen-Spalding
	Canadian Rockies	Assiniboine	N Ridge
	Valais	Matterhorn	Swiss Ridge
	Yosemite	Gunsight	Normal
	Eastern Alps	Grosse Buchstein	W Ridge
	Purcells	Brenta	Normal
F4	Dolomites	Cima Piccola	Normal
	Yosemite	Sunnyside Bench	Normal (S Face)
	Tetons	Grand Teton	Exum
	Valais	Zinal Rothorn	S Ridge
	Selkirks	Uto	SW Ridge
	Canadian Rockies	Louis	Normal
	Mt. Blanc	Dent du Requin	Normal (Colonnes)
	Purcells	Pigeon	Normal (W Ridge)
	Kaisergebirge	Predigtstuhl	N-Kante

NCCS Class	Range	Peak	Route
F5	Tetons	Symmetry Spire	Durrance
	Mont Blanc	Grépon	Mummery Crack
	Dolomites	Campanile Basso	Normal
	Bernina	Piz Badile	N Ridge
	Canadian Rockies	Castle Mountain (Eisenhower)	Brewer Buttress
	Purcells	Bugaboo	Normal
	Cascades	Rainier	Liberty Ridge
	Yosemite	Footstool	E side
F6	Canadian Rockies	Yamnuska	Red Shirt
	Yosemite	Arrowhead Spire	S Ridge
	Tetons	Owen	Summit Knob Direct
	Mont Blanc	Grépon	Knubel Crack
	Purcells	Snowpatch	Vein Pitch
	Cascades	Baring	N Face
	Kaisergebirge	Fleischbank	E Face Dulfer
	White Mountains	Cannon Mountain	Sam's Swan Song
F7	Black Hills	Devils Tower	Wiessner
	Tetons	Grand Teton	N Ridge
	Dolomites	Cima Piccola	Spigolo Giallo
	Yosemite	Washington Column	Direct
	Purcells	Bugaboo	NE Ridge
	Mont Blanc	Petit Dru	N Face, Martinetti Crack
F8	Dolomites	Sass Maor	E Face
	Purcells	N Snowpatch	N Ridge Variant
	Mont Blanc	Aig. Noire de Peuterey	S Ridge
	Tetons	Disappointment Peak	Irene's Arete
	Yosemite	Royal Arches	Arches Terrace

NCCS

Class	Range	Peak	Route
F9	Dolomites	Cima Grande	N Face
	Mont Blanc	Petit Dru	N Face, Allain Crack
	Tetons	Baxter Pinnacle	Gill Route
	Yosemite	El Capitan	Moby Dick
F10	Mont Blanc	Aig. de Blaitière	W Face, Fix Crack
	Dolomites	Marmolada	SW Face
	Tetons	Baxter Pinnacle	N Face
	Yosemite		Crack of Doom

APOLOGY

As the reader will realize, this edition represents a modern revision and correction of its predecessors. Future editions will probably follow; like the present one, their accuracy and usefulness will measure their value. In terms of containing the latest information, any publication like this becomes, in a sense, obsolete even while in the hands of the printer. The scope of the undertaking, moreover, makes unavoidable occasional errors. We ask those who find innacuracies or anachronisms to communicate them to the editors through the publisher.

We urge the users of this guidebook to show greater respect than some of our predecessors for the conservation and perpetuation of the wilderness areas they enter. The expanse of remote country so precious to mountaineers are daily dwindling under the pressure of man and machine. To the limits of our ability, we who frequent the hills should seek to preserve for our successors that which it is still our good fortune to find—the unspoiled grandeur of God's wilderness.

Robert Kruszyna
William L. Putnam

Clear, unscaleable, ahead/Rise the Mountains of Instead, From whose cold cascading streams/None may drink except in dreams.

W. H. Auden

SNOW SUMMITS

FRESHFIELD GROUPS

These groups embrace the peaks on or near the Continental Divide between Howse and Bush Passes, an airline distance of 15 km, but as the Divide runs, about 38. Mount Barnard is the highest summit at 3339m, but there are more than two dozen peaks exceeding 3000m. These groups are noteworthy for their ice and snow features. South drainage is by Blaeberry River while Waitabit and Bluewater Creeks provide W drainage.

The Freshfield Icefield, a principal source of Howse River, occupies a basin 14 km long and 4 km wide. Ice streams 8 and 5 km long, respectively, unite in a tongue more than one km wide, which flows NE 5 km more. The system covers an area of approx 50 sq km. The glacier was discovered in 1859 by Dr Hector of the Palliser Expedition. The first climbing party was that of G.P. Baker, J.N. Collie and *P. Sarbach* in 1897. The glacier was the first one of the N Saskatchewan system to have its movement measured, the retreat 1922–1937 being 400m. A wide gravel flat now occupies the former glacial bed, and near here several ACC camps have been located.

ACCESS

The forest road on Blaeberry River provides access to the Mummery Group and many of the other southerly summits. It was used by the Kauffman party in 1952 and subsequently for the ACC camp in 1958, superseding the former approach over Amiskwi Pass from Field. The road leaves the Trans–Canada Highway at Moberly, 12 km N of Golden, and extends some 45 km up the Blaeberry to Mummery Creek where there is a Forest Service campsite. Although it is generally passable to 4-wheel drive vehicles (1980), and often to passenger cars, washouts can be a problem. Consult the B.C. Forest Service in Golden for current conditions. About one km beyond Mummery Creek, a trail (sign) to Mummery Glacier starts up a logging road and enters the forest at the second switchback. The trail intersects the N terminal fork of Mummery Creek, which must be forded below a gorge choked with slide alder. Cross a ridge to W (markers) to reach open slopes leading toward the tongue of Mummery Glacier. There are campsites below the bluffs, or better, farther up the N fork in open brush or meadows below Mount Cairnes. About 5 km and 700m elevation gain from Blaeberry road; ½ day with full loads.

Beyond Mummery Creek, the road extends another 7 km, after which it becomes a trail which leads to Howse Pass. Some of the peaks of the Conway Group can be reached from the upper Blaeberry over Cairnes or Lambe Glaciers.

The Howse Pass trail is the best approach to the Freshfield Glacier and Icefield and the peaks on its rim. Leave the Banff–Jasper Highway on the steep grade 3 km S of the Saskatchen warden station (trail sign: Sarbach Lookout). Descend into and cross Mistaya Canyon on old road. Branch off road onto trail after crossing River. Leave Sarbach trail and follow Howse Pass trail along E bank of Howse River alternately in trees and flats. Watch for trail cutting back into timber 3 km N of warden cabin (138471). Leave main Howse Pass trail at fork and take branch W to cabin. Go over swampy ground to Lagoon Lake and continue S 2 km to Conway Creek which must be forded. One may either stick with the trail fording Howse River (inadvisable when water high) or skirt the gravel flats to S, fording Freshfield Creek and rejoining trail which leads to tongue of Freshfield Glacier. For climbs at the head of the Icefield a high camp is often made at Niverville Meadow, below SE ridge of Mount Niverville. This area (2200m, wood and water) may be easily reached from Freshfield tongue over the lower glacier (2–3 h). About 30 km to Freshfield Glacier; minimum, one long day. To reach Conway Glacier, stay on Howse Pass trail throughout.

The Freshfield and Mummery Glaciers have become popular areas for ski mountaineering. Parties often approach up the Blaeberry, or by helicopter, skiing over the Divide and out Howse River, ascending peaks en route.

This area is divided on modern maps into five groups, three of which have been of real interest to mountaineers. They are treated separately below.

LITERATURE

Thorington, J.M. "The Freshfield Group, 1922." CAJ **13**-64 (1923). An early expedition which covered much of the ground.

Karcher, P. "A New Shangri-La for Climbers." CAJ **36**-73 (1953). Opening up the Mummery Group.

Mummery Group

This important S wing of the Freshfield Groups extends 20 km into the angle between Blaeberry River and Waitabit Creek. It is dominated by the massif of Mount Mummery and lies entirely on the B.C. side of the Divide. Most ascents have been made from Blaeberry River although approaches to the upper Blaeberry have varied. Good photograph as frontispiece to CAJ 3 (1911).

Map: 82N 10.

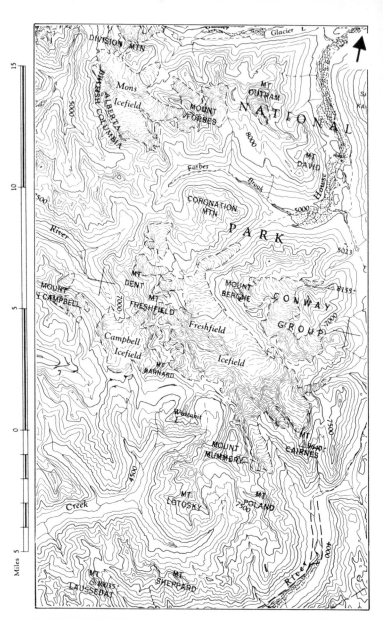

MOUNT LAUSSEDAT (3059m)

13 km SW of Mount Mummery on the crest between Blae-berry River and Waitabit Creek.

FA 1906, C.B. Sissons, A.O. Wheeler, M. Wheeler. From Split Creek campsite, some 20 km up Blaeberry River road, cross river and bushwhack to **SE ridge.** Follow it over rock and a snow couloir to top. 9 h RT from timberline (where FA party bivouacked).

2. N Face, July 1980, D. Waterman, *alone.* From Waitabit Creek to valley to NE. General line follows rock rib considerably right of deep couloir on left side of face. Traverse left from ice slope at foot of face and take 2 V-troughs through steep band. Gain rib at pinnacle visible from below and follow it to summit. Moderate class 5; 7 h up. Descent via easy but very rotten NW ridge in 3 h (CAJ **64**- 91).

MOUNT LOTOSKY (2970m)

4 km SSW of Mount Mummery; overlooking headwaters of Waitabit Creek, 4.5 km E of its forks.

UNNAMED *(Loucks)* (3090m)

2.5 km SW of Mount Mummery on crest extending to Mount Lotosky. FA July 1980, D. Waterman, *alone.* Via **W slopes** from Waitabit Creek in 10 h RT (CAJ **64**-91).

MOUNT POLAND *(M3)* (2840m)

S outlier of Mount Mummery; 3.5 km W of junction of Mummery Creek with Blaeberry River. The nearest to Mount Mummery of four peaks designated by the letter M in CAJ **42**-98, the reference for all of them.

FA July 1958, J. Owen, E. Pigou, A. *Bitterlich.* From camp at mouth of Mummery Creek, ascend **SE ridge,** bypassing over-hanging step on S. Improbable descent down N face on FA. Peak also ascended by ACC party via N glacier to Poland–

Mummery col and then along **W ridge;** this is the descent route of choice.

M2½ (2750m)

1.5 km S of Mount Poland; on spur extending SW from main crest running from Mount Poland parallel to Mummery Creek.

FA July 1958, H. Winstone and ACC party. From basin to S without difficulty after traversing lower SW slopes of M2.

M2 (2720m)

1.7 km SSE of Mount Poland on main crest parallel to Mummery Creek.

FA July 1958, F.D. Chamberlin, D.G. Fish, R. Neave, J. Owen, E. Pigou, S. Spinkova. Approach as for M1, bypassing it on S and W to reach M1–M2 col. Some moderate rock climbing to ascend barrel-shaped tower to summit. Some hardware used on FA for protection and rappels. 8 h up from camp at mouth of Mummery Creek; 6 h down.

M1 (2690m)

2.5 km SSE of Mount Poland.

FA July 1958, Winstone party. From camp at mouth of Mummery Creek via S slopes.

MOUNT MUMMERY (S 3328m; N 3300m)

Large glaciated massif which dominates view up Mummery Creek.

S Peak. FA August 1906, I.T. Burr, S. Cabot, W.R. Peabody, R. Walcott, *G. Feuz, C. Kaufmann*. **SE Ridge.** To follow the original route, it is advisable to camp near the forks of Mummery Creek, below the valley headwall above which hangs the terminus of the Mummery Glacier (3 km from Blaeberry River). Ascend W up talus slopes and cliff bands to reach glacier tongue (*not* the main one) lying left (S) of prominent brown tower

Jones

Karakal

Mummery Glacier

Mummery N

Mummery S

R. Kruszyna

NORTH UP MUMMERY CREEK

(2480m). Cross dry glacier to attain ridge at lowest point. Follow broad snow ridge toward summit, traversing right (E) where necessary. Pass under summit edifice to col between objective and N Peak. Ascend narrow, corniced N ridge to final rocks, the summit being a short distance to S. A classic snow ascent. 10 h up (App **11**-221).

Variant 1. July 1952, A.J. & E. Kauffman, J. Showacre. This is the approach of choice from a camp on the N terminal fork of Mummery Creek, below Mount Cairnes. Ascend ice-scarred bluffs to gain dry part of Mummery Glacier. Cross it in SW direction and then glacier emanating from Mount Mummery itself. Ascend prominent snow couloir, behind brown tower (2480m), which leads to upper glacier and SE ridge route described above. 8 h up (CAJ **36**-76).

Variant 2. July 1952, *H. Gmoser* and ACC party. Instead of passing under the summit edifice to N–S col, climb directly the final steep section of the SE ridge. A sporting climb on exposed, unreliable rock (F3, 3 h), which, when coupled with a descent via the N ridge, makes a good climb even finer.

2. W Face, July 1980, D. Waterman, *alone.* Ascend series of snow/ice gullies directly beneath summit, turning summit head-wall to left. 12 h RT from Waitabit Creek (CAJ **64**-91).

N Peak. FA July 1952, E.K. & P. Karcher (with Kauffman party). As for S Peak, the summit being gained over snow from the intervening col in ½ h (CAJ **36**-77).

UNNAMED *(Karakal)* (2960m)

One km N of Mummery massif; a prominent snow peak when seen from mouth of Mummery Creek.

FA July 1952, E.K. & P. Karcher, A.J. & E. Kauffman, J. Showacre. Via Mummery Glacier from camp below Mount Cairnes. Ascend easy snow slopes to col between objective and next summit to N (Jones). Steep, corniced snow/ice ridge to top. 6 h up (CAJ **36**-75).

UNNAMED *(Jones)* (2990m)

N of Karakal, between it and Nanga Parbat.

FA July 1952, E.K. Karcher, A.J. Kauffman, J. Showacre. As for Karakal, the summit being gained over snow from the intervening col in ½ h (CAJ **36**-76).

While the following peaks are not properly, in a geographic sense, part of the Mummery Group, they are nowadays most readily approached from a camp on the N terminal fork of Mummery Creek. Earlier ascents were often made from Niverville Meadow over the Freshfield Icefield.

GILGIT MOUNTAIN (3090m)

On Divide at head of Mummery Glacier and Freshfield Icefield; N spur divides Freshfield Icefield into two bays.

FA July 1922, H. Palmer, J.M. Thorington, *E. Feuz Jr.* From Divide pass between objective and Nanga Parbat, ascend easy **W snow** to top in ¾ h. 5–6 h to col (CAJ **13**-67).

2. NE Slope, August 1975, J.K. Fox, J.A. Fraylick, S.L. Quinlan. From E basin of Freshfield Icefield via moderately steep snow/ice to upper plateau from which summit is easily gained (CAJ **59**-83).

3. SE Ridge, July 1958, F.L. Cary, L. Coveney, Mr. & Mrs. A.W. Lash. To Gilgit–Helmer col over Mummery Glacier. Then climb rock ridge to top. 5 h up.

MOUNT HELMER (3030m)

On Divide 4 km N of Mount Mummery across upper Mummery Glacier; one km ESE of Gilgit Mountain. S face impressive.

FA August 1949, J. Bishop, D. Greenwell, E.R. LaChapelle, D.M. Woods. **W. Ridge.** Gain Gilgit–Helmer col from Mummery Glacier or E basin of Freshfield Icefield. Ascend along top of steep snow slope on N side of ridge, below cliff. Climb a short open chimney and then an icy gully (loose rock). Some distance beyond, ascend a very steep snow slope. After scrambling a 60m cliff, follow the easy ridge to summit. 4 h from col (CAJ **33**-71).

MOUNT BARLOW (3120m)

On Divide between head of Freshfield and Cairnes Glaciers; 2 km E of Mount Helmer.

FA July 1930, E. Cromwell, J.M. Thorington, *P. Kaufmann.* **W. Slope.** From E basin of Freshfield Icefield, gain Helmer–Barlow col. Skirt lower W peak on its S snow slopes to saddle between peaks, from which higher E peak is attained over snow and final scree. One h from col; 5 h from Niverville Meadow (AAJ **1**-403).

2. S Slopes. July 1952, E.K. & P. Karcher, A.J. & E. Kauffman, J. Showacre. From camp on N terminal fork of Mummery Creek, ascend N over moraines and then E up steep slopes and cliffs to high névé on level with Pyramid Point. Cross névé to low point in Barlow–Cairnes ridge and ascend easy S snow to top. Ascent 5 h (CAJ **36**-74).

MOUNT CAIRNES (3060m)

5 km E of Mount Mummery across Mummery Glacier. A point (2938m) high on the S ridge was occupied by the Boundary Survey.

FA July 1952, E.K. & P. Karcher, J. Showacre. **NW Ridge.** As in Route 2 for Mount Barlow to Barlow–Cairnes saddle. Then follow long snow ridge ("roller-coaster") to final steep pitch leading to sharp summit. 7 h up (CAJ **36**-78).

Variant. FA party. Climb cliffs below Pyramid Point to reach glacier nestled between it and objective. Ascend heavily crevassed glacier and cliffs to Cairnes–Barlow ridge, which is followed as above. Ascent 8 h.

Barnard–Dent Group

These peaks form the rim around the W cirque of the Freshfield Icefield in line S from Bush Pass. The Divide runs 20 km from Nanga Parbat Mountain to Bush Pass traversing almost all the high points. With the exception of Mount Mummery, this group offers the most interest of the Freshfield peaks. Many ascents can be done in combination, as, for example, Mounts Freshfield and Dent or Mounts Pilkington, Bulyea and Walker.

Maps: 82N 10, 82N 15.

NANGA PARBAT MOUNTAIN (3240m)

At heads of Freshfield Icefield and Mummery Glacier; 4 km N of Mount Mummery.

FA July 1922, H. Palmer, J.M. Thorington, *E. Feuz Jr.* **NW Ridge.** Over Icefield to N of mountain. Ascend snow and scree to summit. 6 h up. To descend, follow S ridge until bergschrund on W slope is passed, then go down easy snow to regain approach route. Done in reverse (July 1941) by J. Taylor, A.T. Wiebrecht, *E. Feuz Jr*, who made first traverse by descending **NE ridge** (CAJ **13**-67; **28**-53).

2. NE Ridge, July 1958, P.A. Boswell, I. Keith, R. de Repentigny. From Gilgit–Nanga Parbat saddle, climb elegant corniced snow ridge; 2 h.

3. SE Ridge, July 1980, D. Waterman, *alone*. From cirque at head of Waitabit Creek, climb headwall to snow eminence (3000m) S of peak (also reached from Mummery Glacier); then follow ridge to top (CAJ **64**-91).

MOUNT TRUTCH (3210m)

On Divide one km W of Nanga Parbat.

FA July 1922, H. Palmer, J.M. Thorington, *E. Feuz Jr*. Ascend Freshfield Icefield from Niverville Meadow into high basin below Mount Barnard. Climb prominent **N ridge,** initially over snow and scree. The culminating section offers good climbing on a rocky knife-edge. 2 h from snow basin (CAJ **13**-66).

Variant. April 1980, P. Paul, *alone*. From glacier between

44 THE ROCKY MOUNTAINS OF CANADA/NORTH

objective and Nanga Parbat, ascend 35° snow/ice of NE face to
intersect upper part of ridge. Route lies approximately ⅓ of
the way along face, between seracs and rock buttress.

2. NE Face. July 1980, R.G. Estock, R. Kranabitter. Climb
five pitches of moderate steepness to summit. 3 hours from
base (CAJ **65**-87).

WAITABIT PEAK (3090m)

Minor eminence midway between Mount Trutch and Mount
Barnard; 2 km N of scenic Waitabit Lake.

FA July 1937, E. Cromwell, E. Cromwell Jr., G. Engelhard,
F.S. North, J.M. Thorington. From high snow basin below
Mount Barnard, it can be traversed in either direction along
sharp crest (AAJ **3**-220).

MOUNT BARNARD (3339m)

Highest summit of Freshfield groups, located where Divide
swings from an E–W direction to a NW one.

FA July 1922, H. Palmer, J.M. Thorington, *E. Feuz Jr.* From
Niverville Meadow ascend Freshfield Icefield to high basin at
foot of objective. From base of **SE ridge,** attain crest over a
schrund and steep snow (50m). Follow ridge over two emin-
ences to summit. Ascend 7 h (CAJ **13**-66).

2. S Buttress, July 1980, D. Waterman, *alone.* From Waitabit
Lake, ascend buttress to left of S face to gendarme (3240m).
Descend it on right (S). Follow SW ridge, near top climbing a
deep, ice-filled slot far around to left (W) (CAJ **64**-91).

3. N Ridge. From high snow basin, ascend to col N of peak
and climb steep, corniced ridge. More logical than FA route
(used then for descent).

4. E Face, April 1980, J. Bauer, P. Paul, Ascend 200m of
35–40° snow/ice to minor summit 30m below summit, finishing
along ridge. 1¼ h on face proper.

G. Boles

Mt Barnard

Mt Pilkington

Mummery S

Mt Walker

Mt Trutch

Nanga Parbat

Gilgit Mtn

SE FROM MT. FRESHFIELD

MOUNT BULYEA (3304m)

One km N of Mount Barnard.

FA July 1910, J.E.C. Eaton, *H. Burgener*. **N Ridge.** From snowfield between Mounts Pilkington and Walker (which see), an easy ascent over snow and rock. One h (CAJ **3**-8; **45**-31).

2. E Face, April 1980, J. Bauer, R. Kelly, P. Paul. Climb 200m on 35° snow direct to summit. An aesthetic line. One h on face proper.

MOUNT WALKER (3303m)

Northeast across snow pass from Mount Bulyea; 1.5 km NNE of Mount Barnard. FA July 1910, J.E.C. Eaton, B. Otto, *H. Burgener*. From snow pass at head of Pilkington–Walker névé, ascend **W ridge** over slabs and some snow in one h (CAJ **3**-8).

2. N Face, August 1977, D. Lemon, K. Owens, D. Paterson. A steep snow/ice face climbed directly from névé (CAJ **61**-106).

PRIOR PEAK (3270m)

Between Mounts Pilkington and Bulyea; a minor eminence in SW ridge of Mount Pilkington, rising only 50m above intervening col.

FA July 1937, E. Cromwell, E. Cromwell Jr., G. Engelhard, F.S. North, J.M. Thorington. From Pilkington–Walker névé, traverse from S to NE on broken rock and snow. Has also been done from NE; July 1939, K. Gardiner, *E. Feuz Jr.* (AAJ **3**-220; CAJ **27**-40).

MOUNT PILKINGTON (S 3285m; N 3210m)

2.5 km SSE of Mount Freshfield.

FA July 1910, J.E.C. Eaton, B. Otto, *H. Burgener*. **N Ridge.** Cross Freshfield Icefield from Niverville Meadow to N base of mountain. Climb steep NE snow slope, crossing a bergschrund, to gain N ridge proper. Follow it (snow and loose rock) to N summit (4½ h). Reach the higher S summit along connecting ridge, traversing two slabby gendarmes en route (½ h). Take easy snow of S ridge to névé in one h. **S ridge** ascended in July 1939, K. Gardiner, *E. Feuz Jr.* Easier, but less interesting than FA route (CAJ **3**-7; **27**-40).

2. N Face, August 1977, B. Fairley, J. Harrison. Gain névé basin between Mount Freshfield and objective and ascend steep snow to N summit (CAJ **61**-106).

MOUNT ALAN CAMPBELL (3030m)

7 km W of Mount Freshfield across Campbell Icefield.

FA July 1979, J.A.V. Cade, G. Dougherty, D. Henley, *W.L. Putnam, E. Salzgeber.* From timberline camp 3 km W of objective via **W ridge.** Traverse by SE glacier and S ridge. 12 h RT. Also easily via E ridge, July 1980, D. Waterman.

MOUNT FRESHFIELD (3336m)

Inspiring pyramid which dominates view from tongue of Freshfield Glacier (CAJ **60**-33, photo).

FA August 1902, J.N. Collie, J. Outram, H.E.M. Stutfield, G.M. Weed, H. Woolley, *C. Kaufmann, H. Kaufmann.* **E Ridge.** From tongue of Freshfield Glacier over ice to base of peak (3 h). Round the bank of rocks on the right (NW) and ascend snow slopes to low saddle by which the NE ridge of the mountain is crossed to upper snow slopes facing Mount Pilkington. The remainder of the route follows the E ridge, the climb mainly on rock with occasional short traverses to avoid gendarmes. Ascent 8 h (Collie-266; Outram-321).

2. S Ridge, August 1920, C.B. Eddy, V.A. Fynn, A.L. Mumm, *R. Aemmer, M. Inderbinen.* A variant of the above and now the usual route. From upper snow slopes facing Mount Pilkington, gain S ridge (frozen lakelet, 3200m) which is taken over easy rocks to the summit. From Niverville Meadow, ascent 5 h; descent 2½ h (AJ **35**-43; CAJ **12**-179; **13**-67).

3. SW Face, July 1980, D. Waterman, *alone.* Line generally in center of face, avoiding gullies exposed to rockfall. Class 3; 2 h up, one down from Campbell Icefield (CAJ **64**-91).

4. W Slope & Traverse, July 1910, J.E.C. Eaton, B. Otto, *H. Burgener.* From summit of Mount Dent via intervening col and up easy mixed W slopes. 3 h from Mount Dent (CAJ **3**-10).

MOUNT DENT (3267m)
2 km NW of Mount Freshfield.

FA July 1910, J.E.C. Eaton, B. Otto, *H. Burgener.* **NE Ridge.** Cross Pangman Glacier from Niverville Meadow to base of mountain. Ascend snow, then very rotten rock of ridge to gain upper snowfield. Angle left up steep snow to col SE of summit, between it and snow dome to S. Climb N over mixed terrain to top; 4–5 h (CAJ **3**-9).

2. E Face, July 1969, R. Hornby, P. Roxburgh. Route ascends face of S summit of Mount Dent (snow dome, 3210m). Climb lower third on right, then traverse left between 2 rock spurs and finish up left hand edge. Go N to main summit. RT, with descent by FA route, 18 h (CAJ **53**-74).

PANGMAN PEAK (3170m)
One km NW of Mount Dent, essentially its NW summit rising only 30m above intervening col.

FA 1952, R.C. Linck, *W. Perren.* **E Face.** Over Pangman Glacier from Niverville Meadow to foot of peak (3 h). Climb rock face immediately left (S) of main snow gully on peak. Route begins as a face climb but soon changes into a minor ridge. Rock for initial third is steep but firm; remainder less steep and loose (1½ h). Total time, 4½ h; descent by same route, 3 h. Traverse to Mount Dent appears feasible. Main snow gully, while less steep, is subject to falling stones and avalanches. North subsummits (Peony & Pangman 2) traversed in both directions by ACC parties in 1949. No difficulties. 12 h RT maximum from Niverville Meadow.

UNNAMED *(P2)* (2910m)
One Divide 2.5 km S of Bush Pass; highest point between latter and Pangman Peak.

FA July 1930, E. Cromwell, D. Duncan, A.F. Megrew, J.M. Thorington, *P. Kaufmann*. From Niverville Meadow, go up Pangman Glacier to col S of objective, from which **S snow** slopes are ascended to top. 3¾ h up (AAJ **1**-403).

2. E Ridge, July 1969, M. Foubister, W. Holzer. Sharp snow ridge; 5 h RT from Niverville Meadow.

3. N Face & N Ridge, July 1976, J. Cook, H. Kariel. Via Niverville Glacier to N of peak. Ascend glacier and then rock ridge to top. Descent by N ridge; 4½ h RT from Niverville Meadow (CAJ **60**-83).

MOUNT NIVERVILLE (2960m)

2 km ESE of Bush Pass; N of Niverville Meadow.

FA July 1941, J. Taylor, A.T. Wiebrecht, *E. Feuz Jr*. Via **SE ridge** over broken rock and gendarmes in 4 h from Meadow (CAJ **28**-52).

MOUNT GARTH (3030m)

One km S of Coronation Mountain.

FA July 1934, H.S. Kingman, J.M. Thorington, *R. Aemmer*. From tongue of Freshfield Glacier via S side of Garth–Coronation gully (bush and scree) to SE glacier. Ascend to Garth–Coronation col and climb N ridge (mixed) to summit. Ascent 6 h; descent 3 h (CAJ **22**-214).

CORONATION MOUNTAIN (3170m)

West angle between Forbes and Freshfield Brooks.

FA 1917, Boundary Survey. From camp at head of Forbes Brook, below Bush Pass, via **W ridge.**

2. E Ridge. July 1922, J.M. Thorington, *E. Feuz Jr*. As for Mount Garth to small glacier S of objective. Ascend ice and snow to ridge, the crest of which is followed to the summit. 7½ h RT from Freshfield tongue (CAJ **13**-67).

Conway Group

These are the peaks on the E of Freshfield Icefield bordering its E cirque. More than half are on the Divide which runs from Howse Pass SW to Mount Gilgit. The most common approach has been via the Freshfield Icefield, although Conway and Lambe Glaciers have been used on occasion.

Maps: 82N 10, 82N 15.

MOUNT LOW (3090m)
On Divide at SE head of E bay of Freshfield Icefield, between it and Cairnes Glacier.

FA July 1930, E. Cromwell, J.M. Thorington, *P. Kaufmann*. **SW Ridge.** Via Freshfield Icefield to Low–Barlow saddle. Easy ascent on snow and scree in less than one h. Can be combined with traverse of Mount Barlow; approx 10 h RT from Niverville Meadow (AAJ **1**-403).

MOUNT WHITEAVES (3150m)
On Divide at junction of ridge separating Cairnes and Lambe Glaciers.

FA July 1949, J. Bishop, D. Greenwell, E.R. LaChapelle, D.M. Woods. **NW Ridge & Traverse.** From Niverville Meadow via Freshfield Icefield to Whiteaves–Lambe col (4 h). Easy scrambling along ridge except for exposed 30m traverse on left (N) side (3 h). Descend by SW slopes to Whiteaves–Low col and Icefield (CAJ **33**-70).

MOUNT DE MARGERIE (3000m)
NE of Mount Whiteaves on ridge separating Cairnes and Lambe Glaciers.

FA July 1957, J.G. Kato, D.K. Morrison, J.F. Tarrant, as part of a traverse including Mount Termier (which see). From upper Lambe Glacier climb **E face** in 4 h. Descent can be made at N end of W face (rappel) to regain Lambe Glacier.

MOUNT TERMIER (2850m)

Two km ENE of Mount De Margerie on ridge separating Cairnes and Lambe Glaciers.

FA July 1957, J.G. Kato, D.K. Morrison, J.F. Tarrant. From camp at junction of Cairnes Creek with Blaeberry River, go up through bush along N bank of Cairnes Creek. When below Cairnes Glacier, ascend N along slide alder to rock face which is climbed to col between summits. SE summit is higher; 5 h from camp. Descend to Lambe Glacier by traversing NW summit. This latter route is probably a more reasonable way to climb the peak.

MOUNT LAMBE (3181m)

On Divide between Freshfield Icefield and heads of Lambe and Conway Glaciers.

FA 1918, Boundary Survey. From camp below Conway Glacier, ascend S bay of glacier to Lambe–Solitaire col from which peak is easily attained.

A lesser point (3000m) 1.5 km NE of Mount Lambe was climbed in 1949 by A. Melville and ACC party of 5 from Freshfield tongue via Icefield and Lambe–Solitaire col. 16½ h RT.

MOUNT CONWAY (3100m)

SW buttress of Howse Pass.

FA July 1930, E. Cromwell, J.M. Thorington, *P. Kaufmann*. **SW Ridge.** Gain the Conway Glacier and cross to small glacier on W slope of objective. Ascend snow to lowest point (2700m) of SW ridge. Follow it, encountering moderate rock pitches, most of which can be turned on the W flank. Ascent from W glacier, 3 h. Descent can be made by ribs and gullies of W face to regain glacier (AAJ **1**-335).

2. NE Ridge, July 1949, E. LaChapelle, S. Evans, D. Greenwell, V. Novack, S. Merler, M. Sylvander, D. Wessel. From Howse Pass, follow Divide SW. Some steep snow before E shoulder, but no major obstacles thereafter along crest to top. 11 h up.

SOLITAIRE MOUNTAIN (3270m)

Between Freshfield Icefield and Conway Glacier at head of latter.

FA August 1926, M.M. Strumia, *E. Feuz Jr.* Via Freshfield Icefield and then scree to col SE of peak. Climb **SE ridge** over steep, slabby rock to summit. RT, 10½ h from Freshfield tongue (App **16**-540).

MOUNT BERGNE (3175m)

At W head of Conway Glacier; 4 km ESE across Freshfield Glacier from Niverville Meadow.

FA 1918, Boundary Survey. From camp below Conway Glacier via glacier and upper névé.

2. SW Slope, 1952, M.E., R.C. & R.E. Linck, *W. Perren.* From Niverville Meadow cross Freshfield Glacier and ascend gradual slopes on SW side to col near S peak. It is possible to continue by the ridge, but more interesting to climb steep rock on left to S summit from which main summit is quickly reached. Ascent 5 h; descent 3 h.

MOUNT SKENE (3060m)

S of Freshfield tongue; one km NE of Mount Bergne.

FA July 1930, E. Cromwell, D. Duncan, A.F. Megrew, J.M. Thorington, *P. Kaufmann.* From Freshfield tongue ascend conspicuous gully leading to col between objective and Mount Strahan (3½ h). Summit is easily gained over snow and scree of **NE slopes** in one h more (AAJ **1**-335).

2. N Slope, July 1949, A. Graham, K. Jefferson, D. Lewis, D. Young. From Niverville Meadow to base of gully N of peak (one h). Ascend scree to a series of icy couloirs which lead to notch in summit ridge NE of peak. NE slope is taken for final 300m.

MOUNT STRAHAN (3060m)

NE peak of ridge between Freshfield and Conway Glaciers.

FA July 1930, D. Duncan, A.F. Megrew. **SW Slopes.** As for Mount Skene to intervening col, then easily via SW slopes in less than one h (AAJ **1**-335).

2. W Face, July 1949, V. Novack, S. Merler, D. Wessel. A variant of above in which gully is left at 2400m rather than being taken to Skene–Strahan col. 5½ h up.

The sun as it fell on the mountain was far brighter here than in the plains below, because a smaller extent of atmosphere lay between the summit of the mountain and the sun.

L. da Vinci

On narrowness stand, for sunlight is/Brightest only on surfaces. No anger, no traitor, but peace.

W. H. Auden

UNMISTAKABLE UPLIFT

FORBES–LYELL GROUP

Here are included the compact cluster of peaks surrounding Mount Forbes, the seventh elevation of the entire Canadian Rockies, as well as summits lying on or near the Divide from Bush Pass N to Mount Lyell. Howse River and its tributary, Forbes Creek, bound the group on the E and S, while Arctomys Creek, a tributary of the N Saskatchewan, limits it on the NE. The principal E drainage, however, is by Glacier River, roughly midway between Forbes and Arctomys Creeks. For reasons of access, peaks well W of the Divide—Bush Mountain, etc.—are treated elsewhere.

There are two extensive icefields. The Mons system is bounded on the W by the Divide, although over-topping it in the area between Mons Peak and Division Mountain. This icefield drains entirely to Glacier River, being joined by the W and N Forbes Glaciers. The Lyell Icefield, some 50 sq km in extent, discharges W to tributaries of Bush River and E to Glacier River and Lake. Glacier Lake and River were discovered in 1858 by Dr Hector of the Palliser Expedition. A camp below this main drainage tongue, the SE Lyell Glacier, is the favorite starting point for climbing Mounts Forbes and Lyell and other peaks in the area. Besides these two major systems, there are smaller glaciers to the S and E of Mount Forbes.

ACCESS

The trail on Howse River provides an approach to the S side of Mount Forbes (Forbes Creek) and peaks in the vicinity of Bush Pass. See introduction to Freshfield Groups. After fording Freshfield Creek, cross Forbes Creek also. The trail on its N bank peters out beyond Alpland Creek but the bushwhacking is not unreasonable.

Glacier Lake is the most accessible and most logical base camp in the group. Leave the Banff–Jasper Highway 0.5 km W of Saskatchewan Crossing Store (inconspicuous trail sign). Cross the river on a wooden footbridge and take the excellent trail to and along the Lake. The best campsite ("Glacier Lake Camp") is some 4 km beyond the Lake. Total distance about 16 km; half a day from the highway.

To Mons Glacier. Glacier River must be crossed to its S side and then Mons Creek to its N side as well. This is best done in the valley flats. Ascend slopes toward prominent tree-covered knob, bearing left until it is passed. Then go straight up to a moraine whose crest is followed until it peters out below a buttress on W side of Mons Glacier. An old goat trail leads right, then back left, to the base of the buttress, going around left under the buttress. Drop a short distance onto the Mons Glacier. To reach Forbes Bivouac, cross dry glacier to E to small lake below tongue of Forbes N Glacier. 3–4 h from Glacier Lake camp.

To Lyell Icefield. The SE Lyell Glacier has receded drastically and is now inaccessible. Follow a good trail from Glacier Lake camp along N bank of river. Mount N lateral moraine, following it for nearly 2 km. The trail then cuts up steeply

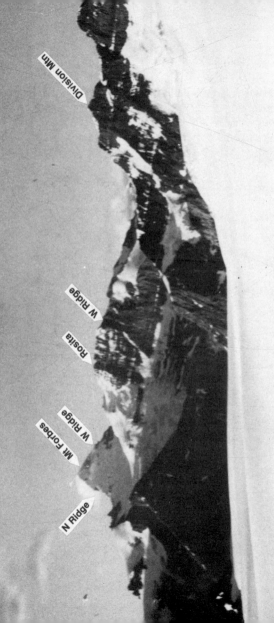

Division Mtn

W Ridge

Rosita

W Ridge

Mt Forbes

N Ridge

FORBES GROUP FROM LYELL ICEFIELD

H. Kruszyna

through timber, gaining rapidly some 500m of elevation. Dip
down to meadows along the creek S of Arctomys Peak and
ascend meadows and talus to slopes below Arctomys. A good
campsite can be found near timberline (Lyell Bivouac); 3 h
from Glacier Lake camp. Above, ascend lower slopes of Arctomys to near W summit, then traverse left (W) to a saddle
through which the Lyell Icefield is gained. Ascend Icefield
initially along N margin, then in center.

Maps: 82N/15W, 82N/14E.

MOUNT DAVID (2780m)
3 km N of intersection of Forbes and Freshfield Creeks.
FA July 1949, ACC parties, easily via **S slopes** from camp
below Freshfield Glacier. 8 h RT.

MOUNT OUTRAM (3240m)
4 km S of inlet end of Glacier Lake.
FA July 1924, F.V. Field, W.O. Field, J. Harris, *J. Biner, E.
Feuz Jr.* From Howse River, go up N bank of creek, draining
Sir James Glacier and reach summit by **SE slopes.** Variations
have been made. 6-7 h up (App **16**-152).

UNNAMED (SE 3090m; NW 3060m)
2.5 km W of Mount Outram; E head of East (Forbes) Glacier.

GOLDEN EAGLE PEAK (3060m)
A nob on long SW ridge of Mount Forbes, 1.5 km S of latter.
No record, but it surely has been climbed.

MOUNT FORBES (3612m)
A striking peak that is prominently seen from many parts
of the range. The normal route, the NW Face and the N Ridge
all are well worth climbing.
FA July 1902, J.N. Collie, J. Outram, H.E.M. Stutfield, G.M.

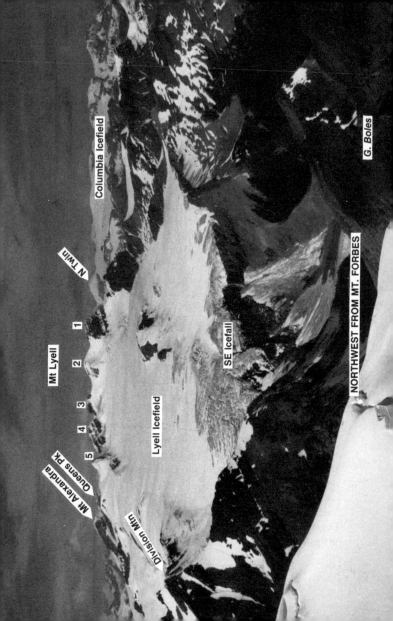

Columbia Icefield

N Twin

1

Mt Lyell

2

3

4

5

Mt Alexandra

Queens Pk

Lyell Icefield

Division Mtn

SE Icefall

G. Boles

NORTHWEST FROM MT. FORBES

Weed, H. Woolley, *C. Kaufmann, H. Kaufmann.* **SW Ridge.** A long, demanding and occasionally loose climb not often repeated. It is facilitated by a bivouac at timberline, reached from Forbes Creek by following up the stream which drains the cirque between the SE and SW ridges. Gain foot of ridge over scree and glacier. Follow the narrow and jagged ridge, turning certain steps to the right (E), to reach the false peak (3450m) where the **SE ridge** joins (6 h from bivouac). Here the ridge becomes more difficult and exposed, some upright cliffs being taken directly as there is scant chance of bypassing them. The final one is the most difficult, beyond which a very narrow, rotten causeway leads to the snowy summit. 10–12 h from bivouac (AJ **21**-370; CAJ **12**-30; Collie-277; Outram-345).

2. W Ridge (normal route), July 1926, A.J. Ostheimer, M.M. Strumia, J.M. Thorington, *E. Feuz Jr.* From Glacier Lake camp to Mons Glacier which is crossed toward Forbes N Glacier. Below tongue is the Forbes Bivouac beside a small lake (ca 2280m, 3–4 h from camp). Ascend N Glacier to base of mountain. The route of choice lies initially on the snow on right side of NW face, angling up and right to join ridge at rock bands approximately halfway up ridge. Continue on ridge to top. The ridge can be followed throughout by climbing through lower cliff bands to W col. 6–8 h RT from bivouac. The climb can be done directly from Glacier Lake camp in about 15 h RT (CAJ **16**-145).

3. NW Face. August 1971, C. Jones, J. Lowe, G. Thompson. As for normal route to foot of peak. The climb goes directly up the center of the face and is recommended as a moderate ice route. 3 h from foot of face; NCCS III (CAJ **55**-87).

4. N Ridge, July 1930, E. Cromwell, *P. Kaufmann.* A little-known route considered first-rate by FA party. Follow normal route to col between N ridge and conspicuous pinnacles to N. Turn the first rock tower on left (E), above which a couloir descending to E Glacier forces a detour on NE face. Climb the last prominent gendarme on left (E) side and take final snow ridge to top. 4 h from col (AAJ **1**-403).

5. SE Ridge. August 1967, W. Holzer, M. Muzzy, *H. Schwarz.* From Forbes Brook ascend E side of Alpland Creek to bivouac near 2200m. Ascend over scree to base of ridge which is followed to junction with SW ridge at false peak. FA route thereafter. 12 h, bivouac to summit.

UNNAMED *(F1)* (2780m)
UNNAMED *(F2)* (2940m)
   3 and 2 km, respectively, NW of Mount Forbes. Training climbs done from Forbes N Glacier by S ridges. 9–10 h RT from Glacier Lake camp (CAJ **49**-187).

UNNAMED *(F3, Rosita)* (3270m)
   2 km W of Mount Forbes; between Forbes N and W Glaciers.
   FA July 1940, R. Bosworth, D.M. Woods and one other. By the usual N Glacier route to Mount Forbes, ascending to W col. Turn W and ascend **NE snow slopes.** 11–13 h RT from Glacier Lake (AAJ **4**-312).
   2. W Ridge, July 1965, L.F. Andrews, H. Gilman, R. Kruszyna, R. Seale. From Glacier Lake camp to Mons Glacier. Gain crest from NW over snow, scree and a steep slab. Follow ridge, a series of short pitches, to top (8 h). Traverse and descend by Route One. 14 h RT; NCCS II, F4. Interesting climb (CAJ **49**-196).

UNNAMED *(F4)* (3150m)
   2 km WSW of Mount Forbes at S head of W Glacier.
   FA July 1965, S. Bezruchka, J. Caldwell, P. Hutchins, W. Joyce, A. Kirn, D. de Montigny, D. Payne, R. Scholes, A. Warnicki. From Glacier Lake camp to Mons Glacier. Ascend Forbes W Glacier to col NE of peak. Climb rock of **NE ridge,** traversing right into 10m chimney which provides key to summit ridge. Descent via W ridge; 8½ h up, 5 down (CAJ **49**-194).

CAMBRAI MOUNTAIN (3134m)
MESSINES MOUNTAIN (3100m)
ST. JULIEN MOUNTAIN (3090m)

These 3 minor summits lie on a W arc of the Divide at the S head of Mons Icefield, 4 to 6 km N to NW of Bush Pass. They are usually climbed in combination from Glacier Lake camp or, better, the Forbes bivouac.

FA of all 3, July 1930. D. Duncan, A.F. Megrew. Ascend Mons Glacier across foot of Forbes W Glacier to upper icefield. Go S close under rocky spur bounding névé on E. Ascend Cambrai by N or **NW ridge** (4½ h from bivouac). Descend to Cambrai–Messines col and climb latter by **E ridge** (2 h). Descend same way and bypass Messines on névé. Climb. St. Julien via **NE face** (2 h). 10 h RT from bivouac; 12–14 h from Glacier Lake (AAJ **1**-338; CAJ **49**-188).

VALENCIENNES MOUNTAIN (3150m)

3 km NW of Bush Pass at head of Mons Creek.

FA July 1934, H.S. Kingman, J.M. Thorington, *R. Aemmer.* From camp on Forbes Brook to Divide, which is followed NW to col E of objective. Climb **ESE ridge,** overcoming steep 100m buttress, to summit snow. 5 h up, 3½ h down (CAJ **22**-215).

ZILLEBEKE MOUNTAIN (3000m)

6 km W of Bush Pass in E angle between Icefall Brook and Valenciennes River.

ARRAS MOUNTAIN (3090m)

8 km WNW of Bush Pass in E angle between Icefall Brook and Valenciennes River.

MONS PEAK (3083m)

On Divide at W head of Mons Icefield; 7 km W of Mount Forbes.

FA July 1902, J. Outram, *C. Kaufmann*. Cross Mons Icefield to N base of peak and ascend snow of **NE ridge.** The final slopes of the summit pyramid are steep and often iced. It is also possible to go higher on the névé below the E face and reach the ridge by a snow ramp leading up right; fewer crevasses. 11–13 h RT from Glacier Lake; NCCS II (App **10**-209; CAJ **27**-180; Outram-311).

2. S Ridge, July 1965, B. Fraser, R. Matthews & ACC party. Ascend Mons Icefield to lowest col on Divide S of objective. Scramble the ridge, 1.5 km long, to summit. 12–14 h RT from Glacier Lake; NCCS II, F3. Descent can be made down NW ridge, circling across easy snow to NE ridge and then descending SE snow ramp to Icefield (CAJ **49**-189).

DIVISION MOUNTAIN (3030m)

At head of Glacier River, separating Mons and SE Lyell Glaciers. Numerous route variants, especially on lower E peak.

FA unknown. Ascend Mons Glacier and Icefield to glacial valley on SW side of main peak. This is the 2nd valley to W, just across Divide. From its head, a short rock scramble leads to top.

2. NW Ridge, 1973, D. Forest, J. Howes, C. Waddell. As above, but continue on to 3rd valley, from which ridge is attained. Thereafter 5 pitches of F4 rock to summit. Ascent 7 h; descent 4 h.

EAST PEAK (3000m)

FA 1918, Boundary Survey. Go up scree and subsidiary glacier of 1st valley. Gain broad col immediately S of peak and climb loose rock of S ridge to top. 10–12 h RT from Glacier Lake (CAJ **49**-189).

2. E Ridge. Before reaching Mons Glacier tongue work W up scree to level part of ridge. Rock ridge is followed throughout. NCCS II, F4.

UNNAMED (3150m)

Between Glacier Lake and Arctomys Creek, 1.5 km ENE of Mount Erasmus. Prominently seen from highway.

FA June 1951, F.D. Ayres, A.E. Creswell. **S Face.** The valley between objective and Survey Peak is approached either by a difficult ford of Saskatchewan River 5 km N of the crossing, or by following Glacier Lake trail and contouring into the valley. Take N shoulder of valley which leads to scree and snow slopes on S side of objective. Climb a long snow-filled couloir in the middle of S face; better early in season. Ascent from highway, 13 h; descent 5 h (CAJ **34**-38, photo; **35**-157).

MOUNT ERASMUS (3265m)

Highest point between Glacier Lake and Arctomys Creek.

Peter Erasmus, Dr. Hector's Indian guide, was the last survivor of the Palliser Expedition.

FA July 1950, F.D. Ayres, J.C. Oberlin. **W Face.** Approach from Glacier River about one km above inlet to Lake. Work up through dense forest into hanging valley between Erasmus–Sullivan ridge and Unnamed 2810m to E, where a camp can be placed (one day from highway). Ascend to obvious saddle (2530m) and turn left (NW) up improbable goat trail which leads to Erasmus–Sullivan ridge. Follow ridge until it is possible to traverse under W cliffs of objective on scree-covered terraces. Route utilizes major cleft in face consisting of 2 narrow couloirs. Start in right (S) one, sometimes climbing on separating rock fin, and eventually finishing in left one. Some iron used on FA. Ascent 11 h; descent 6 h (CAJ **34**-37).

UNNAMED (2810m)

Rock peak 3 km SE of Mount Erasmus.

FA July 1950, F.D. Ayres, J.C. Oberlin. From camp as for Mount Erasmus, climb **S talus** slopes (CAJ **34**-38).

SULLIVAN PEAK (3022m)

2.5 km SW of Mount Erasmus on divide between Glacier River and Arctomys Creek. John W. Sullivan was the astronomer with the Palliser Expedition.

FA 1940, ACC party. **S Slopes.** Approach from Glacier River up gully to SW of peak. Then head NE from top of gully to summit ridge. Uninteresting. 9 h RT.

UNNAMED (2730m)

High point 2 km W of Sullivan Peak along ridge to Arctomys Peak. Of historic interest as it appears to be mountain ascended on September 13, 1858 by Dr. James Hector and Robert Sutherland—in moccasins! This marked the 2nd alpine ascent in the annals of Canadian mountaineering, accomplished without even the primitive equipment of that day.

ARCTOMYS PEAK (2793m)

Between SE Lyell Glacier and head of Arctomys Creek.

FA 1918, Boundary Survey. From Glacier Lake follow the approach to Lyell Bivouac. Easily climb S slopes to round peak on W and so up **W ridge** to top. The more interesting E ridge can also be climbed, the E–W traverse making a pleasant day. 8 h RT from Glacier Lake camp.

MOUNT LYELL

This massif, at the N head of the Lyell Icefield, has five distinct summits separated by cols of approximately 100m depression. The formerly numbered peaks were named in 1972 in honor of the Swiss guides Rudolf Aemmer, Edward, Ernest and Walter Feuz, and Christian Häsler (CAJ **58**-43). The best approach is from Lyell Bivouac; about 5 h to base of peaks, one h additional to any summit. Peaks 1, 2 and 3 are commonly climbed as a traverse as follows: Peak 1 from 1–2 col; return to col; Peak 2 from 1–2 col; descend to 2–3 col;

ascend Peak 3 and return to 2–3 col. Allow 1 h between summits.

RUDOLPH PEAK *(1)* (3507m)

1.2 km NE of Divide summit.

FA July 1926, A.J. Ostheimer, M.M. Strumia, J.M. Thorington, *E. Feuz, Jr.* **S. Ridge.** From Lyell Icefield to 1–2 col and along ridge (CAJ **16**-142).

EDWARD PEAK *(2)* (3514m)

0.7 km NE of Divide summit; highest point of massif.

FA July 1902, J. Outram, *C. Kaufmann.* Simply up **W ridge** from 2–3 col. (FA party approached from Alexandra River via E Alexandra Glacier; see Farbus Mountain).

2. E Ridge, July 1926, Thorington party (above). On traverse from 1–2 col (CAJ **16**-142).

ERNEST PEAK *(3)* (3511m)

On the Divide.

FA July 1926, Thorington party (above). Gain 2–3 col and circle N, crossing a bergschrund before ascending steep **N snow** slopes (CAJ **16**-143).

WALTER PEAK *(4)* (3400m)

0.5 km S of Divide peak.

FA July 1927, D. Duncan, T. Lynes, J. Simpson, *Ern. Feuz.* **S Ridge.** FA party reached 4–5 col by circling S and W of Peak 5, a route now thought impassable because of glacial change. The 4–5 col has been reached directly from the Icefield, but avalanche danger is high on this E approach. From col ascend corniced snow and rock pinnacles above to summit. II F4 (Harvard **1**-60).

2. N Ridge, July 1940, E.R. Gibson and ACC party. Cross Icefield to 3–4 col. The ridge has a rock step and cornices may be encountered higher up. Route of choice.

CHRISTIAN PEAK *(5)* **(3390m)**

1.5 km S of Divide peak.

FA July 1926, Thorington party (see Rudolph). **S Ridge.** From icefield to S shoulder, then by steep snow (CAJ **16**-144).

2. N Ridge, 1973, J.K. Fox, J. Larson, D. MacFarlane. From 4–5 col, the narrow snow ridge and two rock pitches lead to top. (FA party reached col by S–N traverse of Peak 5).

The river had the right of way . . . the river preserved its level but the mountains were lifted up . . . the river was the saw which cut the mountains in two.

J.W. Powell, 1879

I have in vain endeavored to procure accurate maps but have been obliged to makeshift with such sketches as I could trace out from my own observations and that of gentlemen around me.

G. Washington, 1778

OPEN COUNTRY

CLINE GROUPS

This large area, N of the David Thompson Highway and E of the Banff–Jasper Highway, is in turn bounded on the E by the Plains and on the N by Nigel Creek and the Brazeau River. The western portion is in Banff National Park while the eastern part is partially within the disputed boundaries of the White-goat Wilderness, the remainder being Alberta Forest Reserve.

The area can be conveniently split into four groups. The Cline Range, S of the Cline River and E of Sunset Pass; Cataract Group, N of Sunset Pass and W of McDonald Creek; Job Creek Group, being the western half of the First Ranges and the Bighorn Group, the eastern half of the First Ranges. Mount Cline is the highest peak, the entire region being on the Alberta watershed.

The earliest comprehensive chronicler of this region was James Carnegie, Earl of Southesk, who traversed several of the passes in the frontal ranges in 1859 and recorded much of the history of exploration, from Joseph Brazeau and others, in his book. This is the best single historical reference on these parts, although Coleman and Mrs. Schäffer as well give good data on some of the passes near the head of the Brazeau.

Passable trails lead up many of the lateral valleys in these ranges, but often these are not marked. However, the open nature of the forest makes travel quite easy, particularly for those who may have been brought up in the Interior Ranges. In years past a popular trail was from the Brazeau Valley by way of Job Creek and Pass descending on the S via Coral Creek (which becomes more confined in its lower reaches) to the Cline River and Kootenay Plain. Coleman, and Southesk before him, traversed the area via the Cline River and what is now called McDonald Creek. This was "Old Cline's Trail" and ran along what was once called Cataract River, a term now reserved for the headwaters fork flowing SE to join Cline River near Pinto Lake. A trail is currently maintained in Cline River Valley and over Sunset Pass. The trail is signed on the Banff–Jasper Highway 16 km N of Saskatchewan Crossing and ascends 700m to the pass in 8 km. Pinto Lake is another 5 km down the E side. The trail continues down the valley, eventually intersecting the David Thompson Highway along a N leg of the N Saskatchewan. Branch trails running N from the Cline River trail are not maintained.

Cline Range

Bounded by the Banff–Jasper and David Thompson Highways on the W and S, and Cline River and Sunset Pass to the N, this well-glaciated group is fairly easy of access. In addition to the good trail over Sunset Pass and along Cline River, there are game and minor hunting trails in many of the lateral valleys.

Maps: 83C1, 83C2.

MOUNT WILSON (3260m)
6 km NW of Saskatchewan River Crossing; extensively glaciated on N and E (Outram-331).

FA August 1902, J. Outram, *C. Kaufmann*. **N Ridge.** From Banff–Jasper Highway, approach via N bank of Rampart Creek, which lies N of objective. At large waterfall, cross stream and climb 100m rock bank into a lesser valley from which the N ridge of the massif may be gained. Cross to Wilson Glacier on the far side (6½ hours) and ascend to its head. Gain N ridge of main summit over snow and debris and follow snow crest to the top (3 hours) (App. **10**-210).

Variant. NE Slope, July 1927, J. H. Barnes, A. L. Castle, A. L. Castle Jr., *J. Simpson, R. Aemmer*. From a camp on upper Rampart Creek, ascend uncrevassed Wilson Glacier directly to base of N ridge, longer, but more straightforward than above.

2. S Ridge. August 1948, E. & G. Cromwell. From Saskatchewan Crossing go up a long gully to a notch in S ridge. Wilson Glacier once descended to this notch but has now greatly receded, necessitating a 300m loss of altitude in reaching a deep, glaciated trough. Ascend icefall to upper névé just E of main N–S ridge. Traverse the subsidiary S peak en route to main peak; 6 hours up. FA party completed traverse by descending N ridge. From N end of névé, it is possible to swing S and regain route of ascent. The traverse can also be done N to S (AAJ **7**-355; CAJ **33**-148).

3. SW Face. August 1967, F. Beckey, G. Thompson. A winding system of traverses near E edge of face leads to S spur and S summit. One bivouac. Approach up stream from David Thompson Highway.

Wilson Glacier provides a good ski ascent in winter to foot of N ridge. Access to glacier either by S ridge or *Owen* Creek (heavy timber). Summit ridge often icy; 14 hours RT via S ridge.

MOUNT CLINE (3361m)

Highest peak in area, midway between David Thompson Highway and Cline River.

FA July 1927, J. H. Barnes, A. L. Castle, A. L. Castle Jr. *J. Simpson, R. Aemmer*. Approach via W fork of Thompson Creek

(4 km E of Owen Creek along highway) to two small lakes at head of valley (6½ hours). Gain col to W of Mount Cline's SW outlier (Owen, 3120m) and pass it on glacier on NW side to reach SW ridge of objective. Follow the generally broad and easy ridge to the summit. There are two gaps, however: the first is crossed on a keystone lodged some 5m below; the second (70m beyond) overhangs slightly and is 2m across in its narrowest part. Ascent 7½ hours, descent 3 hours.

2. N Ridge. July 1981, B. Hart, O. Miskiw. Approach up N fork of Thompson Creek toward Cline–Resolute col. From col, go up snow and then an ice gully. Follow the ridge, most of the elevation being gained on moderate ice and fair rock. About 6 hours from Cline–Resolute col. Worthwhile route (CAJ **65**-88).

RESOLUTE MOUNTAIN *(Lion; Lioness)* **(3150m)**
A double peak rising out of glaciers 2 km E of Mount Cline.

FA August 1958, A. Hober, E. Hopkins, D.G. Linke. Ascend N fork of Thompson Creek from David Thompson Highway to the Cline–Resolute col, from which the notch between the two summits is easily gained. From here both the E (higher) and W summits can be climbed (CAJ **42**-45).

ELLIOTT PEAK **(2872m)**
Higher of the two summits in SW angle of Cline and N Saskatchewan Rivers. The NW summit is Sentinel Mountain, a landmark of early travellers. The combined ascent of the two peaks offers an enjoyable climb of moderate difficulty (up to F5) and reasonable duration (12–14 hours RT). 2.5 km SSW of Elliott Peak is a lesser crest (2690m) which was ascended in 1858 by Dr. Hector.

FRA, May 1976, B. Hart, O. Miskiw. From David Thompson Highway, traverse Dr. Hector's peak and ascend via **SW ridge** and W face.

2. NW Ridge. August 1979, C.G. Horne. On traverse from

Sentinel Mountain in 3 hours. Descent W via Elliott–Sentinel col.

SENTINEL MOUNTAIN (2600m)

FA October 1975, B. Hart, O. Miskiw. From Cline River tributary, ascend NW ridge, a series of short steps.

WHITE GOAT PEAKS (SW 3080m; C 3210m; NE 3150m)

4 km N of Mount Cline; the three peaks, with intervening cols, extend for more than 3 km (CAJ **42**-43 map). Shortest access to these peaks is up Thompson Creek from David Thompson Highway, (campground at highway) to cross col between Mounts Cline and Resolute, entering head of Shoe Leather Creek.

CENTRAL PEAK

FA August 1958, A. Hober, E. Hopkins, D. G. Linke. From timberline camp below headwall with waterfalls from glaciers N of Mount Cline. From the top of the main waterfall steep scree and snow leads to the col between SW and central peak. A large gully in a cliff band on the **W side** of the objective is ascended via a steep ridge between the gully and a large crack to S. Short pitches and scree to summit (CAJ **42**-43).

SE Ridge. August 1970, P. Ford, C. Smith. From upper Shoe Leather Creek climb scree to gain SE ridge, which is ascended to cliff band below summit. Traverse S until cliff band can be surmounted.

SW PEAK

FA August 1970, A. Daffern, P. Ford, C. Smith. From bivouac cave near small lakes at foot of E Cline Glacier via steep gully in black headwall to col between SW peak and Mount Cline. A long, tiresome scree traverse leads to **NW ridge,** then

Southwest Whitegoat Peak   Central Whitegoat Peak   Northeast Whitegoat Peak

NORTH FROM MT. CLINE

ascended, with three rock pitches and some scrambling to the
summit (CAJ **54**-88).

NE PEAK
   FA July 1980, M. Dahlie, P. Smith. **S Face/SW Ridge.** From
Shoe Leather Creek, ascend prominent snow couloir in S face
to scree ledge ⅓ of the way up. Traverse W to col between
Central Peak and objective. Follow SW ridge (F5) to final cliff
band. Reenter upper part of S snow couloir and ascend it to
a final rock pitch on E side of summit (CAJ **64**-91).
   2. E Face. July 1980, B. Hart, O. Miskiw. Approach via
Thompson Creek over Cline–Resolute col to camp by small
glacier below E face of objective. Ascend face on fair rock, with
some snow/ice, to N shoulder and scramble to summit. 10 hours
RT from camp (CAJ **64**-91).

UNNAMED (3125m)
   6 km E of junction of Alexandra and N Saskatchewan Rivers,
above N head of Rampart Creek.
   FA 1927, Topographical Survey.

UNNAMED (3060m)
   1.5 km NE of above, on Banff Park Boundary.
   FRA September 1976, F. Campbell, P. Vermeulen. From
Sunset Pass trail via SW col and ridge in 3½ hours.

MINSTER MOUNTAIN (3120m)
   7 km E of Pinto Lake; 9 km NW of Mount Cline.

Cataract Group

   These peaks, characterized by extensive shale slopes to the
SW and steep cliffs to the NE, rise on either side of Cataract
Creek and are bounded by Sunset Pass, the Banff–Jasper High-

way, Brazeau River and McDonald Creek. Access is (1) by
Sunset Pass to Pinto Lake and up Cataract Creek, or (2) by
Nigel Pass trail which leaves the Banff–Jasper Highway 4 km
SE of Sunwapta Pass, starting as the old road. It is 6 km to
Nigel Pass and less than a 250m climb. The trail descends
abruptly into the Brazeau valley, from which an old trail can
be traced SE over Cataract Pass (6 km) and along Cataract
Creek to Cline River (16 km more).

Note that Cline Pass is incorrectly marked on the provisional
83C2/W sheet, its correct position is on 83C3 at (998878). A
high pass (006885 on 83C2) immediately above and E of Cline
Pass leads into the W head of McDonald Creek.

Maps: 83C2, 82C3, 83C6, 83C7.

MOUNT COLEMAN (3135m)

East of N Saskatchewan River, opposite mouth of Alexandra
River; N buttress of Sunset Pass.

FA prior to 1907, A.P. Burwash (CAJ **1**-185). An easy ascent
from SW over scree and boulders from Sunset Pass trail in 5
hours. Can also be climbed over NW slopes or glacier from
valley with large lake to N. Splendid view of main watershed
peaks from Mount Lyell to Mount Columbia (CAJ **27**-45).

Winter Ascent. March 1970, P. Ford, G. O'Brien.

UNNAMED (3180m)

5.5 km NW of Mount Coleman; double peak 2 km S of Cirrus
Mountain at end of its high S ridge.

FRA September 1975, F. Campbell, W. Davis, P. Vermeulen.
Via **SW slopes** to S peak and then along S ridge to N peak
which is split by a chasm. 4 hours from camp by lake N of
Mount Coleman.

UNNAMED (3150m)

5 km N of Mount Coleman; 4 km ESE of Cirrus Mountain.

CIRRUS MOUNTAIN (3270m)

Between N Saskatchewan River and Huntington Creek (Cline River). One km to NE is a subsidiary snow peak (3210m) connected by an easy saddle.

FA August 1939, C. B. & H. J. Sissons. **S Ridge.** From the large lake draining Coleman Glacier, go N up a valley filled with broken rock to its end and across into the Huntington Creek drainage. Ascend to Huntington Glacier and cross it, keeping near cliffs to avoid crevasses. Gain ridge mostly on rock and follow it to summit. Ascent 8 hours, descent 4 hours (CAJ **27**-46).

UNNAMED *(Maierhorn)* (3240m)

3 km N of Cirrus Mountain at W head of Cataract Creek.

FA July 1974, W. Costerton, *F. Mair*. **SE Ridge.** From camp by stream W of objective, go up into cirque between objective and Cirrus Mountain and gain ridge over easy slabs. Follow the ridge, bypassing gendarmes on the E, to 100m wall blocking narrow ridge. Climb to a helpful ledge from which the top of the wall is reached. Then take gentle ridge to summit (CAJ **58**-87).

CHRISTIAN PEAK (NW 3134m; SE 3103m)

5 km NW of Cirrus Mountain; 2.5 km S of Cataract Pass.

NW PEAK

FA July 1940, L. Gest, P. Prescott, *C. Häsler Jr*. Leave highway above Panther Falls and work up through timber to W slopes of objective, to gain succession of towers forming **S ridge** (4 hours). Traverse around first tower on left (W) and continue over several towers. Before final tower, traverse right to avoid a cliff and regain ridge, following it to top. Ascent 7½ hours; descent 4½ hours (CAJ **27**-169).

SE PEAK
   FA July 1974, F. Chapple, F. Parker, *W. L. Putnam*. From
camp as for Maierhorn, via SW approach to **S ridge.** III.

UNNAMED (3060m)
   N buttress of Cataract Pass; 5 km E of Nigel Pass.
   FA July 1974. W. L. Putnam & party of 6. III

UNNAMED (3207m)
   3 km NW of Cline Pass at head of W fork of McDonald
Creek.
   FRA July 1974. W. L. Putnam & party of 6. III

AFTERNOON PEAK (3120m)
   5 km NNE of Cline Pass; NE of peak above. Incorrectly
located on 83C7, correct position is (017924). A point (2876m)
N of main summit was occupied as a survey point in 1927. One
of the rottenest peaks in the region, being composed of crumbling red sandstone.

UNNAMED (3120m)
   4.5 km E of Cataract Pass; 2 km NW of Mount Stewart.
   FA July 1974. W. L. Putnam & party of 6. III

MOUNT STEWART (3312m)
   6 km E of Cataract Pass; 12 km NW of Pinto Lake.
   FRA August 1957, F. Burnette, I. & L. Ortenburger, J.
Weicher. From camp on Cataract Creek, scramble SW face to
cliff band (which stopped Coleman in 1902), passing it on **SE
ridge.** Cairn but no record.

UNNAMED (3090m)
   3 km NE of Mount Stewart. Two summits with a third (3060m)
one km NNE. FA of latter, July 1974, W. L. Putnam & party
of 6. III

The remaining peaks in this area, between the southern sections of Cataract and McDonald Creeks, were given the name Cloister Mountains by Professor Coleman (Coleman-223).

MOUNT METAWAMPE (3090m)

4 km SE of Mount Stewart at W head of Berkshire Creek (next E from Cataract Creek).

FA August 1967, J. LaBelle, J. Stengle, H. D. & S. Stidham. From camp in Cataract Valley via cliffs and ledges of **W slope.** Some F3; 6½ hours up (App. **36**-630).

BERTRAM PEAK (3060m)

4.5 km ESE of Mount Stewart at E head of Berkshire Creek.

FA August 1967, LaBelle party (see Metawampe). From Cornice Peak (which see) by intervening ridge in one hour.

CORNICE PEAK (3180m)

6 km SE of Mount Stewart; E of Berkshire Creek.

FA August 1967, LaBelle party (see Metawampe). From camp in Berkshire valley via **SW slopes** to ridge SE of summit; then along ridge. Ascent 5 hours.

SLUMP MOUNTAIN (3090m)

3 km E of Cornice Mountain; prominent landslide on W slope.

FA August 1968, D. & J. P. Robbie, H. D. & S. Stidham. Ascend **W scree slopes** above "slump" to cliff band. Traverse around SE end and onto NE side where a 12m pitch gives access to the summit. 9 h RT (CAJ **52**-62).

UNNAMED (3120m)

One km NE of Bertram. Continuing along the ridge to the NE about 2 km is another peak (3060m).

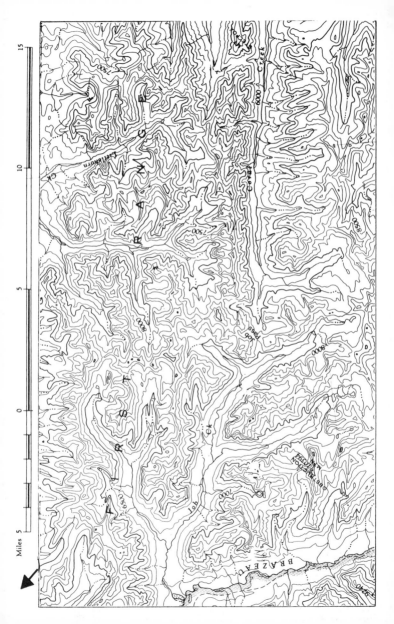

Job Creek Peaks

This little-visited area lies between McDonald Creek on the W and Coral and Job Creeks on the E. It is bounded on the S by the Cline River and on the N by the Brazeau. Best access is by Coral Creek (horse trail) crossing the watershed into the Job Creek drainage by Job Pass. The country is predominantly limestone, with numerous intermittent lakes and streams. Here and there a few summits are of interest, though the quality of the rock is generally poor and one is left with impossibly loose faces or easy scree scrambles. Glaciation is more extensive than the maps indicate. Good fossil country.

Maps: 83C2, 83C7.

UNNAMED (3060m)
9 km N of junction of McDonald Creek with Cline River (197875).

UNNAMED (3060m)
E of terminal forks of McDonald Creek; at W head of Coral Creek (123926).

UNNAMED (3090m)
Three interesting looking summits at the head of Job Creek (105952). Passes to N of these peaks give access to a valley with numerous lakes at the head of a W branch of Job Creek and to the McDonald Creek drainage (098964).

MOUNT FRANCES (2880m)
5 km SE of Mount McDonald in headwaters forks of McDonald Creek.
FA 1902, L. Q. Coleman, *alone,* via SW slopes (Coleman-224).

MOUNT MCDONALD (3116m)

At NW head of McDonald Creek; 8 km SE of Brazeau Lake.

UNNAMED (3090m)

4.5 km NE of Mount McDonald (073016).

OBSTRUCTION MOUNTAIN (3199m)

S angle between Brazeau River and Job Creek (079039).

UNNAMED (3060m)

An isolated summit 5 km E of Obstruction (133043).

HORSESHOE MOUNTAIN (3090m)

6 km SE of Obstruction Mountain, between forks of Job
Creek (122998).

FA August 1973, A. M. & G. M. Daffern. From camp below
Lightning Lake (123968) follow valley N to gain col between
the two summits.

Bighorn Range

East of Coral and Job Creeks is a remote and extensive area
of arid limestone peaks; the E half of the First Range.
Access is difficult and tedious, the best route probably being
Coral Creek and Job Pass.
There appears to be little good climbing apart from some of
the ridges just N of the David Thompson Highway, and
possibly the 2700m peaks on the NE side of Coral Creek.

Maps: 83C7, 83C8, 83C10.

MOUNT ABRAHAM (2820m)

A prominent peak 5 km W of Windy Point above Abraham
Lake. The SE ridge has two large steps and gives a good rock
climb which is in condition early in the season.

FA May 1973, A. M. Daffern, P. Ford. **SE Ridge.** From highway scramble up ridge to start of rock climbing. A small overhang and later a 50m traverse to the W are the keys to the first step. The second step is tackled direct until near the top where the difficulties are avoided by moving right until the ridge can be regained. After the second step the ridge degenerates into a series of pinnacles which are bypassed on the W. 13 hours from road. Descent by avalanche gully to the E (snow early in the season).

CORAL MOUNTAIN (3125m)
3 km E of Job Pass (3125m); at head of Bighorn River.
FA 1928, Topographical Survey.

UNNAMED (3120m)
8 km ESE of Coral Mountain; W of Littlehorn Creek (277966). A double peak with subsidiary to NE reaching 3090m.

UNNAMED (3060m)
3 km NE of Coral Mountain (218022).
FA August 1973, A. M. Daffern by way of **W Ridge.** Summit 2940m to the W also climbed.

UNNAMED (3090m)
A group of 4 rocky peaks 4.5 km N of Coral Mountain encircling a small glacier. Immediately to the NE are 3 summits of about 3050m and a further one 2 km NE (240083).
FA August 1973, Mr. & Mrs. A. M. Daffern from the S.

OPABIN MOUNTAIN (3097m)
At head of Opabin Creek (165167); 8 km E of mouth of Job Creek.

But the altars are behind and higher/Where the great hills raise their naked heads/Pale agonists in the reverbrance/of the pure air and the pitiless God.

R. Jeffers

BACKWATER

ALEXANDRA GROUP

Northwest along the Divide from Mount Lyell to Thompson Pass rises a spectacular escarpment whose cascading glaciers feed Alexandra River, a major tributary source of the North Saskatchewan. Set off to the E of the main uplift, in the S angle of the N Saskatchewan and Alexandra Rivers, is a secondary group dominated by Mount Amery. West of the Divide, bounded on the S by Lyell Creek and on the W by Bush River, is another ridge of lesser summits. This is one of the more scenic areas in the Rockies, offering splendid icefalls and flowered alps in abundance. However, although the routes are generally easy, once reached, approach is difficult and tedious.

ACCESS

Alexandra River. Formerly, this approach was used to climb Mount Alexandra and its nearby satellites, but glacial recession has made it less desirable. However, the head of Alexandra River does give access to the impressive NE cirque from Mount Lyell to Mount Spring Rice and the East Alexandra Glacier can be ascended to the Divide to reach Mounts Farbus and Oppy, and also Mount Lyell. The trail begins on the old road some 8 km N of the Alexandra–North Saskatchewan junction, just N of a group of vacant buildings on the W of the Banff–Jasper Highway. The road descends from a pullout at Coleman Creek (sign), crosses the river and goes about 6 km S before turning W up Alexandra River. The fire road continues 14 km up the river to near the confluence of Castleguard River. Cross the Alexandra to its S bank and then recross shortly beyond the Castleguard junction. Follow up the N bank, avoiding a canyon, to gravel flats and a glacial lake below the glacier snouts. Allow one long day from the highway.

To reach Mount Alexandra, etc., ascend the E Rice Glacier, outflanking the main icefall on outsloping, scree-covered ledges on the N, to gain Trident Col (2860m) and the S Rice Glaciers. This approach is not suitable for heavy backpacking, but for a fast party, lightly encumbered, with only one or two objectives in mind, it should not be discounted.

Thompson Pass–Rice Brook. This long, roundabout route is nevertheless probably the optimum way to place a climbing camp in the heart of the group. It also has the advantage of giving access to Mount Bryce along the way. Follow the Alexandra River approach to Castleguard River. The trail continues up the N bank of the Castleguard, the creek from Castleguard Meadows being crossed on a tree. Farther on, the trail splits, the right fork going up steeply over a hogback to W of creek from Meadows and then through bush to Castleguard Meadows, which lie in the valley between Castleguard and Terrace Mountains. The left fork soon presents a difficult ford of the creek draining Castleguard Glaciers, best made in early morning. The trail passes N of Watchman Lake, its continuation to Cinema Lake requiring close watching. 1½ days to Thompson Pass.

From the Pass, an ancient, indistinct trail (blazes) follows Rice Brook to the W for 5 km to near the junction of S Rice

Brook. Cross and bushwhack along the E bank of S Rice Brook, fording it at some flats. Then ascend alongside the branch to right of prominent waterfall to alplands, which are traversed to upper cirque below peaks. A hard day from Thompson Pass.

Bush River–Lyell Creek. As logging operations are extended up Bush River and its tributaries, this approach may soon become the route of choice. Check with B.C. Forest Service in Golden for current conditions. In 1976, it was possible to drive up Bush River as far as a washout at Goodfellow Creek, where a canoe was needed to regain the road one km beyond. Pack along road, which leads up into Lyell Creek valley. About one day to end of road. A horrible bushwhack along S bank leads to terminal forks in one day more. To place a camp at timberline on the N fork requires another half day. Mount Alexandra can then be climbed via the Alexandra–Whiterose col (CAJ **60**-25). The 1951 Hendricks party reached the same site from Glacier Lake via the Lyell Icefield; emphatically *not* recommended. They then packed over the Alexandra–Whiterose col to the upper cirque of S Rice Brook. In 1980, a small party helicoptered to upper S Rice Brook in 30 minutes from Golden. Not easy to get to!

LITERATURE

Wexler, Arnold. "Cross-Country Mountaineering in the Canadian Rockies." (CAJ **35**-115 (1952).

Maps: 82N14, 83C/2W, 83C3.

OPPY MOUNTAIN (3330m)

Next N of Farbus Mountain on Divide.

FA August 1947, R. Davis, J. C. Oberlin, D. M. Woods. **SE Ridge.** Traverse Farbus Mountain by its SE and N ridges. Ascend two shelves and then work up to near the left side of the prominent couloir/chimney which splits the final cliff from top to bottom. Cross couloir to right side at about mid-height and climb a series of easy ledges to snow slopes. Recross couloir near its head and go left to turn cornice at its weakest point. A long snow ridge leads to top. Ascent from head of Alexandra River, 11 h; descent 7 h (AAJ **24**-268, CAJ **31**-100).

2. W Ridge. From Douai (which see) over easy snow. Descent may be made to Lyell Creek by a ridge to W and a steep couloir.

DOUAI MOUNTAIN (3120m)

One km SE of Mount Alexandra.

FA July 1951, E. Cammack, S.B. Hendricks, D. Hubbard, J. Smith, A. Wexler. **E Ridge.** From camp on N fork of Lyell Creek go up moraine and talus to rock wall which guards the lower slopes of objective. Climb wall easily on left and continue directly up snow to broad col on Divide between Douai and Oppy. Pass the rock step on the ridge by an icy chimney to left. 5 h from Lyell Creek (AAJ **26**-251; CAJ **35**-119).

MOUNT ALEXANDRA (3388m)

Massive, brooding summit at head of Alexandra River.

FA August 1902, J. Outram, *C. Kaufmann*. **SW Slopes.** From a camp in upper cirque of S Rice Brook ascend bluffs below W Alexandra Glacier and gain same by a right to left zigzag. After reaching col at base of mountain, ascend simple SW snow slopes to summit. 7 hours up (Outram-400; CAJ **25**-25).

QUEENS PEAK (3350m)

N peak of Mount Alexandra; 0.5 km N of main peak.

FA July 1978, M. Dahlie, P. Smith. **N Ridge.** Gain W Alexandra Glacier, as above. Climb to Divide and ascend sharp, corniced crest, a traverse to W being required to outflank a rock buttress. FA party approached from E, up dangerous icefall of Alexandra Glacier, not recommended (CAJ **62**-90).

FRESNOY MOUNTAIN *(Consolation)* (3240m)

On Divide 2 km NW of Mount Alexandra; between E and S Rice Glaciers.

Queen's Peak

Mt Alexandra

MT. ALEXANDRA FROM WEST

R. Kruszyna

FA August 1902, J. Outram, *C. Kaufmann*. **N Ridge.** The ridge rises from Trident Col (see introduction), which is gained by either E or S Rice Glacier. A straightforward mixed climb. 1½ h from col (Outram-397).

2. SW Ridge. August 1961, B. DeVos, E. Hopkins, J. Mares, P. Payne, R.E. Scholes. Ridge rises from the col between Fresnoy and its 2940m outlier to SW, approached from S Rice or W Alexandra Glacier. Easy snow and rock lead to the top. 4½ h from S Rice Brook (CAJ **46**-68).

MOUNT SPRING RICE (3275m)

2.5 km N of Fresnoy Mountain across Trident Col.

FA August 1923, J. W. A. Hickson, *E. Feuz Jr*. **S Ridge.** From S Rice Glacier to Spring Rice–Queant saddle, from which easy snow leads to summit. 4½ h from S Rice Brook. Can also be approached via E Rice Glacier and Trident Col (CAJ **14**-6).

MOUNT AMERY (3329m)

Massive, fortresslike mountain in SW angle between Alexandra and N Saskatchewan Rivers.

FA August 1929, L. S. Amery, B. Meredith, *E. Feuz Jr*. **W Face.** After fording Alexandra River, work up Amery Creek. The route goes up the most broken section of the buttresses that lie on the face, where detours are used to bypass difficulties. The exact line is unclear from the description of the first and apparently only ascent. The route finishes on crest S of actual summit (CAJ **18**-3).

UNNAMED (3120m)

3 km S of Mount Amery along its crest, with a ridge extending E, 3 points of which exceed 3000m.

FA of most easterly of above, a rock pinnacle (3060m), July 1981, M. Dahlie, P. Smith. **N Face/N Ridge.** From near Sunset Pass turnoff on Banff–Jasper Highway, ford N Saskatchewan and go up creek leading toward objective. Initially the route

goes up the prominent snow/ice couloir splitting the N face.
Exit right on terraces and ascend to deep cleft on N side of
summit block. Pass through cleft and finish climb on N ridge
and NW face. Excellent F6 climbing near top (CAJ **65**-87).

MOUNT WILLERVAL (3180m)

4 km WSW of Mount Amery across Amery Creek.

FA July 1951, F. D. Ayres, A. E. Creswell. Leave Alexandra
River trail and ford river above junction with Amery Creek.
Bushwhack up Amery Creek and follow valley to head of
cirque. From upper end of scree slopes, work along narrow
ledges to reach hanging glacier between Mounts Willerval and
Monchy. Climb it to col between them. Route then traverses
completely under **W flank** of summit edifice to gain a snow
saddle joining N corner of summit to subsidiary tower on NW.
Pass through saddle and ascend a broken area to snowfields
and so to summit, the route having almost completely circled
the mountain. An approach from Ridges Creek may be preferable. 13 h up from Amery–Alexandra junction; 5 down (CAJ
35-40).

MOUNT MONCHY (3210m)

1.5 km S of Mount Willerval; a double summit with one km
long crest exceeding 3100m. S summit named **Mount Hooge.**

FA July 1948, F. D. Ayres, J. C. Oberlin, D. M. Woods. **E
Slopes and S Ridge.** As for Mount Willerval to hanging glacier.
Cross it to SE and traverse ledges to reach long, hanging glacier
on N side of objective. Continue E along glacier and climb to
saddle on S Ridge which leads easily to summit. 10 h up from
camp on Amery Creek; add approximately 2 h from Alexandra
River (CAJ **32**-16).

FARBUS MOUNTAIN (3150m)

On Divide 2 km NW of Mount Lyell; at head of E Alexandra
Glacier.

FA July 1937, E. R. Gibson, S. B. Hendricks. **SE Ridge.** From a camp at head of Alexandra River ascend the E branch of Alexandra Glacier to the Farbus–Lyell col in 4½ h. In the narrow upper section of the glacier, there is danger from avalanching ice cliffs of N Lyell Glacier and the summit mass of Farbus. Follow easy quartzite ridge to summit. Total time, about 9 h (AAJ **10**-151; CAJ **25**-98).

2. N Ridge. A steep, corniced snow ridge descended and reascended en route to Oppy Mountain, which see.

QUEANT MOUNTAIN (3120m)

One km SW of Mount Spring Rice, rising from S Rice Glaciers.

FA August 1937, K. Gardiner, L. Gest, *E. Feuz Jr, C. Häsler.* As for Mount Spring Rice to saddle, then take sharp **N ridge** (snow) to summit. One h from saddle (CAJ **25**-24).

UNNAMED *(Rice East, Turret Peak)* (3060m)

2 km NE of Mount Spring Rice on Divide.

FA August 1902, J. Outram, *C. Kaufmann.* **S Ridge.** An uncertain, improbable route from Trident Col, skirting under the SE cliffs of Mount Spring Rice. Not repeated, nor recommended. The variant below is to be preferred.

Variant, August 1972, J. K. Fox, R. A. Lambe, D. R. DeMontigny. From a camp at head of Alexandra River, gain the rocky **S ridge** over ice and moraines of E Rice Glacier. Generally easy climbing, the final 100m being rather more difficult. 17 h RT.

2. W Slopes. 1918, Boundary Commission. From Thompson Pass over shale and easy ledges (Outram's descent route) (ABC **2**-51).

WATCHMAN PEAK (3009m)

SE buttress of Thompson Pass.

FA 1918, Boundary Commission, via **W scree slopes**; 3 h (ABC **2**-51).

MOUNT WHITEROSE (3060m)

3 km SW of Mount Alexandra at S head of S Rice Brook.

FA 1918, Boundary Commission. Approach as for Mount Alexandra, gaining glacier on **N slopes** of objective. Easy snow to summit; variations possible. 8 h RT from camp near head of S Rice Brook (ABC **2**-60).

COCKSCOMB MOUNTAIN (3180m)

A crenellated N–S ridge with several lesser summits; 5.5 km SW of Mount Whiterose.

FA July 1951, E. Cammack, S. B. Hendricks, D. Hubbard. **N Ridge.** From camp at head of S Rice Brook go W over alps and a flat glacier to a low saddle overlooking the W fork of Lyell Creek. Swing around this valley and gain glacier at base of minor peak N of objective. Ascend to divide overlooking Bush River and pass minor peak by a ledge system on its W side. From col climb a yellow cliff band and take snow ridge to top. Good route. 9 h up; 7 h down (AAJ **8**-252).

Glaciers fulfill three purposes. They polish rocks, supply ice to hotels and provide chasms for tourists to tumble into.

E. Whymper

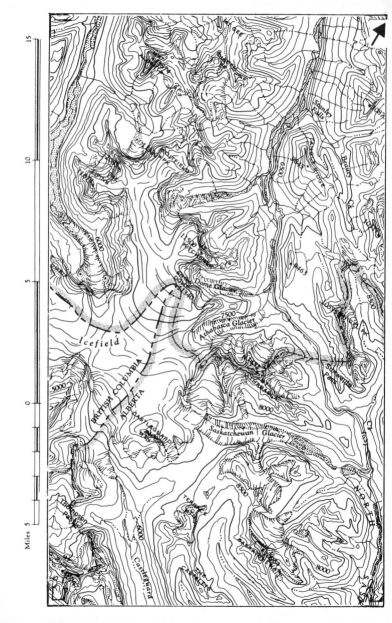

APEX OF AMERICA

COLUMBIA ICEFIELD GROUP

Included in this group are fully one fourth of the 50 highest peaks in the Canadian Rockies. Four of the 8 highest rise here, the others being widely scattered. The region offers excellent climbing of all grades on both rock and snow/ice, much of it readily accessible from the Banff–Jasper Highway. The S boundary of the group is Thompson Pass while the N limit is the confluence of the Athabasca and Sunwapta Rivers. On the W, the arbitrary division between this and the Chaba Group is the low glacial pass (2220m) on the Divide, connecting the W headwaters of Athabasca River with Wales Glacier and the N headwaters of Sullivan River.

The Columbia Icefield, occupying the central part of the group, including its subsidiary glaciers, is some 280km² in extent, the largest in the Canadian Rockies. Its discovery in 1898 by Collie and Woolley marked one of the great moments in North American mountaineering. "A new world was spread at our feet; to the westward stretched a vast ice-field probably never before seen by human eye, and surrounded by entirely unknown, unnamed, and unclimbed peaks." (Collie-107). The Icefield drains into 3 distinct watersheds: the Arctic (Athabasca River), the Atlantic (North Saskatchewan River), and the Pacific (Bush River). It is thus the hydrographic apex of the North American continent (see Snow Dome). The higher peaks of the group include Mounts Columbia and North Twin, the second and third elevations in the range, as well as such striking summits as Mounts Alberta, Bryce, King Edward and Athabasca. The N wing of this group, from the Twins N to the Athabasca–Sunwapta angle, is the Winston Churchill Range.

ACCOMODATIONS

There are no huts in the group, the former Saskatchewan Hut having sadly been undermined by the river. The most popular campsite among climbers is the Icefields Campground, located immediately E of the Icefields Chalet. It is well situated for day climbs in the vicinity of Mount Athabasca. However, it is often filled to capacity with tourists, especially in good weather. A new, larger campground a short distance down the road has not alleviated the crowded conditions. It is advisable to arrive early in the day and to investigate "doubling up" with other climbers.

APPROACHES

The following approaches to various parts of the group are listed from S to N and are referred to in the climbing descriptions. They represent the best known routes, but this is not to imply that some of them are not long, easy to lose, or involve wild river crossings.

Alexandra River. This gives access to Castleguard Meadows and Thompson Pass. For a detailed description, see under Alexandra Group.

Saskatchewan Glacier. An alternative to the Alexandra River and a generally preferred way to reach Castleguard Meadows or Thompson Pass. The trail starts from the highway at the

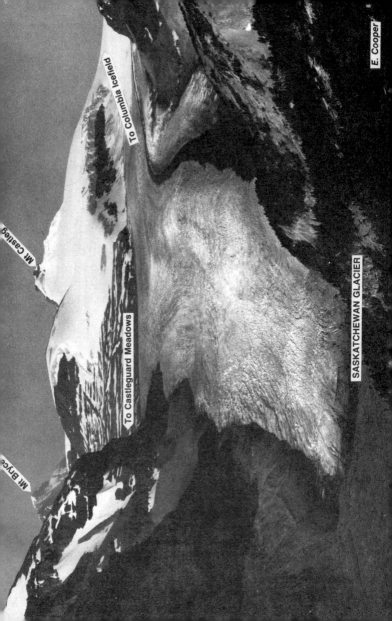

To Columbia Icefield

Mt Castleg

To Castleguard Meadows

Mt Bryc

SASKATCHEWAN GLACIER

E. Cooper

sweeping bend below (S) the long final climb to Sunwapta Pass,
and may be seen in the edge of the trees on the S side of the
bend. Leave cars on the old road that branches off at the S
end of the bend and which bridges the river. The trail goes
through the canyon where the Saskatchewan Glacier stream
emerges. When the trail peters out walk on moraine to the
glacier tongue. Leave the glacier after 5 km and follow flats of
black moraine to descend to Castleguard Meadows. To reach
Thompson Pass, stay on trail to W of creek emerging from
Meadows. Descend a hogback steeply to trail on Castleguard
River and difficult ford (see Alexandra River). Allow 6–8 hours
to Castleguard Meadows, a minimum of one full day to Thompson Pass if lightly encumbered.

Athabasca Glacier. Probably the most used of all approaches,
as it leads into the heart of the Icefield and the regular routes
on Mount Andromeda and the major Icefield peaks. Park at
snowmobile parking lot. The most common route in summer
crosses to the N side, toward Snow Dome, while in winter,
parties on skis usually travel up the center. Once on the Icefield,
a high camp is often placed on the S slopes of Snow Dome,
from which peaks such as Mount Columbia and the Twins are
readily approached.

Woolley Shoulder. This is the most commonly used approach at the N end of the Icefield. Although originally pi-
oneered as an approach to Mount Alberta, this route also gives
access to the N end of the Icefield and to peaks at the head of
Athabasca River such as Mounts Columbia and King Edward.
The canyon leading W to the 2900m Shoulder between Mount
Woolley and Unnamed (*Engelhard*) is the first major one some
5 km N of Tangle Creek. Ford the Sunwapta River opposite
the canyon, the place being marked by a small "island" of trees
immediately W of the highway. Follow a now well-trodden trail
along the S side of the creek to a vast morained basin (campsite
at last greenery). Hike NW to gain glacier descending from
saddle and follow its margin close under Mount Woolley. As-

cend tortuous scree and nasty cliffs to Shoulder. 7–8 hours from highway. For Mount Alberta, descend in NW direction to pass Little Alberta on N. To reach Athabasca River, descend SE to pleasant meadows and then drop down into the valley of Habel Creek, passing Little Alberta on the S. (While it is also possible to reach Habel Creek by passing Little Alberta on the N, the descent of the headwall is problematical.) Follow Habel Creek (occasional vestiges of ancient trail) to its junction with Athabasca River; a long day from highway. From the pleasant meadows mentioned above, one can round the head of Habel Creek and ascend the glacier flowing between the two peaks of Mount Stutfield, thus gaining the Icefield.

Gec–Nelson Col. This gives access to the mountains N of Diadem Peak and leads to pleasant campsites in the cirque surrounding the NW branch of Lynx Creek. The canyon mouth is opposite a viewpoint ("Sunwapta River") on the highway, where a sign points SW to Diadem Peak. Ford the Sunwapta near the viewpoint and work up the valley NE of Diadem Peak. After leaving timberline, moraine slopes lead to cliffs at the base of the high pleateau glacier that runs NW from Diadem Peak, eventually to terminate E of Gong Lake. Climb out of head of canyon on N side where cliffs are easiest. Travel NW on glacier for some 3 km and cross the 2700m col between Mounts Gec and Nelson. 500m of descent and a traverse W bring one to the NW fork of Lynx Creek where good campsites abound. Allow 2 full days from highway.

Athabasca River. This is the preferred approach to peaks in the Gong Lake area and a reasonable alternative to Woolley Shoulder as a way to reach peaks at the head of Athabasca River, such as Mounts Columbia and King Edward. The trail, initially in good condition, begins at the Sunwapta Falls canyon and follows the E bank of the Athabasca until it peters out near the confluence of Chaba River (13 km). For Gong Lake, continue some 2 km along the Athabasca, then bushwhack SE up to the lake (18 km from Sunwapta Falls, one day).

Mt King Edward

Mt Columbia

S Twin

N Twin

R. Kruszyna

HEADWATERS OF ATHABASCA RIVER FROM NORTH

It is feasible to continue along the E bank of the Athabasca using stretches of open gravel flats and occasional vestiges of ancient horse trail (exceptionally scenic). Some tedious bushwhacking around the junction of Lynx Creek. The junction of Habel Creek is some 35 km distant from Sunwapta Falls; 1½ days. While this approach is longer in time than Woolley Shoulder, it does not involve the gain and loss of 1300m of elevation, being essentially level. To reach the E headwaters under Mount Columbia, stay on the E bank. For the W vicinity of Mount King Edward, ford the Athabasca near the Habel Creek junction and follow gravel flats into the W headquarters. Recross at junction of stream from hanging valley W of Mount King Edward and ascend true right bank (E) of same through bush to King Edward Camp; a partial day from Habel Creek.

Athabasca Valley to the Icefields. Apart from actual climbs of peaks, there are three reasonable routes from the Athabasca Valley to the Icefields.

2220m Pass. This provides a route to the peaks S and W of Mount King Edward. It is reached from the W terminal fork of Athabasca River. The glacier at the head of the valley ("Toronto Glacier") is followed W and then S to the 2220m pass on the Divide; 4 hours from valley. From the Divide the Wales Glacier descends on the W.

King Edward–Triad Col. This is the broad saddle (2650m) on the Divide SW of Mount King Edward, and provides the usual approach to that peak and the W face of Mount Columbia.

Columbia Glacier. From the E headwaters branch, ascend glacier to near the Icefield, then break off left (NE) to rocks W of subsidiary glacier entering Columbia Glacier from the NW. Climb cliffs and later get onto the subsidiary glacier. This is emphatically *not* recommended as a connection from the Icefield to the head of Athabasca Valley, as the complex route is not evident from above.

Ski Mountaineering. The extensive Columbia Icefields are an ideal area for ski travel, with May being the most popular month for ski mountaineering. A camp is usually placed near the Snow Dome, from where the Twins, Stutfield, Kitchener, etc. are ski ascents (Mount Columbia probably requires ax and crampons.) Good conditions will often be found from February through June, and several climbers maintain that skis are the best means of travel even in the summer, although they have to be carried up the lower part of the Athabasca Glacier. At the present time alpine skis with bindings, such as Silvretta, are more usual than cross-country gear; if cross-country equipment is used, overboots should be carried as conditions can be harsh. In brief, cross-country equipment will generally allow easier travel, though mountain boots may have to be carried. As of this writing, alpine equipment is heavier but more dependable. It should be emphasized that skiing on the glacier demands the use of the rope at all times: there has been at least one fatality on the Athabasca Glacier recently due to skiing unroped.

Rock Climbing. South of Sunwapta Pass and close to the Banff–Jasper Highway are a number of short rock routes which can be done when the weather rules out the higher summits. Just N of the "big bend" in the highway (on gravel flats where the N Saskatchewan River comes in from the W) rises an extensive rock face on the S side of Parker Ridge. The original *Big Bend* route (F6) was climbed in 1971 by H. Fuhrer and D. White in 2 hours (CAJ **55**-88). Also in 1971, P. Charkiw and R. Kelly climbed *Dragonfly* (F6) in center face. Many other routes have since been done and additional possibilities still seem to exist. The rock is generally sound limestone. Farther S, on the E side of the highway, the **Weeping Wall** rises below Cirrus Mountain. *Stolen Beer* (F7, 5 pitches with rappel descent), 100m N of Weeping Wall parking lot, was climbed by S. Otto, D. Pors, and B. Tinge. Other possibilities exist on this cliff (CAJ **64**-90).

LITERATURE

The following articles contain a wealth of information, maps and photographs, giving a historical and physical feeling for the region.

Collie, J. N. "Climbing in the Canadian Rocky Mountains." AJ **19**-441 (1899). Discovery of the Columbia Icefield and various first ascents.

Ladd, W. S. & J. M. Thorington. "A Mountaineering Journey to the Columbia Icefield." CAJ **14**-34 (1924). First ascent of North Twin and other peaks.

Ostheimer, A. J. "From the Athabasca River to Tsar Creek." CAJ **16**-16 (1928). The account of an amazing 2 months, 1000 km, 25 first ascent trip!

Wilts, C. H. "First Ascents from Lynx Creek Valley." CAJ **35**-28 (1952). Best account of Lynx Creek peaks.

Maps: 82C5; 82C6; 83C3.

MOUNT BRYCE (SW 3507m; C 3370m; NE 3300m)

A magnificent, isolated massif with a sweeping N face; 5 km W of Thompson Pass. First two routes are approached by either Alexandra River or Saskatchewan Glacier.

FA July 1902, J. Outram, *C. Kaufmann*. **NE Ridge.** A classic route, highly recommended. The climb may be made from a camp at Cinema Lake, but because of its length, most parties prefer to start from a bivouac at the foot of the ridge (c 2800m). From Cinema Lake work W and then N up a boulder-strewn basin below the glacier on the E side of Mount Bryce, to the low point of the ridge, immediately S of the Divide (bivouac site, 3½ h). Climb ridge over mixed scree and snow to smooth gray buttress, which gives a good 25m pitch. Easier going over mixed terrain leads to the NE summit (4 h from bivouac). Descend to intervening col and climb central peak over mixed rock and ice (2 h). Repeat above to gain main SW summit. Return by same route, bypassing central peak on S névé. 17 h RT from bivouac (AJ **21**-464; Outram-412; CAJ **55**-39, detailed account).

Note: FA party bypassed central peak on S. Its FA was made from col between it and main peak, reached by Route 2 below, July 1961, S. Bucher, R. Fierz, J. G. Kato (CAJ **45**-12). First complete traverse, August 1971, G. Boles, D. Forest, M. Toft.

2. S Glacier/SE Face, July 1937, K. Gardiner, L. Gest, *E. Feuz Jr., C. Häsler Jr.* The glacier is bounded on the W by the S ridge, emanating from the main peak, and on the E by a ridge which descends S from the upper névé (not the small glacier under the SE side of the massif). Start from a camp near the junction of the N and S forks of Rice Brook and bushwhack to the foot of the glacier where a bivouac is usually made. The steep glacier gives rapid access to the upper plateau, where a large gendarme stands at the col at the head of the glacier. Cross the col and turn up the SE face of the main peak, a final 300m of cliffs partly snow covered, or, alternatively, go to the col between the main and central peaks and climb the NE ridge. 4–6 h from foot of glacier (AAJ **3**-155; CAJ **25**-25).

3. N Face, July 1972, Jas. Jones, E. Grassmann. This soaring 1000m face on Mount Bryce's main (SW) peak offers one of the great ice climbs of Canada. Approach via Saskatchewan Glacier, Castleguard Meadows and Castleguard Glacier, descending into the upper reaches of Bryce Creek. A very long day. The lower part of the N side of Bryce consists of trees, cliffs and scree and the ice itself is not reached for 8 h. Claw directly up the face, which starts at 45° and steepens to 55° near the top. 7 h on the face (CAJ **56**-14).

4. NW Face, Central Peak. August 1977, D. Hale, R. Winner. From Castleguard Glacier, instead of descending to Bryce Creek, traverse left along a hanging glacier which gives access to base of face. Start in dihedral to left of prominent waterfall. After 70m in dihedral (F7), traverse into gully and ascend avalanche debris to initial ice slope. Pass first seracs on right (W) and, higher, make a 65° ice traverse below second group of seracs. Thereafter, frontpoint up 55° slope to summit. 7 hours up (AAJ **52**-551; CAJ **61**-106).

Mt Bryce

N Face

Mt Bryce Centre P

Freshfield Gro

NE Ridge

Mt Bryce East

G. Boles

SOUTH FROM MT. COLUMBIA

Mount Bryce has apparently also been climbed from the W, starting at Bryce Creek. Long and not recommended.

THE CASTELETS (2280m)

Three pinnacles N of junction of Alexandra and Castleguard Rivers. No mountaineering interest (ABC-45).

TERRACE MOUNTAIN (2940m)

8 km NE of Thompson Pass across Castleguard valley.

FA July 1923, J. M. Thorington, *C. Kain*. **SE ridge** can be reached from a camp in Castleguard Meadows via glacier which descends from col between Terrace and Unnamed 2840m to S. Follow ridge over easy shale and boulders to top; 3 h from camp. **W ridge** has been taken in descent (CAJ **14**-39).

MOUNT SASKATCHEWAN (3342m)

Massive mountain in angle of Alexandra and N Saskatchewan Rivers; prominent in view from highway.

FA July 1923, W. S. Ladd, J. M. Thorington, *C. Kain*. **S Face.** Approach from Castleguard Meadows over N shoulder of Terrace Mountain (or bushwhack up Terrace Creek). The SW side of the mountain is divided into 2 cirques by a subsidiary ridge. Gain this ridge from the W cirque and follow it to cliff bands. Move right (E) 100m into S cirque to surmount the initial band. Continue to work E and upward by chimneys to top of a minor buttress (cairn). Scramble down-tilted scree and ascend snow slopes to main ridge and thus to the summit. 8 h from Meadows (CAJ **14**-41, marked photo).

2. W Ridge, September 1963, R. Fierz, J. G. Kato. Take trail to Saskatchewan Glacier for approx one km; then turn S up canyon which descends from N side of Mount Saskatchewan, staying W of creek. Gain col (2650m) at end of ridge (4 h; bivouac on FA). Good climbing on ridge. 4 h above col, turn a prominent gendarme with a horizontal roof on the left (N). Immediately above, pass an overhang on the right (W; piton

on FA). One pitch higher the difficulties ease. 8 h from col.
Descent by Route One and return to col, 5½ h. Recommended
(CAJ **47**-57).

UNNAMED (2940m) *(Cleopatra, Lighthouse Tower)*
   A striking pinnacle 2 km E of Mount Saskatchewan; well
seen from the highway (ABC 2-50).
   FA 1964, G. Boehnisch, L. Mackay. Follow creek that enters
Saskatchewan River some 5 km N of Alexandra River; then
gain E scree ridge on which Cleopatra sits. Round objective on
S and climb 80m rockband, then 80m pinnacle itself. F7; 8 h
from highway.

CASTLEGUARD MOUNTAIN (3090m)
   At S head of Saskatchewan Glacier; a fine viewpoint and
good ski ascent.
   FA 1919, Boundary Commission. **N Ridge.** A simple snow
climb, frequently done on ski to foot of steeper snow (ABC **2**-
64).
   2. E Ridge. July 1922, T. Frayne, U. LaCasse, W. S. Ladd,
J. M. Thorington, *C. Kain.* Take snow and shale to the top in
3 h from Castleguard Meadows (CAJ **14**-39).
   3. N Slopes. 1938, ACC party. Scree to summit.

UNNAMED (3330m)
5 km N of Castleguard Mountain, at N head of Saskatchewan
Glacier.
   FA July 1924, F. V. Field, W. O. Field, L. Harris, *J. Biner,
E. Feuz Jr.* **S Ridge.** Take long shale and snow ridge to summit
(App. **16**-145). Other routes have been done on ski, in partic-
ular, the N ridge.

UNNAMED (3240m)
   High point on long SE ridge of Unnamed (*Andromeda*); 2½
km E of foregoing.

FA July 1978, G. Boles, L. Kubbernus. **SE Ridge.** Ascend Saskatchewan Glacier beyond base of ridge. Angle up to a snow cirque between S and SE ridges and climb to its head to gain S ridge and then main SE crest. 7 h up, 4 down (CAJ **62**-38).

UNNAMED *(Andromeda)* (NE 3450m; SW 3450m)
2 km W of Mount Athabasca. A deservedly popular peak, well seen and easily accessible from the Icefields campground via the road to the snowmobile parking lot.
FA July 1930, W. R. Hainsworth, J. F. Lehman, M. M. Strumia, N. B. Waffl. **S Ridge.** Approach over Athabasca Glacier to col between objective and Unnamed (3330m). Snow and scree to summit. 6–7 h from parking lot (CAJ **19**-152). Now used almost exclusively as a descent route.
2. Skyladder. This is the elegantly curving snow/ice face that leads to the W shoulder of the peak. July 1960, J. Fairly, B. Parks. From snowmobile parking lot work across moraine and cross N glacier to foot of face (2–3 h). The angle steepens, then lessens in the upper part. Difficulties depend on the amount of ice exposed, thus times from foot of face have varied between 3–9 h. A classic route, highly recommended (CAJ **44**-87; **55**-88).
3. W Shoulder Direct. 1973, J. Lowe, *alone*. The mixed rock and ice N face leading directly to top of the W shoulder also gained by Skyladder. Angle averages 50–55°, with short, steeper sections. It is usually possible to belay from rock; 4–6 h on face (AAJ **48**-163).
4. NW Bowl. August 1972, D. Hamre, J. Glidden, G. Lowe. A difficult ice climb lying left of W Shoulder Direct. Approach as for Skyladder. Route ascends steep face just right (W) of ice overhangs in middle of bowl. The steepest ice (70°) comes at the top. 11 pitches, III (CAJ **56**-80).
5 N Bowl. August 1976, R. Boisselle, R. Ware. To left of above. Start under seracs in middle of bowl, traversing slightly

E. Cooper

Skyladder

W Shoulder Direct

NW Bowl

MT. ANDROMEDA FROM NORTH

Snow/Ice Gullies

E Ridge

right (W) to foot of a short, vertical ice wall. Above, follow a ramp leading between seracs to summit plateau (CAJ **60**-83).

6. N Face. 1966, J. Gow, C. Raymond. Left of Route 5. This route makes for the saddle between the summits of Andromeda. It lies between the ice overhangs in the middle of the bowl and rock bands to left (E).

7. N Ridge Couloir. August 1975, T. Sorenson, W. Strugatz. Route apparently starts near base of N ridge leading to NE summit. 500 m of 50° ice in central chute, with 10m of rotten vertical ice. Rockfall danger most days. Then along ridge to summit. 10 h RT; III (CAJ **59**-83).

8. Snow/Ice Gullies. On the rocky NE face which lies below the NE summit and across from the NW ridge of Mount Athabasca, there are 3 gullies which offer good practice climbs of 150–300m length. The leftmost is the shortest while the other 2 are in the form of an inverted V.

9. E Ridge. July 1938, ACC party led by *E. Feuz Jr.* Approach by glacier that flows NW from Athabasca–Andromeda col. Follow narrow rock and snow ridge to broken rock, above which snow slopes lead to the top. 6 h from snowmobile parking lot. Athabasca–Andromeda col has also been reached from the Saskatchewan Glacier via the SE-flowing glacier.

10. SE Ridge. September 1981, G. Boles, L. Kubbernus. From site of former ACC hut, ascend Saskatchewan Glacier and bypass Unnamed (3240m) on W to gain col between it and objective. Easy shale to top; 13 h RT.

Traverse. E and S ridges are often combined as an enjoyable traverse. Better E to S.

MOUNT ATHABASCA (3491m)

A magnificent peak 4 km SW of Sunwapta Pass, from which the 1898 party discovered the Columbia Icefield. Justly popular and very accessible, it is probably the most-climbed major peak in the Rockies.

FA August 1898, J. N. Collie, H. Woolley. **N Ridge.** Usually

MT. ATHABASCA FROM NORTH

- Athabasca–Andromeda Col
- NW Ridge
- N Glacier
- Silverhorn
- N Face
- N Ridge
- A2
- E. Cooper
- NW Ridge Trail

gained at saddle (2750m) to S of subsidiary peak between Athabasca and highway. Approach either via N glacier, skirting subsidiary peak on W, or by "Boundary Glacier" (see below). Follow ridge over variable-quality rock to prominent snow shoulder. Above, the summit cliffs are negotiated by a chimney to right (W) of the ridge (Collie-105).

Variant A. Approach as for N face, then climb rock and/or snow to snow shoulder below summit cliffs.

Variant B. The Boundary Glacier flows toward the Banff–Jasper Park Boundary at Sunwapta Pass and was, in part, followed by the 1898 party. From Pass, go up to a small lake, then ascend to glacier. Take it to its head and continue up to snow shoulder on N ridge.

2. E Face. 1969, K. Baker, L. Mackay. The face rises above the glacier that descends E from the mountain and from which Hilda Creek (sign) springs. Leave highway at Hilda Creek and walk up glacier to foot of face. Start by climbing a snow/ice slope, then continue on rocks (sometimes snow-covered) directly toward the summit. Turn the summit cliffs on the right (N) thus joining the N ridge just above the shoulder. III.

3. E Ridge. August 1945, T. Dowler, E. R. Gibson, P. Methuen. Gain ridge from the SE by striking up from the Saskatchewan Glacier some 3 km above its tongue. Head for a prominent col (2860m) below which are three small peaks on the ridge. Ascend ridge close to crest, sometimes bypassing, sometimes climbing gendarmes. About 300m below summit, the rocks steepen into a series of down-sloping slabs connected by short cliffs, which are climbed to a final snow ridge leading to the top. Inadvisable except under dry conditions. It is possible to avoid this upper section by traversing on steep snow across E face to join N ridge at the shoulder. 8 h up (CAJ **29**-299; **48**-126).

4. W Ridge. As for Andromeda E Ridge to Athabasca–Andromeda col, then to summit. This route is commonly taken in descent as an alternative to coming down the normal N

Glacier route. Has been done from Saskatchewan Glacier as well.

5. NW Ridge. Descends toward the Icefield Chalet and provides a good rock scramble. August 1938, ACC party led by *E. Feuz Jr.* Approach as for N glacier, ascending E flank of ridge to col at its foot. The first tower is soon reached and the climb continues over towers until the saddle (3170m) on the normal route is gained. 9 h, road to summit.

6. N Glacier (normal route). August 1920, J.W.A. Hickson, E. L. Redford, *E. Feuz Jr.* The route goes up the glacier descending toward the Icefield Chalet. Approach via W moraine, reached by leaving the snowmobile access road just beyond the point where the glacier stream is crossed. Follow trail and gain glacier. Work generally left (E), making for the snow col below Silverhorn. Before reaching it, make a rising traverse right (W) to gain the prominent saddle (3170m) between Silverhorn and the towers of the NW ridge. From here snow and scree lead to the forepeak and snow to the summit itself. 3–6 h from road. The 1898 party used this route in descent (CAJ **12**-37).

7. Silverhorn. August 1947, E. R. Gibson, G. G. Macphee, N. E. Odell, F. S. Smythe. As for the normal route to the rising traverse, Then continue left to snow col at base of this prominent snow/ice slope which sweeps down from the forepeak. Cross bergschrund on left and climb moderately steep snow/ice to the forepeak. An elegant route; 4–6 h from access road (CAJ **31**-81).

8. N Face–W Summit. August 1971, D. Rau, D. Soper. Approach as for Silverhorn, crossing snow col at its base and continuing into basin beyond. The route lies entirely on snow/ice, just right of the high rock bands under main summit, and offers a fine ice climb on slopes up to 55° (AAJ **18**-142).

9. N Face. August 1973, S. Wunsch and a companion. Approach as for foregoing route. The face steepens toward a narrow right-slanting ice couloir (60°), the key to the climb, which leads through the summit rock band. Several alternate lines have been taken up the rock band. There is a sheltered bivouac ledge to right (W) of couloir. 600m on face; 4–12 h from access road, depending on conditions and amount of belaying.

UNNAMED *(A 2)* (3060m)

Tower one km NE of Mount Athabasca.

FA August 1938, V. R. Fritz, E. Knowlton, A. D. Macpherson, D. Smith. From Sunwapta Pass, take the Boundary Glacier and reach the notch between A2 and A3 by a snow gully. Climb some snow/ice gullies and follow the NE ridge to the top.

2. S Ridge. The more commonly climbed route, and usual descent, leads simply up from the Athabasca–A2 col (2950m) which is gained from the Boundary Glacier.

UNNAMED *(A3, Hilda)* (3060m)

2 km NE of Mount Athabasca. A popular, short day climb.

FA July 1938, Mr. & Mrs. E. C. Brooks, R. P. Cross, W. E. Marples. **W Face.** From Sunwapta Pass take Boundary Glacier to base of face. Ascend a snow couloir, zigzag up scree-covered slabs and climb final rock tower. Unpleasant even on descent; 4 h from Sunwapta Pass.

2. E Ridge. From Hilda Creek parking lot 3 km SE of Sunwapta Pass, take the prominent ridge to the top. The upper part offers exposed climbing (F3–F4) on somewhat loose rock. A good warm-up climb. 4 h up.

SNOW DOME (3451m)

An uninteresting bump on all sides save the N, but unique in that it is the hydrographic apex of the Columbia Icefield, a tri-oceanic watershed (see Introduction).

FA August 1898, J. N. Collie, H. E. M. Stutfield, H. Woolley. A snow walk (or ski ascent) up any side of the peak, reached via Athabasca Glacier.

2. NE Buttress. August 1967, C. Raymond, D. Vockeroth.

From parking lot at base of Athabasca Glacier tongue cross to Dome Glacier. The route follows the left-hand (E), more prominent buttress of the two. Some 750m of rock climbing on the prow of the buttress, concluding with a 50m ice cliff at the top. FA party took 1½ days; IV, F7, A2 (AAJ **16**-170).

3. NE Ridge. 1938, R. C. Hind, P. Prescott, P. M. Purves. Gain the broad col ("ski saddle," 2520m) on the ridge from Athabasca Glacier, preferably starting from the snowmobile parking lot. Class 3 and 4 climbing along ridge, which melds into Columbia Icefield 2.5 km E of Snow Dome summit. 4½ h from parking lot to Icefield.

UNNAMED (3170m)

Minor eminence on S margin of Columbia Icefield; 4 km SE of Mount Columbia.

FRA May 1970, D. Forest, K. Ricker. Via N. slopes.

MOUNT COLUMBIA (3747m)

A majestic mountain at W of Icefield; the second elevation of the Canadian Rockies. Use Athabasca glacier approach and (most usually) place a camp on the Icefield for the first two routes. In former times, these were approached from Castleguard Meadows, but this made for an exceedingly long day and increased the likelihood of a bivouac.

FA July 1902, J. Outram, *C. Kaufmann*. **E Face** (normal route). A straightforward snow/ice climb on face to right of SE rib, which is also commonly climbed. 3 h from schrund (Outram-376).

2. S Ridge. July 1924, M. Brooks, F. V. Field, W. O. Field, L. Harris, C. Smith, E. Stenton, *J. Biner, E. Feuz Jr*. An alternate to the normal route should that be iced up. Snow with some rock pitches. Longer but in a more splendid ambiance than Route One. 5 h from bergschrund (App. **16**-150).

3. W Face. August 1951, G. I. Bell, D. Michael. See Athabasca River approach. From a camp in the hanging valley W of Mount

Columbia Icefield

E Face

W Face

N Ridge

MT. COLUMBIA FROM NORTH

R. Kruszyna

King Edward, swing S around latter and cross Icefield toward Mount Columbia. Ascend snow up the middle of the face. Move right (S) at the first cliff band until a chimney appears which permits access to the sloping shelf below the next band. Again go right to another chimney. The third band is climbed diagonally right to strike the S ridge some 200m below the summit. 3–4 h from base (AAJ 8-259).

4. N Face/Ridge. August 1970, C. Jones, G. Thompson. On the N side, Mount Columbia rises to its full stature, towering more than 2000m above the headwaters of the Athabasca River. This route is one of the finest mixed climbs in the Rockies, a major undertaking in remote surroundings. Use Woolley Shoulder approach, then follow Habel Creek to the Athabasca. Follow up to its source and cross on snout of Columbia Glacier. Ascend W side of N ridge, crossing E to below rock towers (bivouac). Allow 2 full days for approach. The lower snow slopes immediately left of the ridge lead to a narrow ice gully which connects to the upper slopes. A snow arête joins the ridge and several pitches of rock climbing lead toward the top of the prominent final tower. Pass this on ledges to the right (W) to gain cracks that lead up to final rocks. FA party took 2½ days; V, F7 (AAJ 17-292).

Note: There exists a traverse ledge on the NW face at approximately 2900m which makes it possible to descend the W face and return to a camp below the N ridge, rather than descending to the Icefield and exiting E to the highway. Exposed, loose, but straightforward. August 1975, A. Higbee, A. Spero, D. Waterman.

MOUNT KING EDWARD (3490m)

A fine peak 5 km W of Mount Columbia, above SW headwaters of Athabasca River. See Athabasca River approach for all routes.

FA August 1924, J. W. A. Hickson, H. Palmer, *C. Kain.* From King Edward Camp, ascend glacier S to Divide pass (2620m) and swing SE around to S base of peak. Scramble S slopes, passing cliffband on E to a couloir which leads to summit ridge. S peak is higher (AJ **37**-306).

2. NE Ledges. 1973, H. Michell, *alone.* From forks at head of Athabasca River, head up to the moraine leading to the intersection of the N and NE faces. Work up NE face by a right-leading ramp and then a long ledge that leads back left. Ascend an open book to a second ledge. Details lacking, but it appears route thus gains Icefield between objective and Mount Columbia, from which summit is reached over steep snow. III, F5.

3. NW Ridge. July 1975, D. Waterman, *alone.* From King Edward Camp, scramble lower part of ridge to steep section (crux). Traverse left (E) onto N face and climb an obvious crack. Ascend a steep face to a ledge. Difficulties ease as one gets higher, the upper part being much shattered and requiring care. III, F5; 12 h RT with descent by Route One (AAJ **50**-469).

The following peaks lie W and SW of Mount King Edward on or near the Divide and are topographically part of the Columbia Icefield Group.

UNNAMED *(Toronto)* (2940m)
   3.5 km WNW of Mount King Edward.
   FA August 1975, P. Benson, A. Maki, H. Microys, M. Rosenberger. **S Ridge.** From King Edward Camp, ascend glacier S toward Divide, then swing W and NW to gain ridge over glacial slopes. Go simply to the top. Ascent 5 h.

TRIAD PEAK (3030m)
   On Divide 3.5 km SW of Mount King Edward.
   FA July 1936, E. Cromwell, E. Cromwell Jr., F. S. North, J. M. Thorington. Start as for Toronto above, crossing ridge connecting it with Triad to reach glacial basin to W. Ascend

to its S head and cross Divide pass between Triad and Omega. Take SW snow slopes to summit. FA party gained glacial basin directly from W headwaters branch of Athabasca River (AAJ **3**-61).

OMEGA PEAK (3060m)

On Divide 4.5 km SW of Mount King Edward; W of Triad Peak.

FA August 1975, P. Benson, A. Maki (Route One), H. Microys, M. Rosenberger (Route 2). Approach as for Triad Peak.

NW Ridge. Principal difficulty is crossing moat to gain ridge. Easy scrambling thereafter; 6 h up.

2. E Ridge. Same day as above. 200m of F3 rock to top; 6 h up.

UNNAMED *(Watershed)* (S 3150m; N 3090m)

On Divide 6 km W of Mount King Edward.

S Peak. FA July 1931, E. Cromwell, N. W. Spadavecchia. **W Ridge.** From W headwaters branch of Athabasca River, take 2220m pass approach but turn S down glacial basin paralleling Divide. One hour of rock climbing on ridge (App. **18**-354).

N Peak. FA July 1931, E. Cromwell, N. W. Spadavecchia, J. M. Thorington. **NW Ridge.** Sharp slabs below summit. 3 h from near 2220m pass (App. **18**-351).

UNNAMED *(Aqueduct)* (3180m)

W rim of glacial basin W of Divide, 6.5 km S of 2200m pass.

FA August 1978, H. G. Kruszyna, R. Kruszyna, A. Maki, H. Mutch, P. Vermeuler, D. Whitburn. **N Ridge.** From a camp in E terminal fork of Sullivan River, ascend E edge of spectacular icefall to gain glacial basin above (N). Cross to W to gain ridge which is followed over snow and rock to forepeak. Continue along horizontal section (gendarmes) and finish up a steep snow/ice crest. 12 h up; II, F4 (CAJ **62**-7).

2. S Ridge. July 1979, J. Petroske and 3 sons. From camp at 2220m pass on Divide, go SSW on glacier for some 6 km. Cross SW ridge, traverse SW glacier, and gain S ridge. Easy scree to top. Ascent 6 h (Mazama 1979-19).

UNNAMED (3090m)

N of Aqueduct; 4.5 km SSW of 2220 pass on Divide.

FA July 1936, E. Cromwell, E. Cromwell Jr., F. S. North, J. M. Thorington. **N. Ridge.** From 2220m pass ascend icefall between objective and unnamed peak (2970m) just to N. From saddle ascend snow, then narrow rock ridge. Party also climbed peak (2970m) by S slopes from saddle. Ascent 6 hours for both (AAJ **3**-60).

2. S Ridge. J. Petroske and 3 sons. From col between objective and Aqueduct climb primarily snow to top. 4 h from 2220m pass (Mazama 1979-19).

We return now to the N extension of the Columbia Icefield to describe routes on the peaks situated N and NW of its apex at Snow Dome.

MOUNT KITCHENER (3480m)

3.5 km N of Snow Dome.

FA July 1927, A. J. Ostheimer, *H. Fuhrer.* **W Slopes.** Approach via Athabasca Glacier. An easy ascent, but good as a ski mountaineering objective (CAJ **16**-21).

Note: The FA was part of a remarkable *tour de force.* At 1:00 A.M., they left a camp in the E fork of the Athabasca River, climbed the Columbia N Glacier and icefall to the Icefield (11:00 A.M.); North Twin (7:00 P.M.); Stutfield Peak (9:00 P.M.); Mount Kitchener (midnight); Snow Dome (4:00 A.M.) and were headed for Mount Columbia when worsening weather caused them to return to camp (midday), 36 non-stop hours after leaving it.

2. NE Face/Right. As one approaches the Columbia Icefields from the N, along the Banff–Jasper Highway, the brooding

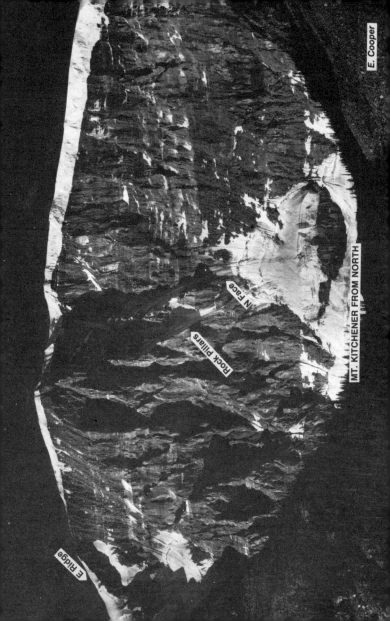

E. Cooper

MT. KITCHENER FROM NORTH

N Face

Rock Pillars

E Ridge

NE face of Mount Kitchener dominates the scene, much as the N face of Mount Temple towers over the Lake Louise area. August 1971, C. Jones, J. Lowe, G. Thompson. Cross the Sunwapta River at a narrow gorge just below the upper gravel flats and go over a shoulder into the basin below the face (5 h). A rock buttress splits the 1200m face into two ice slopes, of which the right is taken. Cross the schrund on either extremity and climb easily to ice slope proper. Ice extends some 600m, then 2 rock pitches lead to rightward-trending ice ramp. Follow ramp to summit. A very serious undertaking; 2 bivouacs on FA. V, F7 (AAJ **18**-66).

3. NE Face/Rock Pillars. July 1972, B. Beale, G. Homer, B. Greenwood, R. Wood. This route lies on rock immediately to left of the left-hand ice slope. Approach as for route above. Cross schrund at E extremity and ascend snow/ice, initially, keeping just to side of rock. Once on upper ice slope, traverse to rock on left, which is frequently steep and demanding, and of variable quality. Near summit, traverse left to avoid verglas-coated rock. V; 2 bivouacs on FA.

4. E Ridge. July 1955, F. D. Ayres, D. G. Claunch, R. K. Irvin. From toe of Athabasca Glacier cross moraine and ascend Dome Glacier. Gain a prominent saddle on E ridge over tedious scree slopes. Continue up an elegant snow/ice ridge to an unexpected and invisible 25m gap. Descend out-shelving ledges, then cross cornice *(au cheval)* to opposite wall (piton). Climb steep, loose pitch to summit snow. 7 h from parking area; II, F4 (AAJ **10**-123).

UNNAMED *(K2)* (3090m)
Minor eminence on E ridge of Mount Kitchener, 2 km from latter.
FA July 1938, ACC party led by *C. Häsler Jr.* By way of Dome Glacier and SE slopes (CAJ **26**-52).

THE TWINS
   At NW extremity of Columbia Icefield. The normal routes on The Twins are usually approached via Athabasca Glacier,

parties placing a high camp SW of Snow Dome, from which other peaks, such as Kitchener and Stutfield, may also be reached. It is also possible to approach via Woolley Shoulder, the E head of Habel Creek, and the glacier between the 2 peaks of Stutfield. There is a good bivouac site on rock on the SW slope of Stutfield W; a long day by either approach.

S TWIN (3580m)

FA July 1924, F. V. Field, W. O. Field, L. Harris, *J. Biner, E. Feuz Jr.* **N Ridge.** Gain the broad saddle (3230m) E of N Twin and from there the col between The Twins. Follow the narrow snow ridge to the top. 2 h from col between The Twins (App. **16**-147).

2. S Couloir. This couloir, which drains to the lake at the tongue of Columbia Glacier, rises to the col between S Twin and Unnamed (3360m) immediately NW. July 1975, D. Waterman *alone*. From Athabasca River, gain bench (approximately 2200m) which runs across W side of Twins massif. Traverse S and ascend couloir to col at its head, from which N ridge is easily reached. This route offers a rapid descent to treeline from the vicinity of The Twins (AAJ **50**-469).

UNNAMED (3360)

One km NW of S Twin, culminating complex W ridge of Twins massif.

FA July 1975, D. Waterman, *alone*. E slopes from plateau between objective and S Twin.

N TWIN (3730m)

Third highest peak in the Canadian Rockies; often reached on ski from SE.

FA July 1923, W. S. Ladd, J. M. Thorington, *C. Kain.* From the 3230m saddle to E, summit is gained over snow of **E slopes.** 2 h from saddle (CAJ **14**-40).

2. S Ridge. July 1924, F. V. Field, W. O. Field, L. Harris, *J. Biner, E. Feuz Jr.* From 3230m saddle to col between The

"Son of N Twin"

Twins Tower

N Twin

Stutfield W

Columbia Icefield

Habel Creek Valley

ACROSS "BLACK HOLE"
FROM MT. WOOLLEY

Twins. 2 h to top. Usually used on a traverse between The Twins (App. **16**-147).

3. NW Ridge. July 1965, H. L. Abrons, P. Carman, R. Millikan. A climb of nearly 2000m in wild surroundings. Use Woolley Shoulder approach, skirting Little Alberta on E to reach E head of Habel Creek (one day). The initial, and principal, problem is to gain the "pocket" glacier below the prominent tower (3270m) rising W of objective. Its icefall presents a difficult and dangerous obstacle, which in 1979 was surmounted on its far right (W) side. Then work through glacier to ridge proper, which presents no serious difficulties until a notch near the summit. At the notch, climb a hard 50m pitch, after which mixed rock and snow lead to the top. One bivouac on FA; IV, F7 (AAJ **15**-30).

4. N Face. The most fearsome wall in the range; the Rockies' equivalent of the Eiger Nordwand. The climb requires several days, presents difficult and treacherous rock, snow and ice, offers scant opportunity to retreat, and is subject to changeable weather. August 1974, C. Jones, G. Lowe. Approach as for NW ridge above. Climb bottom rock band on left to snow flanking hanging glacier. Traverse up and W 500m to schrund below left upper lobe of glacier. Climb second band near crest of rib immediately left of main lobe of hanging glacier. Continue up to grey rock of upper wall. Difficulties become serious and continuous, with considerable aid climbing required. Poor protection possibilities. Finally work left toward an ice runnel leading up toward ice slope below summit. Traverse into runnel and climb straight up on 60° snow/ice (15 pitches) to summit of Twins Tower. Reach summit of N Twin via connecting ridge. 6 bivouacs on FA, which was accomplished during a period of storm. VI, F9, A3 (AAJ **49**-1).

TWINS TOWER (3640m)

This is the N summit of N Twin, not to be confused with the 3270m tower mentioned in NW ridge description.

FA July 1938, C. Cranmer, F. Wiessner. Attain the notch between objective and N Twin either by descending from latter or by traversing from the 3230m saddle across a bench on E slope of N Twin. Snow/ice to summit. This summit is traversed by both the NW ridge and N face routes on N Twin (AAJ **3**-366).

UNNAMED *(Son of N Twin)* (3270m)

Striking tower on complex NW ridge of Twins massif; 0.7 km NW of Twins Tower.

FA August 1979, A. Spero, D. Waterman. **W. Ridge.** Approach as for NW ridge of N Twin to Pocket glacier. To reach notch to W of objective ascend right (W) of 2 couloirs, switching to left ⅔ of the way up. Traverse left to large snowpatch and ascend gullies to large ledge on ridge proper. Climb rock on end to left of ridge (2 pitches of F6). Near the top the angle eases but the rock is very loose.

STUTFIELD PEAK (W 3450m; E 3390m)

Double-summited peak at NE extremity of Columbia Icefield; summits 2 km apart.

W Peak. FA June 1927, A. J. Ostheimer, *H. Fuhrer.* A simple snow climb via **S slopes.** Approach same as for normal route on N Twin (CAJ **16**-20).

E Peak. FA August 1962, W. J. Buckingham, W. W. Hooker. From E Head of Habel Creek, ascend glacier flowing from between the 2 peaks of Stutfield, then follow the **NW ridge** (AAJ **13**-499).

2. SW Slopes. August 1973, G. Boles, F. Campbell, D. Forest, M. Simpson. Easily reached from summit of W Peak in 2½ h, return 1½ h.

UNNAMED (3120m)

Outlier one km E of Unnamed *(Cromwell)*. No specific information, but it has likely been climbed.

UNNAMED *(Cromwell)* (3330m)
  At E head of Habel Creek; 2 km N of Stutfield Peak East.
  FA August 1936, E. Cromwell, E. Cromwell Jr., F. S. North, J. M. Thorington. **S Ridge.** Follow Habel Creek E to glacier which is its source. Ascend this glacier, which flows between the two summits of Stutfield, and gain col between objective and Stutfield East. The ridge is a simple climb on mostly rock. 9 hours from camp near junction of E and N branches of Habel Creek (AAJ **3**-61). A snow couloir in SE flank of mountain has been descended into Sunwapta drainage, August 1974, C. Jones, G. Lowe.
  2. N Face. Winter 1980, J. Elzinga, C. Miller. No details available.

UNNAMED *(Engelhard)* (3270m)
  Immediately S of Woolley Shoulder.
  FA July 1930, W. Hainsworth, J. F. Lehmann, M. M. Strumia, N. D. Waffl. **NE Ridge.** Use Woolley Shoulder approach and when near the glacier tongue traverse horizontally SE to base of ridge. Follow ridge easily to within 100m of summit where a notch is encountered. Turn the notch on the left (E) side and the top is soon at hand. 6 h from foot of ridge. The peak may also be climbed over N ridge directly from Woolley Shoulder; the two routes join before the difficult notch (AAJ **1**-307).

UNNAMED *(Little Alberta)* (2970m)
  3 km SE of Mount Alberta.
  FA August 1924, J. W. A. Hickson, H. Palmer, *C. Kain.* **W Face.** Climb straight up from glacier tongue to W of peak, via several chimneys, to reach summit ridge between two peaks. The S summit is higher. 3 h from glacier (AJ **37**-315).

MOUNT ALBERTA (3619m)
  One of the finest peaks in the Rockies, a singular uplift that is difficult on all sides. The first ascent by the Japanese party

N Face

R. Kruszyna

E Face

MT. ALBERTA FROM EAST

Habel Creek

was a notable achievement, marking the end of the era of first ascents of the major peaks in the Canadian Rockies. A spirited account of the historic FA may be found in AAJ 8-466.

FA July 1925, S. Hashimoto, H. Hatano, T. Hayakawa, Y. Maki, Y. Mita, N. Okabe, *J. Weber, Hy Fuhrer, H. Kohler.* **E Face.** Approach via Woolley Shoulder, skirting Little Alberta on the N, where there is a small campsite. The line taken varies somewhat, but in general begins on the lower-angled SE slopes, where good bivouac sites may be found at approximately 2700m (snow melt water). One long day from the highway. An hour of scrambling takes one to the base of the black rock of the SE buttress. Traverse on easy ledges around to right (N), choosing a line that will lead to the summit ridge at the first prominent notch from its S end. Some parties have had success by aiming for the second notch. Serious route-finding problems on steep black rock. Follow the narrow summit crest N to a further 20m notch, where a rope is often left for return, and so to the top. 8 h from bivouac. Descent is usually made by a series of long rappels (10) starting from the southernmost notch. IV (AJ **37**-316; 374; AAJ **7**-124, marked photo; CAJ **32**-1).

2. N Face. One of the finest modern climbs yet established in the Rockies. Steep ice followed by steep rock. August 1972, J. Glidden, G. Lowe. Approach via Woolley Shoulder and pass N of Little Alberta to gain shoulder on NE ridge (one day from highway). Descend a chimney to the glacier N of Alberta and cross to the foot of the face. Some 600m of ice climbing leads to the upper rocks, which initially are loose and moderately steep. The steep upper wall requires about 10 pitches, with some aid, to reach the summit icefields. FA party bivouacked twice; V, F9, A2 (CAJ **56**-35).

MOUNT WOOLLEY (3405m)
3.5 km E of Mount Alberta.
FA July 1925, Y. Maki's party from Mount Alberta. **S Slopes.** Round mountain on S from Woolley Shoulder and climb snow

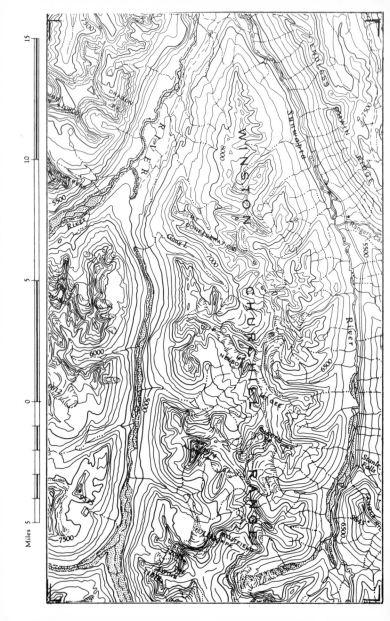

slopes and poorly-defined ridge. Mostly snow with rock pitches (App. **16**-408).

2. N Ridge (Normal Route). August 1947, J. Ross, D. Wessell. From camp near tongue of glacier descending E from Mount Woolley, work up to the steep snow couloir lying between the Woolley–Diadem icefall and the rocky buttress of Mount Diadem. Climb couloir to icefield and Woolley–Diadem col, then take snow/ice ridge to top. 6 h from camp. Woolley and Diadem are usually climbed in the same day from their connecting col (CAJ **32**-13).

DIADEM PEAK (3371m)

Immediately NE of Mount Woolley. Incorrectly marked on 83C/6, where Unnamed *(Mushroom)* appears as Diadem Peak.

FA August 1898, J. N. Collie, H. E. M. Stutfield, H. Woolley. **SE Ridge.** From camp placed as for Mount Woolley N ridge, cross glacier to ridge. Stay on rib, avoiding loose rock, to reach "diadem" of snow on summit (Collie-128; AJ **19**-461).

2. S Ridge. August 1962, W. J. Buckingham, W. W. Hooker. As for Route 2 on Mount Woolley to Woolley–Diadem col. Take S ridge to summit; one hour from col (AAJ **13**-499).

UNNAMED *(Mushroom)* (3210m)

2 km E of Diadem Peak.

FA August 1947, N. E. Odell, *alone*. From camp placed as for Woolley and Diadem, cross glaciers and a small icefall to steep boulder slopes on **W flank** of peak. Scramble 500m over boulders and then 150m on scree to summit (CAJ **31**-80).

MOUNT GEC (3130m)

3 km NNW of Diadem Peak.

FA July 1948, G. Harr, C. Wilts, E. Wilts. Use Gec–Nelson col approach to high plateau glacier, but branch off to gain the S pass between objective and Diadem Peak. Follow the S ridge and W face (Class 4 at end) to top (CAJ **32**-131).

MOUNT NELSON (3150m)

5 km NNW of Diadem Peak.

FA August 1951, D. & F. Ebersbacher, G. Roberts, C. & E. Wilts. From camp in Lynx Creek ascend **W face** to gain summit ridge S of main (N) summit (CAJ **35**-33).

MOUNT SMYTHE (3240m)

A fine double-summited peak immediately N of Mount Nelson at NE head of Lynx Creek basin.

FA August 1951, G. Roberts, C. & E. Wilts. **W Ridge.** From camp in Lynx Creek, ascend snow gully to top of buttress on S side of objective. Traverse left (W) across hanging glacier and slabs to W ridge. Several Class 5 pitches, with traverses onto N face at second and third steps, to reach summit (CAJ **35**-31).

UNNAMED (3030m)

Most S of peaks in cirque surrounding NW fork of Lynx Creek. FA July 1927, Harvard Mountaineering Club party. Easily via **S slopes** (CAJ **37**-107).

UNNAMED *(Palmer)* (3150m)

Double summit at NW margin of Lynx cirque; 5 km S of Gong Lake.

FA July 1953, G. Harr, J. & R. Mendenhall, G. Roberts, R. Van Aken. **E Ridge.** From camp on Lynx Creek, a snow couloir is taken to reach the ridge, which is then followed to the top (CAJ **37**-107).

UNNAMED *(Thorington Tower)* (3150m)

A large rock tower between Unnamed (Palmer) and Unnamed (Smythe), at head of NW fork of Lynx Creek valley.

FA September 1967, D. Lashier, C. Raymond. **E Ridge.** From E end of Gong Lake, reach a glacier just N of peak. This leads to a 300m snow couloir which is ascended to a notch in the E ridge. Easily gain the base of an imposing cliffband. Start 10m to left of ridge and work up and left. 100m of hard climbing gives way to easier rock leading to the summit. III, F7 (AAJ **16**-170).

UNNAMED *(Gong)* (3120m)

A bell-shaped summit at head of valley draining N and W to Gong Lake.

FA July 1936, E. Cromwell, E. Cromwell Jr., F. S. North, J. M. Thorington. From camp near Gong Lake, follow N margin of timber to glacier at head of valley. Cross glacier to U-shaped notch at S base of peak. Ascend **S slopes** over downtilted strata and snow patches to top. 8 h up (AJ **48**-292).

UNNAMED *(McGuire)* (3030m)

One km NE of Gong.

FRA August 1971, H. & L. Fuhrer, B. Martin. **SE Ridge.** Approach from Icefields Highway for fording Sunwapta River one km N of Jonas Creek; a difficult ford. Follow game trails on S side of creek which flows from cirque formed by objective and Unnamed *(Weiss)* to camp in open valley below moraines (a short day). Gain glacier and follow it S to col E of intended ridge. Climb NE-facing rock (F3) to SE ridge. Ascend ridge to summit, passing over a final tower (F4). 5 h from camp (CAJ **55**-92).

UNNAMED *(Weiss)* (3090m)

2.5 km NNW of McGuire.

FA August 1971, H. & L. Fuhrer, E. Martin. **SE Ridge,** on traverse from McGuire (2 h). Traverse was completed by descending NE ridge over several sharp towers (F4). 13 h RT (CAJ **55**-93).

MOUNT MITCHELL (3040m)

5 km E of Gong Lake.

FA July 1970, Park Wardens. **N Glacier/E Ridge.** Ford Sun-

wapta River 2 km N of Poboktan Creek Warden Station. Follow
W side of creek descending from Mitchell–Weiss cirque, past
lakes. The climb initially goes up the glaciers of the N face and
thus to the E ridge. Near top, a traverse on the N face and
then one on the S face are required to pass overhangs (CAJ
54-88).

UNNAMED (3090m)
   3 km E of Mount Confederation.
   FA 1938, Topographical Survey via **W slopes** from Gong
Lake.

MOUNT CONFEDERATION (2969m)
   N of Gong Lake. The peak repulsed 6 attempts before the
successful ascent.
   FA July 1947, J. & R. Mendenhall. **N Ridge.** Approach along
Athabasca River and bushwhack into cirque W of peak. Ascend
to lowest notch in NW ridge and continue along easier half of
ridge to a square-topped mass. Gain platforms halfway up final
tower by a traverse left (E) followed by exposed rock climbing.
Start the final steep section to right (W) of ridge and finish up
the couloir which splits the final towers. 18 h RT from camp
in W cirque (CAJ **31**-55, marked photos).

MOUNT MORDEN LONG (3040m)
   3.5 km NE of Mount Confederation. Apparently climbed by
S ridge from camp at Gong Lake.

Whence it is evident, that the Earth is considerably flatted towards the poles.

P.L.M. De Maupertuis, 1737

BETWEEN

CHABA GROUP

These peaks rise generally in a U-shaped formation about the head of Chaba River. The Group is seldom visited, due in part to the greater prominence of the adjacent Columbia and Clemenceau Groups, and in part to the difficulty of access. However, the Chaba region offers several fine summits, among them Sundial, Dais, Quincy and Ghost Mountains, and may well repay the effort to reach the area.

The S boundary, by which the Chaba is separated from the Columbia Icefield Group, is arbitrarily taken as the low glacial pass (2220m) some 7 km W of Mount King Edward, connecting the W headwaters of Athabasca River with the Wales Glacier. The W limit of the group is the Alberta/British Columbia Divide N to Apex Peak, and Clemenceau Creek thereafter. The summits on the Divide SE of Apex Peak are assigned to the Chaba Group although, as far as is known, they have to date been climbed only from the Clemenceau (W) side. Fortress Lake delimits the Chaba peaks on the N.

ACCESS

Possible base camps: on the S shore of Fortress Lake, in either of the terminal forks of Chaba River (although the W fork has been reported as rugged going because of canyons and slides), and on Athabasca River. **For Fortress Lake and Chaba River,** start at Sunwapta Falls as for Athabasca River (see Chapter 5, Columbia Icefields). Near the junction of the Chaba (13 km), it is necessary to make a hazardous ford, preferably one river at a time. Then follow the Chaba (old, indistinct trail) to Fortress Pass and Lake (8 km); a long day. The forks of the Chaba are another ½ day farther. Several ascents in E wing of the group have been done from Athabasca River, the major problem being the fording of the stream. Peaks at the extreme S end can be reached from the W headwaters fork of Athabasca River or the 2220m Divide Pass (2½–3 days).

LITERATURE

Ostheimer, A. J. "From the Athabasca River to Tsar Creek." CAJ **16**-16 (1928). The account of Ostheimer and Fuhrer's grueling summer.

Thorington, J. M. "Up the Athabasca Valley." CAJ **20**-30 (1932). Several minor ascents around the W headwaters of Athabasca River.

Maps: 83C4; 83C5.

The following peaks are those that lie generally to the E of Chaba River, bounded in turn on the E by Athabasca River from which, with the exception of Mount Quincy, they are usually approached.

MOUNT QUINCY (3150m)

At N of group; name misplaced on 83C5.

FA July 1927, A. J. Ostheimer, *J. Weber, H. Fuhrer.* **SW Slopes/ Central S Ridge.** From the Chaba valley the W-facing cirque to the S of the peak is climbed to the 2600m level (5½ h). Then take the right (E) of two couloirs to the central of the three ridges descending from the summit. The highest point is to the E. Ascent 8 h (CAJ **16**-22).

UNNAMED *(Blackfriars)* (3210m)

2 km N of Quincy Creek; 3 km E of Mount Quincy.

FA July 1953, G. E. Landt, A. MacIntosh, *W. Perren.* **N Ridge.** From Athabasca River, ascend to timberline and traverse around the NE ridge. Cross the bowl of the N face on a ledge system from E to W and climb a snow couloir to reach a saddle at the foot of the ridge. Initially the ridge is steep but well broken, but soon the angle eases and the top is reached without great difficulty (CAJ **37**-101).

UNNAMED *(Massey)* (2940m)

Between Quincy and Warwick Creeks.

FA June 1927, A. J. Ostheimer, *H. Fuhrer.* From the Athabasca River, ascend a slide to timberline and gain the rock of the **S ridge,** by which the top is reached in 3–4 h from timberline. FA party descended W slopes to névé E of Dais Mountain (CAJ **16**-18).

DAIS MOUNTAIN (3300m)

The outstanding summit between Athabasca and Chaba Rivers.

FA June 1927, A. J. Ostheimer, *H. Fuhrer.* **SE Face/S Ridge.** From Warwick Creek, ascend to timberline and cross moraines of E Dais Glacier to round the SE ridge. Cross S Dais Glacier to gain the SE face of the final pyramid at 3000m. Work left in the most-westerly snow couloir to gain the partly knife-edged S ridge, and so to the top. Ascent 12 hours (CAJ **16**-18).

SUNDIAL MOUNTAIN (3182m)

5 km S of Dais Mountain at W head of Warwick Creek.

FA 1919, Boundary Commission. **W Slopes,** reached from

SUNDIAL MOUNTAIN FROM NORTH

N Face

the W by ascending beside a creek flowing down to Chaba Glacier or from the S from the W headwaters fork of Athabasca River over S glaciers. Recently the peak has also been reached from Warwick Creek.

2. N Face. August 1975, D. Waterman, *alone*. A steep snow/ice route of approximately 200m (AAJ **50**-469).

WARWICK MOUNTAIN (2906m)

Minor point W of Habel–Athabasca junction.

FA 1919, Boundary Commission. **SE Slopes,** straightfor-wardly from Athabasca valley (ABC **2**-58).

UNNAMED (3120m)

1.5 km SW of Warwick Mountain.

FA July 1931, E. Cromwell, N. W. Spadavecchia. **SW Face.** From camp in W headwaters of Athabasca River, ascend S-flowing glacier that issues from cirque between objective and Unnamed (3090m). Gain col (2860m) on W ridge and climb this, joining SW face higher up. Several chimneys near the summit provide good climbing. Ascent 7–8 h (CAJ **20**-34).

2. S Ridge. August 1975, A. Maki, D. Whitburn. From lake SE of Warwick Mountain, ascend to base of ridge. Follow ridge, bypassing a vertical step on W face, to final airy section and summit. 5 h up.

UNNAMED (3090m)

2 km SE of Sundial Mountain.

FA July 1931, E. Cromwell, E. Cromwell Jr., N. W. Spada-vecchia, J. M. Thorington. From camp as for Route One above, ascend glacier and **W slopes** (CAJ **20**-34).

UNNAMED *(Chaba)* (3150m)

The original Mount Chaba named by Jean Habel, whose summit record was found in 1936 by Dr. Thorington and party. 2 km NE of present Chaba Peak.

FA August 1901, F. Ballard, D. Campbell, J. Habel. Take the **W ridge** from the col between objective and Chaba Peak (AAJ **3**-59; App. **10**-36).

CHABA PEAK (3210m)

At extreme head of Chaba River drainage.

FA September 1928, E. Schoeller, *J Rähmi*. **S. Ridge.** The ridge is reached from Chaba River up the E Chaba Glacier or from the Chaba Icefield itself, and presents little difficulty (AAJ **3**-59). It has also been reached from the S by crossing the Divide between objective and Wales just N of some rock spires. These latter *(Demon Horns)* offer some interesting rock work up to F5; July 1979, B. & J. Petroske (Mazama 1979-21).

UNNAMED *(Wales)* (3120m)

On the Divide 2 km SSE of Chaba Peak.

FA August 1927, J. DeLaittre, W. R. Maclaurin, J. Weber. The snowclad **W side** of the peak is a simple climb, with an approach over the Chaba Icefield (CAJ **16**-40).

The following six minor peaks lie on the Chaba–Clemenceau Divide, reaching from W of Chaba Peak up to just N of Apex Peak. So far they have always been climbed with an approach from the Clemenceau (W) side. FA of Eden and Noel, August 1927, A. J. Ostheimer, *J. Weber, H. Fuhrer.* (CAJ **16**-37). FA of the other four, in one day, July 1927, A. J. Ostheimer, *H. Fuhrer* (CAJ **16**-32).

EDEN PEAK (3180m)

4.5 km WSW of Chaba Peak.

The shale of the **NW ridge** is followed to the top in 1½ h from the col.

NOEL PEAK (3150m)

1.5 km N of Eden.

W ridge, approached from the SW and climbed in ½ h.

GRAY PEAK (3180m)
1.5 km W of Noel.

NW ridge, climbed in one h from col. FA party traversed from Lawrence.

LAWRENCE PEAK (3090m)
2.5 km E of Apex Peak. W–E traverse of this inconspicuous bump in one h, col to col.

WALCOTT PEAK (3150m)
NE of Apex Peak. **E Ridge.** This interesting rock and snow ridge is climbed from the Walcott–Lawrence col in ¾ h.

YOUNGHUSBAND PEAK (3150m)
1.5 km N of Apex Peak. From the Apex–Younghusband col, climb a couloir to the **S ridge,** which gives good climbing; 2 h.

LISTENING MOUNTAIN (3150m)
In forks of Chaba River.

FA July 1951, A Fabergé, P. Prescott. **S Slopes.** A small lateral glacier on the E side may be reached from E fork of Chaba River, the peak being ascended from the 2700m pass at its head (CAJ **16**-36).

UNNAMED (*Amundsen*) (3150m)
On Divide 4.5 km N of Apex Peak; 3.5 km SSE of Brouillard Mountain.

FA August 1927, J. DeLaittre, W. R. Maclaurin. **NW Slopes,** reached from Chaba Icefield over high pass (2950m) on Divide immediately N of objective (CAJ **16**-36).

UNNAMED (*Peary*) (3120m)
One km WNW of Amundsen.

FA July 1927, J. DeLaittre, A. J. Ostheimer, *H. Fuhrer.* From the S, ascend on the W flank of a small tributary glacier to gain the **W ridge** at 2700m. Snow and shale lead in one h to the top (CAJ **16**-30).

BROUILLARD MOUNTAIN *(Misty)* **(3210m)**

At S head of Chisel Creek drainage, across Clemenceau Creek from Mount Clemenceau.

FA August 1892, A. P. Coleman, L. Q. Coleman, L. B. Stewart. **NW Ridge** (this is most probably Coleman's route). Approach either up the glacier descending into Chisel Creek (Chaba Icefield) as did the Colemans, or from the W as in 1964. Ascend rock and snow to top (Coleman-155).

2. S/SW Ridge. July 1927, W. R. Maclaurin, A. J. Ostheimer, *H. Fuhrer.* Ascend the glacier on the S side of the peak and then the shale S ridge to 2950m. Descend to left (W) to gain SW ridge 100m lower down. Climb this ridge to summit. FA party completed traverse by descending SE ridge (CAJ **16**-26).

UNNAMED *(Franklin)* (3210m)

On Divide 3 km NE of Brouillard Mountain.

FA July 1927, W. R. Maclaurin, A. J. Ostheimer, *H. Fuhrer.* **S Ridge.** Approach over the Chaba Icefield or from the W fork of Chaba River. Loose shale (CAJ **16**-27).

GHOST MOUNTAIN **(3204m)**

At W head of Chisel Creek.

FA July 1927, A. J. Ostheimer, *H. Fuhrer.* **NW Ridge.** From timberline camp above Clemenceau Creek on W slopes, ascend to ridge below third tower from N. Climb the ridge, passing difficulties initially on the N and later on the W, to reach the summit over several humps. 5 h from camp (CAJ **16**-25).

2. NE Ridge. September 1979, D. Waterman, *alone.* From camp on Chisel Creek, gain glacier in SE cirque of peak. Ascend couloirs to ridge below final step and continue to top. Entire ridge ascended on FA; not recommended.

3. S Ridge. August 1927, W. R. Maclaurin, J. Weber. From a camp W of Brouillard Mountain, gain the subsidiary SW ridge, bypassing a prominent gendarme on the left. Once attained, the knife-edged S ridge gives good and exposed climbing. 5 h from point of attack (CAJ **16**-36).

CHISEL PEAK (3049m)
S of W end of Fortress Lake.

FA 1920, Boundary Commission. From camp on Wood River, most probably by long W spur (ABC **2**-85).

Anything worth having is worth cheating for.

W. C. Fields

If one loves sausage, and one respects the law, one ought not to watch either product being made.

O. von Bismarck

High objects, it is true, attract the sight, but it looks up with pain in craggy rocks and barren mountains . . .

J. Dryden

LAST FRONTIER

CLEMENCEAU ICEFIELD GROUP

The peaks in this remote and spectacular group rise W of the Alberta/British Columbia Divide, most of them located on the margins of the Clemenceau Icefield (100 km²). The dominant peak is Mount Clemenceau, the fourth highest of the Canadian Rockies and an outstanding objective. In addition, several other peaks in the region offer considerable mountaineering interest, among them Mounts Tsar, Shackleton and Tusk. The climbing is predominantly on snow and ice, but there are also occasional ridges of fair to good rock. Because of its remoteness, few parties had visited this region until some 10 years ago. Helicopter transportation and the new Alpine Club of Canada hut (below) however, are helping to open it up. The situation is analogous to that of the Columbia Icefields Group after the completion of the Banff–Jasper Highway in the late 1930's.

The group is bounded on the E by Wales Glacier, the Divide, and Clemenceau Creek. Wood River limits it on the N. On the

W and S sides, the group descends to low valleys leading to Columbia River.

There is some uncertainty regarding elevations in this group. Traditionally, Mount Clemenceau has been listed at 12,001 feet (3658m), but recent maps show 11,900 feet (3630m) as the highest contour. Glacial recession in the past 50 years could easily account for this difference. The map gives Tusk Peak as 11,000 feet (3350m) and Mount Shackleton as 10,900 feet (3320m) but, having recently stood on both summits, one editor is convinced that Mount Shackleton is slightly higher.

ACCESS

Nowadays, most parties enter the region from the W and by helicopter, flying from the vicinity of Mica Dam. While relatively expensive, this saves the 4–5 days of backpacking required by the alternative E approaches. For these, first refer to the Athabasca River approach (Chapter 5) and the Fortress Lake/Chaba River approach (Chapter 6). After fording the Athabasca and reaching Fortress Pass (one day), there are two alternatives. The first, and probably better, is to continue up Chaba River and take its W fork to reach, ultimately, the W Chaba Icefield. Cross the Divide at the 2650m saddle 1.5 km SW of Unnamed (Franklin), connecting the Chaba and Chisel valleys. Swing SW and cross the 2860m col 0.7 km SE of Mount Brouillard, thus entering the Clemenceau drainage. The other alternative is to skirt Fortress Lake on the N, ford Wood River in the vicinity of Serenity Creek, and climb up the lower slopes of the NW ridge of Ghost Mountain, to the E of Clemenceau Creek. Then contour near 2000m on the W flank of the ridge to gain Clemenceau Glacier, thus avoiding the heavy brush in Clemenceau Creek. In either case, 4–5 days from the Banff–Jasper Highway. For greater detail and additional routes, see CAJ **65**-89 (1982).

ACCOMMODATIONS

The Lawrence Grassi Hut of the Alpine Club of Canada,

erected in 1981, sits at 2070m on "Cummins Alp" (323810), some 8 km SSW of Mount Clemenceau. This spacious hut accommodates 20, with propane and Coleman stoves, dishes and utensils, and oil-fired heater. Propane and heating oil must be brought in; consult ACC office in Banff. Other sites for camps include: on the SE slopes of Mount Clemenceau (370874); in scrub E of Clemenceau Glacier (390878); at the end of the S ridge of Mount Shackleton (392803); E of Unnamed (Ellis) (443783).

LITERATURE

Boles, G. et al. "The Clemenceau Area." CAJ **56**-80 (1973). Account of the 1972 ACC camp when much was done in the area.

DeVilliers–Schwab, H. B. "Mount Clemenceau." CAJ **14**-18 (1924). The historic first ascent of Mount Clemenceau.

Hendricks, S. B. & G. I. Bell. "West of the Divide." AAJ **8**-250 (1952). Several first ascents and important routes.

Ostheimer, A. J. "From the Athabasca River to Tsar Creek." CAJ **16**-16 (1926–27). Peak storming with Ostheimer and Fuhrer.

Maps: 83C4, 83C5. Minor W portions are on 83D1 and 83D8.

UNNAMED *(Odell)* (3150m)
4.5 km SSW of Tsar Mountain.

TSAR MOUNTAIN (3424m)

A striking pyramidal peak at the S end of the group, usually approached from the N by way of the Clemenceau Icefield.

FA August 1927, A. J. Ostheimer, *H. Fuhrer, J. Weber.* **NW Face.** This route is no longer practicable because of ice retreat (CAJ **16**-38).

2. N Ridge. July 1951, G. I. Bell, W. V. G. Matthews, D. Michael. The prominent ridge is followed throughout, except

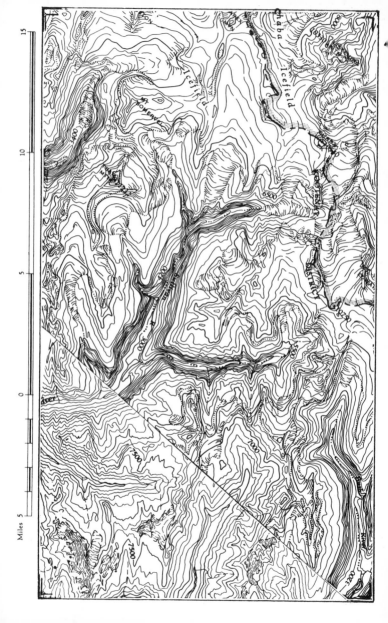

that the summit glacier is passed on the right by way of the W ridge. Recommended (AAJ **8**-258).

Variants. August 1972, G. Boles, D. Forest and ACC party. Gain the Tsar–Somervell col and work up onto the subsidiary W spur of the main N ridge (as in the 1927 FA). Follow the spur to its juncture with the main ridge. Above, it is possible to climb on the E flank, parallel to the ridge, regaining the crest below the summit edifice via a steep snow/ice slope (CAJ **56**-82).

MOUNT SOMERVELL (3120m)

5 km N of Tsar Mountain.

FA July 1951, G. I. Bell, J. R. Rousson. **S Ridge.** Ascend a couloir on the E face to gain ridge between objective and a subsidiary peak one km to S. Take easy ridge to top (AAJ **8**-258; CAJ **37**-101).

UNNAMED *(Ellis)* (2970m)

2 km NE of Mount Somervell.

FA August 1972, G. Boles, R. Matthews, R. Parsons, J. Pomeroy. Traverse from S to NE in 2½ h (CAJ **56**-82).

UNNAMED *(Norton)* (3060m)

A undistinguished N–S snow ridge; 2 km S of Apex Peak. FA August 1927, A. J. Ostheimer, *H. Fuhrer, J. Weber.* The summit may be reached via the **N ridge** in one h from the Apex–Norton col, while several other routes are possible from the W (CAJ **16**-37).

APEX MOUNTAIN (3240m)

Just W of Divide at N of Clemenceau Icefield.

FA August 1922, A. Carpé, H. S. Hall. The gently-sloping **S ridge** is simply reached by the Clemenceau Glacier. Take scree and rock to top (CAJ **13**-90).

2. SW Ridge. August 1972, H. Butling, J. Christian, I. Newberry, J. Peck. Follow the snow ridge, gaining the summit by traversing left (N) to the NW face (CAJ **56**-83).

3. N Ridge. August 1964, L. & V. Mondolfo, L. Roloff. Climb ridge directly from col to N of peak (CAJ **48**-117).

Mounts Stanley, Livingstone and Rhodes rise in a compact grouping some 5 km SE of the Grassi Hut. All 3 peaks may be climbed in one day by a fast party. From the hut, cross the dry glacier to E and descend over moraines into the "Pit." Ascend and gain the W glacier tongue. Part way up this glacier, cross intervening rock rib and continue up E glacier to snow pass below Livingstone–Rhodes basin (approximately 2520m).

MOUNT RHODES (3060m)

S summit of massif; one km S of Mount Livingstone.

FA August 1972, G. Boles, J. Christian, D. Forest, P. Roxburgh, G. Scruggs. **N Ridge.** Ascend much-crevassed glacier from 2520m snow pass to Livingstone–Rhodes col. Follow ridge to summit in one h; good scrambling (CAJ **56**-82).

2. W Face. August 1980, ACC parties. From snow pass, ascend steep snow couloir of W face (CAJ **64**-93).

MOUNT LIVINGSTONE (3090m)

SW summit of Mount Stanley.

FA August 1927, D. Hoover, A. J. Ostheimer, *H. Fuhrer.* **W Ridge.** From 2520m snow pass, gain the sharp ridge and follow it over steep and broken rock to the top. 5 h from pass (CAJ **16**-40).

2. S Ridge. August 1972, Boles party (see Rhodes). Reach the Livingstone–Rhodes col as for latter. After an easy initial section, overhangs on the ridge may be turned via ledges parallel to the crest on the left (W) side. 2 h from col (CAJ **56**-82).

MOUNT STANLEY (3120m)

N and principal summit of massif.

FA August 1972, M. Kingsley, R. Lidstone, J. Mellor, R. Reader, P. Robinson. **N Ridge.** From a high camp at end of S ridge of Mount Shackleton, attack ridge connecting objective and Pic Tordu from E at its weakest point. After climbing 100m of rock to reach a depression in the ridge, ascend ridge to a subsidiary peak (*Speke,* 2980m) and continue on to summit. On descent, rappels have been used to regain glacier from depression in ridge (CAJ **56**-82).

2. S Ridge. August 1972, Boles party (see Rhodes). From summit of Mount Livingstone, descend its N ridge to intervening col and then climb ridge to Mount Stanley. The main difficulty is an overhang that can be tunneled through. 1½ h from summit of Mount Livingstone (CAJ **56**-82).

PIC TORDU (3210m)

An amazing uplift of twisted and contorted strata rising some 3.5 km E of the Grassi Hut.

FA August 1972, M. Kingsley, R. Lidstone, J. Mellor, R. Reader, P. Robinson. **E Face.** From a high camp on S ridge of Mount Shackleton, cross bergschrund and climb the most southerly of a series of rock ribs. The N ridge is gained some 100m below the summit and is taken to the top (CAJ **56**-82).

2. W Ridge. August 1972, H. Microys, M. Rosenberger. Given the location of the Grassi Hut, this long, interesting and difficult ridge offers the route of choice on the mountain. Climb the ill-defined introductory ridge to the subsidiary W peak (3090m). The ridge now becomes exposed and serrated. The rock is variable in quality because of the vertical alignment of the strata, but in general is surprisingly good. 7 h from base of ridge to summit (CAJ **56**-84).

In a remarkable *tour de force*, Microys and Rosenberger continued the traverse by descending the N ridge, making the FA of Cowl Mountain (which see), and then traversing all 3 summits of Mount Shackleton (which see).

UNNAMED *(Cowl Mountain)* **(3060m)**

A minor snow eminence on the ridge connecting Pic Tordu with Mount Shackleton.

FA August 1972, H. Microys, M. Rosenberger, on **traverse** from W to E (CAJ **56**-84).

2. S Face. August 1972, Lidstone party (see Tordu). From camp at base of Mount Shackleton S ridge, ascend snow directly to top (CAJ **56**-82).

MOUNT SHACKLETON (W 3310m; C 3330m; SE 3320m)

A splendid wedge-shaped snow massif with 3 peaks, located in the center of the group. It is exceedingly well protected from all directions save perhaps the SW. The central and W peaks are normally climbed together. Highly recommended.

FA **(C and W Peaks),** July 1951, G. I. Bell, D. Michael. **NW Ridge.** The primary problem lies in working a route through the spectacular and dangerous icefall which descends N between Mounts Tusk and Duplicate. In 1972, two climbers were killed here by falling seracs. The best lines lie generally to the left (E), on or near a dark streak. Once in the basin below the mountain, climb steep snow to gain the NW ridge some 200m below the W summit, which is then attained over a steep snow crest. The ridge connecting to the central and highest point, while narrow and exposed, is straightforward. Unaccountably, few cornices are normally encountered on this route (AAJ **8**-255).

Variant. August 1982, R. Kruszyna, A. Maki, J. E. Taylor. This long and nontrivial approach makes it possible to climb Mount Shackleton from the Grassi Hut. Climb rock headwall to right (S) of icefall dropping from glacier lying between Pic Tordu and Shipton–Irvine ridge; rock climbing to F5 on steep, friable rock (2½ h from hut). Cross glacier to Shackleton–Irvine

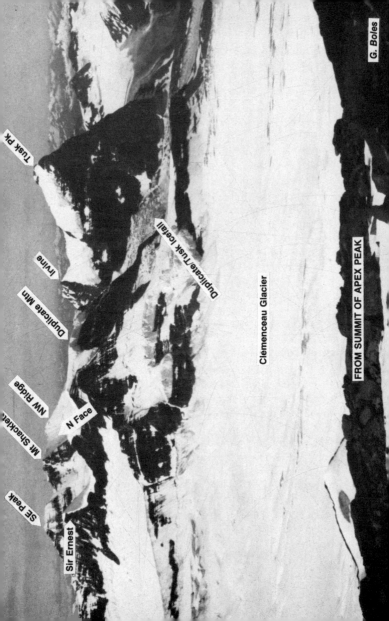

Tusk Pk

Irvine

Duplicate/Tusk (icefall)

Duplicate Mtn

NW Ridge

N Face

Mt Shackle...

SE peak

Sir Ernest

Clemenceau Glacier

FROM SUMMIT OF APEX PEAK

G. Boles

col (1½ h). Attack step on its W side, then at midheight move
to N side, in order to reach shoulder on NW ridge where FA
route is joined. Steep, loose rock (F4) mixed with ice and snow.
III; 8 h hut to summit. This approach also seems to give access
to the Shackleton–Tordu col. It is possible to reach the Shackleton–Irvine col by descending snow and unpleasant downshelving slabs from the Irvine–Tusk col.

2. N. Face. August 1971, M. Heath, W. Summer. The route
on this face of the central summit lies just to the right of a
prominent rock-ribbed buttress. It may be reached by traversing in from the Shackleton–Irvine col (as in the FA) or by
the Duplicate–Tusk icefall. 400m of 55–60° water ice gives a
fine climb. III–IV (AAJ **46**-140).

3. SW Ridge. August 1972, H. Microys, M. Rosenberger.
The Shackleton–Cowl saddle is most readily reached from the
S by ascending Cowl, or on a traverse from Pic Tordu. Ascend
ridge directly to Shackleton W peak, from which the main
summit is easily gained. There is one difficult vertical step near
the top of the ridge. 2–3 h from saddle (CAJ **56**-84).

SE PEAK

FA August 1972, H. Microys, M. Rosenberger. Via **NW ridge**
on traverse from Central Peak. A large rock gendarme just
beyond the main summit constitutes a formidable obstacle.
Traverse a narrow band on gendarme's N side and work into
col beyond (from which it could be climbed). Ascend a short
vertical rock step and continue along a more-or-less level section of ridge. From ensuing col, climb 2 pitches of ice/snow to
top. 3 h from Central Peak. Descend snow and steep rock of
E ridge to Shackleton–Sir Ernest col in 3 h more (CAJ **56**-84).

UNNAMED *(Sir Ernest)* (3150m)

An attractive snow peak between Mounts Shackleton and
Duplicate.

FA July 1936, E. R. Gibson, S. B. Hendricks, R. C. Hind, J.

Southard. **W Face.** A straightforward snow climb from the Shackleton–Sir Ernest col in one h (AAJ **3**-48).

2. NE Ridge. August 1972, ACC party. A clean and enjoyable route from the Duplicate col (CAJ **56**-83).

DUPLICATE MOUNTAIN (SW 3140m; C 3150m; NE 3120m)

A flat-topped massif 2 km NE of Mount Shackleton.

FA July 1936, E. R. Gibson, S. B. Hendricks, R. C. Hind. J. Southard. **S Ridge.** Reach the Duplicate–Sir Ernest col either via the Duplicate–Tusk icefall or from the S via Clemenceau Glacier, and ascend the simple ridge in ½ h (AAJ **3**-43).

NE Peak via N Ridge. August 1972, H. Microys, M. Rosenberger, T. Turner. Avoid the vertical lower section on the right (W) and then climb the rock ridge which offers several steep pitches. Snow/ice slopes lead to the top. A traverse may be made by descending the **S ridge.** 13 h RT from camp below Mount Clemenceau (CAJ **56**-84).

UNNAMED *(Shipton)* (3030m)

The most westerly of 3 peaks on ridge running SW from Tusk Peak; 3 km NE of Grassi Hut.

FA August 1964, F. & H. Largiader, L. Mondolfo. **E Ridge** from Shipton–Chettan col (CAJ **48**-117).

2. N Ridge. August 1972, H. Mutch, B. Sanford, on descent as part of a traverse. An enjoyable and exposed scramble on the ascent. 4 h from hut (CAJ **56**-83).

UNNAMED *(Chettan)* (3040m)

Next E of Shipton.

FA July 1936, E. R. Gibson, S. B. Hendricks. R. C. Hind. J. Southard. From glacier in Shipton–Tusk cirque, ascend directly the **N slope.** 4 h from base of glacier (CAJ **24**-59).

2. E–W Traverse. August 1964, C. Fay, R. Kruszyna, W. T. Sharp. As above, but ascend to minor point *(Tilman)* E of ob-

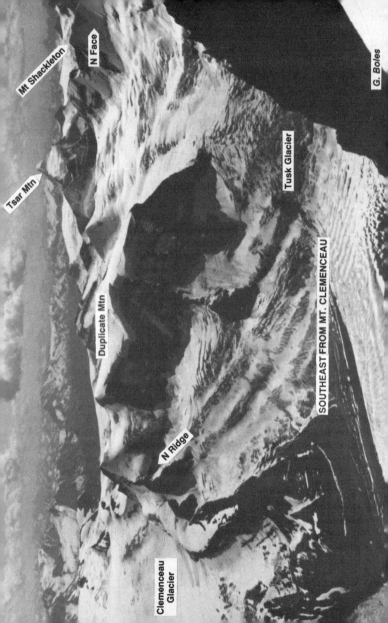

Mt. Shackleton

N Face

G. Boles

Tsar Mtn

Tusk Glacier

Duplicate Mtn

SOUTHEAST FROM MT. CLEMENCEAU

N Ridge

Clemenceau Glacier

jective. Follow enjoyable snow ridge to top and descend rock to Shipton col. 5 h from base of Tusk (CAJ **48**-117).

UNNAMED *(Irvine)* (3060m)

1.5 km S of Tusk Peak.

FA July 1927, J. DeLaittre, W. R. Maclaurin, A. J. Ostheimer, *H. Fuhrer.* **E Slopes.** The original approach via the Duplicate–Tusk icefall to the Shackleton–Irvine col and then to the Tusk–Irvine col is no longer sensible. Instead, ascend a snow couloir from the Tusk–Shipton cirque to the latter col, from which the summit is readily attained (CAJ **16**-33).

TUSK PEAK (3360m)

An outstanding pyramidal peak; one of the prizes of the region. FA July 1927, Ostheimer party (see Irvine). Gain the Tusk–Irvine col as for Irvine (above). Two variants are possible. Climb the rock of the **S ridge** (one difficult step) or swing out onto the snow of the **SE slopes.** 2 h from the col in either case; 10 h RT from Grassi Hut (CAJ **16**-33).

2. NW Ridge. July 1951, G. I. Bell, J. R. Rousson. A long rock route. Poor rock in the lower sections, but with better and much-exposed climbing in the top 300m (AAJ **8**-257).

Note: Various segments of the Tusk–Shipton ridge have been traversed in both directions, affording enjoyable but easy climbing. First complete traverse, August 1972, H. Microys, M. Rosenberger, who started with the NW ridge of Tusk and finished on the N ridge of Shipton; 16 h total from camp E of Mount Clemenceau (CAJ **56**-84). Shipton–Irvine segment takes 12 h RT from Grassi Hut.

MOUNT CLEMENCEAU (3658m)

The outstanding peak in the area, and the fourth highest summit in the Canadian Rockies.

FA August 1923, D. B. Durand, H. S. Hall, W. D. Harris,

Tusk PK

Mt Shackleton

Duplicate/Tusk Icefall

Duplicate Mtn

Tusk Glacier

FROM EAST SIDE OF MT. CLEMENCEAU

H. B. DeVilliers–Schwab. **W Face.** A classic snow and ice route of great character. From the Grassi Hut, approach across the Cummins and Tusk Glaciers to the SW corner of the mountain. The route then goes up the Tiger Glacier, which covers the W side of the peak, from lower right (SW) to upper left (NW). Pass through the lower band of cliffs and crevasses to gain a great basin. Work left up a steep slope to reach a "col" just above a small snow hump on the subsidiary W ridge. Continue up to a broad bench which lies below and parallel to the main summit crest. Traverse left (N) along this bench to the NW ridge, which is followed to the top. 12–15 h RT (CAJ **14**-18).

2. S Ridge. August 1964, F. & H. Largiader. Initially follow route above to near great basin, until it is possible to work right (S) and ascend steep snow to the prominent shoulder of the S ridge. Take the heavily-corniced ridge to the summit. 9 h from base of peak (CAJ **48**-116).

3. NE Ridge. August 1980, D. Eberl, P. Jensen, T. Kelly, G. Thompson, J. Wilson. This is the curving ridge which extends eastward from the summit and then turns and drops northward. Approach from E across valley of Clemenceau Creek to place a camp on alp below ridge. Ascend a 500m ice face to gain ridge proper. Continue along ridge, easily at first, to a flat area suitable for a bivouac. The final part of the ridge is heavily corniced to the N and very steep on the S, and the snow is unlikely to be stable. Near the summit, there is a pitch on a 5m vertical knife edge of snow. The route compares to the Wishbone or Emperor Ridges on Mount Robson. V; one bivouac (AAJ **55**-123).

MOUNT MORRISON (2880m)

On "Reconnaissance Ridge," which runs N–SE between Cummins Glacier and the Clemenceau massif; 2.5 km N of southernmost high point.

FA August 1972, R. Lidstone, J. Mellor, R. Parsons, R. Reader,

P. Robinson, P. Roxburgh. Gain the summit ridge, a knife edge of solid rock, by the **E flank** from glacier to E (CAJ **56**-83).

MOUNT SHARP (2910m)

On Reconnaissance Ridge, one km N of Mount Morrison.

FA August 1972, Lidstone party (above). **SE Ridge.** Gain ridge either by a traverse of Morrison (as in FA), or at Sharp–Morrison col (CAJ **56**-83).

UNNAMED *(Cresswell)* (2970m)

One km N of Sharp.

FA August 1972, W. J. Hurst, *alone*. **SW Ridge.** Ascend Cummins Glacier until it is possible to climb a rock ramp from the SW corner of objective to the ridge proper. Take ridge over crumbling rock to top (CAJ **56**-83).

The peaks to the NW of Mount Clemenceau are most readily ascended from a high camp or bivouac located on a bench above (N) of the glacier ("Bruce Glacier") which flows E between them and Mount Clemenceau. Mounts Mallory, Farrar and Bruce can all be climbed in a single day, as on the FAs.

UNNAMED *(Bruce)* (3090m)

8 km NW of Mount Clemenceau, at N end of Reconnaissance Ridge.

FA August 1927, A. J. Ostheimer, *H. Fuhrer*, on traverse from Mallory, via **NE ridge.** Gain col to E of objective and round latter on glacier to N. Ascend easily to ridge and summit; 2 h from col. FA party descended **S ridge** to Bruce Glacier (CAJ **16**-35).

UNNAMED *(Mallory)* (3270m)

7 km NNW of Mount Clemenceau, at N head of Bruce Glacier.

FA August 1927, A. J. Ostheimer, *H. Fuhrer*. From camp

above Bruce Glacier, ascend shaley ridge N toward objective and cross small glacier to Mallory–Farrar col (2½ h). Then ascend **SW ridge** simply to top in ½ h more. FA party descended **W face** en route to Bruce (CAJ **16**-34).

UNNAMED *(Farrar)* **(3240m)**
A wedge-shaped peak one km SE of Mallory. It is well guarded on all sides save the N.

FA August 1927, A. J. Ostheimer, *H. Fuhrer.* **N Ridge.** Reach the Mallory–Farrar col, as above. Ascend the ridge, making a traverse of 50m on the E just above the col. The ridge offers good rock climbing in chimneys and overhangs. 2 h from col (CAJ **16**-34).

MOUNT BRAS CROCHE (3286)
The northermost peak in the Clemenceau Group, bounded on the E by Clemenceau Creek and to the N and W by Wood River.

FA August 1927, J. DeLaittre, A. J. Ostheimer, *H. Fuhrer.* From camp above Bruce Glacier, descend NE to timber until it is possible to round the end of SE ridge of Farrar and gain the glacier between Farrar and objective ("Bras Croche Glacier") (5 h). Cross glacier and ascend shale and snow of **S slopes,** the final part of the climb being on snow/ice (6 h). Descent by same route in 5½ h (CAJ **16**-35).

Perched on the loftiest throne in the world, we are still sitting on our own ass.

Montaigne

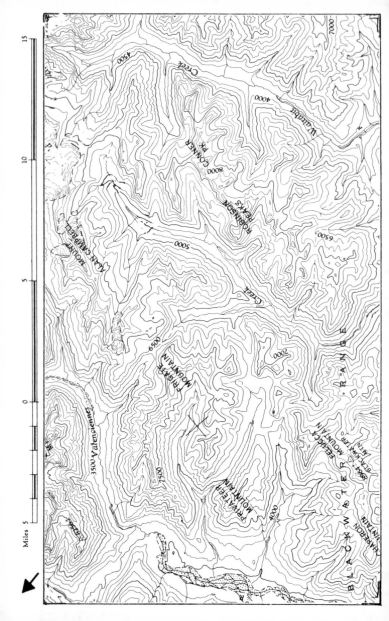

WEST OF THE DIVIDE

Here are collected isolated summits and massifs which rise W of the main chain of the Rockies. Approaches have been from the Columbia River valley and, in recent years, generally by air.

Blackwater Range

This subsidiary to the Divide peaks is centered 30 km W of Freshfield Icefield. These scattered minor summits lie N of Bluewater Creek and S of Bush and Valenciennes Rivers, entirely within B. C. and the Hamber Provincial Forest. The highest point is Frigate Mountain (2880m). Logging roads reach close to timberline in many of the tributaries of Bush River and extend into the Bluewater valley as well.

Maps: 82N 11, 82N 14.

FRIGATE MOUNTAIN (2880m)
11 km W of Mount Alan Campbell.
FA July 1979, W. L. Putnam, *E. Salzgeber* and larger party.

Via **SW ridge,** after tourtuous approach from E. Same party also ascended several high points between Mount Alan Campbell and Frigate Mountain, as well as most along Bush–Bluewater Divide.

Waitabit Ridge

An area of alpine country between Bluewater Creek on the N and Waitabit Creek on the S, much resembling the Blackwater Range above. The highest point (2940m) is 18 km N of the Trans–Canada crossing of Columbia River.

Map: 82N 11.

Bush Mountain

This impressive massif is located 10 km W of Mons Peak (Forbes–Lyell Group). It and its satellites are bounded by Valenciennes River and its tributary, Icefall Brook, on the S and E and by Lyell Creek on the NW. The ridge extending N from Bush Mountain toward Mount Lyell carries three lesser summits, Kemmel, La Clytte, and Lens Mountains.

ACCESS

The initial attempt to reach this region was up the notorious Bush River by the party of J. N. Collie in 1900. To quote, ". . . we had an excellent view of the promised land which we were about to enter. It looked anything but promising."

Nevertheless, in 1936, W. N. M. Hogg and party succeeded in making the FA of the highest peak, Rostrum, after 4 days of boating and bashing up the Bush to the base of the massif. See introduction to Chapter 4, under Bush River–Lyell Creek, for current situation of approaches from W. Approach from the E was made in 1954 by the Hendricks party, which started

from Glacier Lake (see Chapter 2 introduction), ascended the
Lyell Icefield, crossed the Divide to the SW Lyell Glacier, and
contoured S above and parallel to Icefall Brook. Any overland
approach requires several days of backpacking and bushwhacking, while the helicopter trip from Golden takes 20 minutes.

Map: 82N 14.

ROSTRUM PEAK (3300m)
Southernmost and highest of Bush Mountain massif.
FA September 1936, W. N. M. Hogg, *C. Häsler Jr.* **NW Gla-
cier/NE Ridge.** From camp on creek that descends from the
W cirque of objective to its head. Climb steep snow/ice couloir
to notch in ridge, to left (N) of which rises the rock tower of
Bush Peak. Climb along NE ridge to summit. Ascent, 9½ h.
FA party descended SE to dry glacier between S and E ridges,
a roundabout route but, perhaps, safer in the late afternoon
than the snow/ice couloir (CAJ **24**-43).

BUSH PEAK (3090m)
The sharp central and lowest peak of Bush Mountain. (AJ
20-479; **39**-60).

ICEFALL PEAK (3210m)
N summit of Bush Mountain.
FA July 1954, S. B. Hendricks, D. Hubbard, E. K. & P.
Karcher, A. E. Peterson. **NE Face.** From timberline camp E of
Kemmel Mountain, cross several intervening ridges to glacier
on E side of massif. Climb the steep snow/ice of the NE face
to the final summit ridge. 12 h RT from camp (CAJ **38**-20).

KEMMEL MOUNTAIN (3120m)
6 km N of Bush Mountain.
FA July 1954, Hendricks party (see Icefall) plus J. Showacre.

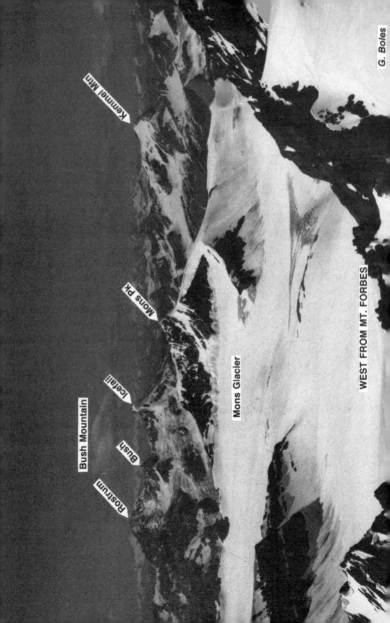

Kemmel Mtn

Mons Pk.

Bush Mountain

(cefall)

Bush

Rostrum

Mons Glacier

WEST FROM MT. FORBES

G. Boles

Easily climbed by any of several routes from timberline camp
to E (CAJ **38**-23).

LA CLYTTE MOUNTAIN (2910m)

2.5 km next NW of Kemmel Mountain.

FA July 1954, E. K. & P. Karcher, J. Showacre. From La
Clytte–Lens col via **NE ridge** without difficulty (CAJ **38**-23).

LENS MOUNTAIN (3150m)

6 km SSW of Mount Lyell on W margin of SW Lyell Icefield.

FA July 1954, S. B. Hendricks, D. Hubbard. Via SW Lyell
Glacier to col at base of **E ridge** and so to summit (CAJ **38**-
21).

Peaks West of Bush River

Although not connected geologically or geographically with
the main mass of the Rockies, the following three massifs are
contiguous and some peaks may afford significant mountaineering interest. Approach has been exclusively by helicopter.

Maps: 82N/14W, 82N/13E.

GOAT PEAK (2810m)

S point of long ridge W of S-flowing Bush River; 5 km W
of mouth of Lyell Creek. Ridge extends some 20 km and supports small glaciers and many points above 2700m.

VERTEBRAE MOUNTAIN (2880m)

16 km N of mouth of Bush River, the ridge next W of above.
It extends 20 km in a NW direction, parallel to main range.
Considerable glaciation and several peaks in the 2700m class.

KITCHEN RANGE (2970m)

Ridge next W of above, parallel to Columbia River and some 8–10 km distant therefrom. The three central peaks and several others were ascended in 1977 by W. L. Putnam, *H. Gmoser* & party.

Chess Group

In the angle formed by the headwaters of Bush River and the E headwaters fork of Sullivan River rises this attractive cluster of heavily-glaciated summits which geologically belong to the Rockies. The principal summits are 14 km W of Mount Bryce and 12 km S of Mount King Edward. Four major peaks, rising in an E–W line, are drained by the cascading Chessboard Glacier whose icefalls constitute the principal climbing problems in the area. Two other large peaks rise to the E and W, respectively, of the head of Prattle Creek, which drains the massif on the S. Access by helicopter, although it is possible (4 days at minimum) to approach via the W terminal fork of Athabasca River, the 2220m pass on the Divide, and the glacier flowing S from there (see Chapter 5, Approaches). All ascents listed made from camp (1980m) at tongue of Chessboard Glacier (CAJ **52**-6).

Maps: 83C/3W, 83C/4E.

THE PAWN (3100m)
Rounded snow dome E of head of Prattle Creek.

ROOK MOUNTAIN (3100m)
Castle-shaped rock peak at W head of Prattle Creek.

KING MOUNTAIN (3120m)
Easternmost and highest of peaks at head of Chessboard Glacier.

King Mtn

Bishop Pk Knight Pk Queen Mtn

Chessboard Glacier

CHESS GROUP FROM NORTH

R. Kruszyna

FA July 1978, H. G. & R. Kruszyna, A. Maki, H. Mutch, P. Vermeulen, D. Whitburn. Ascend hard, compacted moraine on true right (E) side of Chessboard Glacier and then work up through icefalls, bearing left, to gain upper glacier below objective. Ascend to broad saddle W of peak and take snow of **W ridge** to top. 6 h up.

BISHOP PEAK (3060m)
Fluted snow peak W of King Mountain.

FA July 1978, Kruszyna party (above). From King Mountain via **E ridge** (snow, then rock) in one h. Descent to W col and return to camp in 3½ h.

KNIGHT PEAK (3060m)
Next W of Bishop Peak.

FA August 1978, H. G. & R. Kruszyna, H. Mutch. From Bishop–Knight col via steep snow of **E face** in one h.

QUEEN MOUNTAIN (3110m)
Westernmost and most impressive of group.

FA August 1978, H. G. & R. Kruszyna, H. Mutch. **E Face.** Approach as for King Mountain to upper glacier, then swing W below Bishop and ascend through icefall into basin defined by Queen, Knight and Bishop. An enormous crevasse cuts across the entire E face, from lower right to upper left, and provides the line of ascent. Enter crevasse and traverse left on wedged blocks into a huge ice cavern, 30m high, 30m wide and 100m long. Exit through a window at far end to a balcony. Climb a groove and surmount overhanging upper lip. Work through a few more crevasses and then take snow of N ridge to summit. Ascent 6 h, descent via easy broken rock of SE ridge to glacier.

2. S Ridge. August 1978, A. Maki, D. Whitburn. From head of Prattle Creek valley, reached over saddle W of King Mountain, climb rock ridge.

West of Athabasca Pass

In the large area between Athabasca Pass and Canoe River, there are few peaks of interest.

Map: 83D8.

UNNAMED *(Dunkirk)* (3030m)
16 km NE of Big Bend from which it is visible; 21 km SW of Athabasca Pass, between Harvey and Dawson Creeks (031908).

FA August 1940, H. S. Hall, *E. Feuz Jr.* Boat now necessary to reach Harvey Creek, up which the approach is made. Work up stream descending from pocket glacier S of objective. Climb through **SW cliffs** (400m) by a narrow chimney to broken rock which leads easily to summit. Ascent, 11 h from Harvey–Canoe junction (AAJ **4**-314; CAJ **27**-213).

UNNAMED (3090m)
At N head of Baker Creek (991017); 20 km W of Athabasca Pass.

The offer contained in the final lines of page 73 of the previous edition is hereby withdrawn.

W.L. Putnam

Isn't that the secret wish of all mountaineers, to remain at the summit, never to return again to the world that one has just left behind?

R. Messner

LAKES

MALIGNE RANGES

Here are included peaks in the extensive district E of Athabasca River and its Sunwapta tributary and N of the Brazeau River as far as the line of the Canadian National Railroad. On modern maps this large area is referred to as the Queen Elizabeth Range. The highest peaks lie from 24 to 29 km E of the Divide, entirely on the Alberta slope, along the irregular Saskatchewan–Athabasca watershed, separating Brazeau River from Rocky and McLeod Rivers. The region is noteworthy as containing some of the most beautiful lakes in Canada, Maligne (1673m) being the largest in the range, 21 km long and upwards of 2 km wide. Maligne River, rising at Maligne Pass 21 km S of the lake, enters it about 8 km from the lower end. The stream emerging from the lake flows 13 km N to Medicine Lake, 6 km long, bordered on the NE by jagged limestone peaks. This lake has no visible outlet, Maligne River flowing underground (except in times of flood) for 14 km before reappearing in its remarkable canyon (60m in depth) and debouching into the main Athabasca valley.

The highest peak, Mount Brazeau, stands SE of Maligne Lake at the head of Brazeau Icefield, 50 sq km. The most impressive peaks of the region are situated in this vicinity and may be approached from camps at the SE extremity of Maligne Lake.

As early as 1800, Duncan McGillivray crossed from Brazeau Lake to Athabasca River, possibly by Poboktan Pass. The Mount McGillivray of Arrowsmith's map (1862) accompanying D. G. F. MacDonald's *British Columbia* appears to be identical with the present Mount Brazeau. Maligne River is shown by this name on Waddington's map of 1868 (Proc RGS 38-118), and Maligne Lake was visited by H.A.F. MacLeod as early as 1875 (see map accompanying Sandford Fleming's *Report on Surveys and Preliminary Operations on the Canadian Pacific Railway.* Ottawa, 1877.)

In 1902, A. P. Coleman reached Brazeau Lake and attained an elevation about 3200m on the Brazeau snowfield. The country E of Maligne Lake was traversed in 1859 by James Carnegie, Earl of Southesk, who ascended Embarras River and the head of McLeod River, thence crossing a low divide to Rocky (Medicine Tent) River. Near the source of the latter he built Southesk Cairn at an elevation of 2540m. He then followed down Southesk to Brazeau River, up Job Creek and down Coral Creek to Kootenay Plain and the North Saskatchewan. Siffleur River was then ascended to Pipestone Pass, and Pipestone and Bow Rivers descended. Mountain names given by Southesk are Cheviot, Lindsay and Dalhousie. A mountain 6 km S of Southesk Cairn was reserved for his own name.

LITERATURE

Crawford, C.G. "The Maligne Lake Camp." CAJ **19**-56 (1931).

Peaks East of Icefields Highway

In this section we describe three minor groups of peaks which run roughly parallel to the Icefields Highway between Sun-

wapta Pass and Jasper. The most southerly group lies immediately N of Sunwapta Pass from whose vicinity most of its
peaks are approached.

Maps: 83C3, 83C6.

NIGEL PEAK 3211m)

3 km N of Sunwapta Pass.

FA 1918, Boundary Commission. **W Slopes, N Ridge.** Gain
Wilcox Pass via trail from Icefields Campground. Pass N around
end of outlying ridge into basin containing lake. Go up scree
of W face, working left below summit edifice to gain N ridge
which is followed over snow to top.

Variant. 1920, Mr. & Mrs. C. Raymond. As above to base of
summit edifice. Then ascend directly up huge gully to summit
by series of ledges. "More interesting than on ridge."

2. W (Gerda) Ridge. 1966, G. Smythe, *H. Fuhrer.* As in FA
route to long outlying ridge, which is gained by steep scree.
Follow ridge around bend of glacier, approaching peak from
SW. Finish by Route One variation. Traverse from highway in
14 h.

3. S Side. August 1979, H. & R. Kruszyna. From Campground to alps below Wilcox Pass. Work S 2 km to reach couloir
cleaving S cliffs. Climb scoured slabs to amphitheater from
which scree and snow are ascended to SW ridge. Finish by
Route One variation. RT from highway, 9 h.

MOUNT WILCOX (2884m)

Between Wilcox Pass and Sunwapta River.

FA 1893, H. Woolley, *alone.* Readily ascended by SE slopes
from Wilcox Pass. Also easy from other directions. Excellent
view of Columbia Icefield peaks. Winter ascent (CAJ **29**-187).

UNNAMED (3033m)

W buttress of Nigel Pass.

FA 1928, A. J. Gilmour, *alone,* presumably from trail on Nigel
Creek via S slopes.

UNNAMED (3145m)
 5 km NE of Wilcox Pass; 5 km S of Jonas Pass.
 FA July 1893, A. P. Coleman, L. Q. Coleman, L. B. Stewart. From camp near head of Brazeau River, up subsidiary valley to NW, ascending scree and steep limestone. Ascent 4 h (Coleman-183).

TANGLE RIDGE (3000m)
 Between Tangle and Beauty Creeks.
 Waterfall Climb: Distant Blue, 4 pitches, Grade 3, March 1980, R. Doege, P. Monkonnen. On N buttress; 4 km approach along Beauty Creek from Icefields Highway.

SUNWAPTA PEAK (3315m)
 Major peak in SE angle between Sunwapta River and Jonas Creek.
 FA 1906, J. Simpson, *alone*. From highway by **SW slopes.** Can also be climbed by S slopes in 4½ h from Beauty Creek.
 2. N Face, August 1976, O. Miskiw, D. Pors. Go up creek valley 4 km N of Beauty Creek to toe of N glacier. Ascend toward ice towers, turning left below them and continuing to N ridge. Follow it briefly, then traverse below upper ice wall to gain NW ridge which is taken to top. "Better than standard route on Athabasca." Asecnt 6 h (CAJ **60**-83).
 3. N Ridge, July 1972, J. Cumberbatch, J. Creore, W. McIntosh. Approach from trail on Poboktan Creek, taking S fork into Jonas Creek drainage. Cross creek to reach basin with lake, NE of subsidiary peak at end of N ridge. Gain ridge and traverse subsidiary peak to col beyond (or, as on FA, avoid peak by descending S into valley and climbing back up to col). Follow ridge (snow/ice), staying mainly on left side, to summit. Approach from trail, one day. Ascent proper, 7 h; descent 4 h. 7 h more to return to Poboktan Creek (CAJ **56**-85).

UNNAMED *(Screed)* (3060m)
  3.5 km NNW of Sunwapta Peak.
  FA August 1976, R. Funk, G. Hrabar, W. Kelly, O Miskiw.
Via **SW slopes** in 7 h RT from highway (CAJ **60**-83).

In the area SW of Jonas Creek and Pass are many "writing
desk" mountains other than those specifically listed above, several exceeding 2900m.

WATERFALL PEAKS (2950m)
  On Poboktan–Jonas divide, 2.5 km SW of warden's cabin on
Poboktan Creek.
  FRA 1939, L. Gest, P. Prescott, who found the summit record
of a party led by *J. Weiss*. Cross Poboktan Creek at warden's
cabin and follow N side of waterfall stream to small glacial
basin. Ascend **E face** to N peak, traversing to higher S peak
(AAJ **4**-314).

N of Poboktan Creek, the **Endless Chain Ridge,** a structur-
ally-controlled dip slope, extends NW some 40 km to Hardisty
Creek. The few peaks of climbing interest rise at its N end and
are readily approached from the highway. They are listed below from N to S. Map 83C/12.

MOUNT HARDISTY (2700m)
  6 km NE of Athabasca Falls.
  FA Dominion Survey. Easily done by S or W slopes.
  2. N Ridge. August 1972, G. Irwin, *H. Fuhrer*. From Horseshoe Lake ascend through rockslide area and ascend NW face
to N ridge. Climb good quartzite to top, the final buttress being
especially fine. 6 h up (CAJ **56**-84).

MOUNT KERKESLIN (NW 2950m, SE 2936m)
  Massif with substantial glacier on E, located 5 km SE of
Athabasca Falls; incorrectly located as next peak to S on 83C/
12.

FA August 1926, F. H. Slark, J. Weber. **N Ridge.** Starting from highway about 2 km N of Athabasca Falls, work up through forest along a NW spur onto NW face. Gain N ridge near 2500m and follow it to prominent black band. Climb this steep section, 70m high (F4), and continue to summit. 7 h up; descent, rappelling black band, in 4 h. A good climb of the short and accessible variety.

2. SW Side. July 1946, E. R. Gibson, R. C. Hind. Leave highway about 4 km S of Athabasca Falls and follow up a stream bed which develops into a canyon. Exit to N and proceed to head of canyon. Traverse right on steep grass and easy rock, then head straight up to noticeable dip in S ridge. A steep pitch of 70m leads through the black band to the ridge some distance S of the summit. Follow it, overcoming two 3m overhangs, to top. Ascent 6½ h; FA party completed traverse by descending Route One (AAJ **6**-448; CAJ **30**-42, compass directions thoroughly confused).

WINDY CASTLE (2820m)

4 km SE of Mount Kerkeslin; incorrectly labeled as "Mount Kerkeslin" on 83C/12.

FA August 1947, A. Bruce–Robertson, M. Finley, N. E. Odell, J. Ross, F. S. Smythe. Approach from highway by stream leading to saddle between objective and SE summit of Mount Kerkeslin. Ascend a chimney to scree slopes below final cliffs. Move left to NW corner and climb another chimney and a last limestone wall (CAJ **31**-75).

Immediately SE of Jasper, in the angle between Athabasca River and Maligne River (Medicine Lake), rises a group of minor summits called the **Maligne Range** (not to be confused with the major peaks at the S end of Maligne Lake). This area is served by the Skyline Trail, which runs from Maligne Canyon over Shovel Pass to the outlet end of Maligne Lake, a distance of about 50 km. Although popular with hikers, this area offers no challenge to climbers with the exception of the Watchtower, next described. Map 83C/13.

THE WATCHTOWER (2791m)

6 km SW of Medicine Lake; 5 km N of Shovel Pass.

FA August 1951, R. K. Irvin, J. Mowat, R. Strong. Leave Jasper–Medicine Lake road 2.5 km below (NW) outlet of lake. FA party was able to follow an abandoned trail which begins just S of Excelsior Creek (and eventually reaches Shovel Pass). Work up into valley to NW of objective and gain its **N ridge.** This narrow, exposed crest is followed thereafter over 2 false summits to the peak. Ascent, 5 h; descent by same route, 4 h. The greatest difficulty is in returning over the first false summit (CAJ **35**-99).

Winter Ascent, February 1977, O. Miskiw, D. Pors.

Le Grand Brazeau

Here are listed the peaks rising to the SE of the Lake Peaks, in an area roughly bounded by Poboktan Creek on the SW, Brazeau River on the SE, and Southesk River on the N. The group has not engendered much interest among technical climbers and is seldom visited. Most of the high peaks are ranged around Swan Lake (825202), which lies at the head of the N fork of Brazeau River. The rock is largely limestone of Cambrian Age with many fossils, and is of extremely variable quality. The timber, however, is open and going is generally good. Streams often flow underground and karst topography abounds.

The most commonly used access to this region is by the Poboktan Creek Trail, which leaves the Icefields Highway at the ranger station 70 km S of Jasper. It is well maintained over Poboktan Pass (27 km) to Brazeau Lake (37 km) where it joins with the trail in Brazeau River. This latter runs from Nigel Pass NE to this junction (22 km) and then onward to meet the

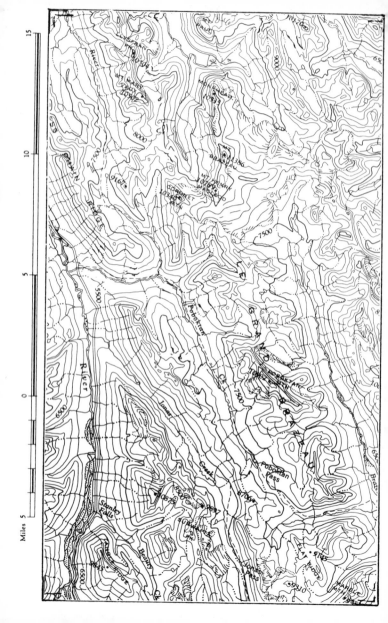

Southesk River trail. Warden cabins are maintained at half-day intervals along these back country trails.

Recent parties have approached **Swan Lake** (6.5 km ESE of Mount Brazeau) using game trails in open bush along the E side of the tributary to Poboktan Creek next E of Poligne Creek (along which latter runs the Maligne Trail to Maligne Pass). Take the E fork of this tributary to col (2630m) which leads over to lake-studded Valley of All The Lakes. Follow this valley out to N fork of Brazeau River and go upstream 4 km to Swan Lake. One and a half days with full packs. It is also possible to reach Swan Lake from Maligne Lake via Warren Creek. No time advantage, and the disadvantage of ascending on glacier with heavy loads.

Maps: 83C/6, 83C/11.

To the N of Brazeau Lake, in the SW angle between Brazeau and Southesk Rivers, there are a number of named points exceeding 2900m, including **Mount Aztec, Mount Olympus** (FA 1928), **Chocolate Mountain, Arête Mountain,** and **Mount Dalhousie.** There are also at least three peaks in this area which exceed 3300m in elevation, for which there are no records of any ascents.

POBOKTAN MOUNTAIN (E 3323m; W 3313m)

Large massif lying between Poboktan Creek and N fork of Brazeau River; magnificent NE escarpment.

FA 1928, Topographical Survey, via **SW slopes.**

UNNAMED (2970m)

3.5 km NNW of Poboktan Mountain; S of Valley of All The Lakes, which drains NE into N fork of Brazeau River.

FA July 1971, J.A.V. Cade, F. Chapple, E. Johann, G. Hintriger, D. von Hennig, L. R. Wallace, *H. Gmoser, W. L. Putnam.* From camp in center of Valley, ascend rock and snow of **N**

ridge. II, 4 h up. Same group also climbed other minor peaks surrounding Valley to W and NW and found no difficulties on obvious routes (CAJ **55**-91).

The following nine peaks are most readily approached from a camp near Swan Lake (see Introduction). They are listed from SE to NW.

UNNAMED (3190m)
Double summit 7 km SE of Swan Lake; 5 km NW of Chocolate Mountain (891166).

UNNAMED (3000m)
5 km ESE of Swan Lake (876185).

FA July 1971, J.A.V. Cade, D. von Hennig, G. Hintriger, *W. L. Putnam.* From Swan Lake, enter Valley to NW of objective, passing S of lake therein. Ascend snow gullies and scree to upper part of glacier. Traverse E across ice (bare late in season) to summit. 4½ h up; II, F4 (CAJ **55**-91).

UNNAMED (3180m)
5 km E of Swan Lake (877197).

FA August 1970, Putnam party (see Cornucopia). As for above, into valley to W. Ascend scree gully to col W of summit; then take steep **W scree** slopes to top in one h more. 8 h RT; III, F4 (AAJ **17**-386; CAJ **54**-89).

UNNAMED (3150m)
3 km ENE of Swan Lake (857210).

UNNAMED (3120m)
3.5 km NE of Swan Lake (855225); N of peak above at head of same valley, which drains into Brazeau River below Swan Lake.

FA July 1971, J.A.V. Cade, F. Chapple, D. von Hennig, *W.*

L. Putnam. Enter open valley leading toward objective, passing
a lake on NW. Work NW to gain glacier and follow it to **W
ridge.** Climb ridge to summit; E point is higher. FA party left
fixed rope to return to W point. III, F5 (CAJ **55**-91).

UNNAMED (2910m)
    1.5 km NE of Swan Lake (834215).
    FA, same as above. Follow route above to col NE of objective
and climb **N ridge;** II, F6.

UNNAMED (3090m)
    3 km NE of Swan Lake (842227).
    FA July 1971, F. Chapple, E. Johann, L. R. Wallace, *H.
Gmoser.* **NW Slope.** From Swan Lake, gain glacier to W of
objective. Climb W rock buttress to upper snowfield which leads
to summit. 6 h up; III, F6 (CAJ **55**-91).

UNNAMED (3150m)
    4 km N of Swan Lake (820245).

UNNAMED *(Cornucopia)* (3210m)
    5 km N of Swan Lake (823253).
    FA Topographical Survey, date unknown.
    S Glacier. August 1970, G. Boss, M. Broman, F. Mettrick,
L. Putnam, W. L. Putnam, A. Wexler. From Swan Lake, ascend
S glacier and then SW ridge. 8 h RT (AAJ **17**-386; (CAJ **54**-
89).

UNNAMED (3240m)
    Highest point to E of Le Grand Brazeau; in W angle of forks
of Southesk River; 6 km SSE of Southesk Lake (895266).
    FRA August 1971, M. H. Benn, T. Sorenson. This remote
peak entails a long approach. While the trail on Southesk River
offers a possible route, it is probably better to approach via
Maligne Lake and Warren Creek. Take the E terminal fork of

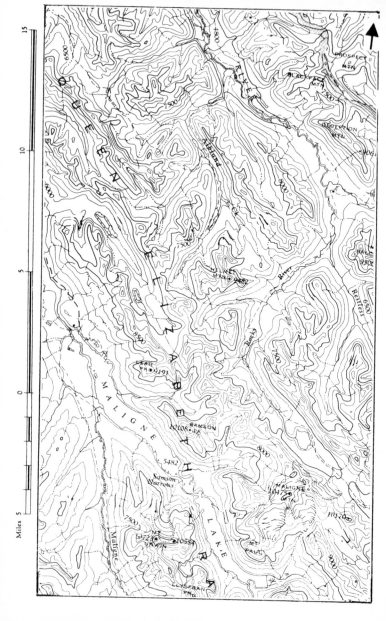

the latter to a col (2800m) which leads over to a major SW tributary of Southesk River. Follow glacier down to campsite by large lake 4 km W of objective; one day from Warren Creek delta. The climb itself poses no difficulties; 1200m of scree on the **W ridge.** Cairn but no record. 4 h up; 2 h down (CAJ **55**-90).

Lake Peaks

Here we describe those routes commonly approached from campsites on or near Maligne Lake. Climbers are required to check in with the Warden who is located near the outlet (NW end) of the Lake, at the end of the paved road from Jasper. Charter boat service is available from this point to any other on the lake shore, without prior reservation. Camping is restricted in immediate vicinity of the Lake. There are two designated campsites; one is at the S end of the Lake near the outflow of Coronet Creek. The ACC camps of 1930, 1950, 1962, and 1979 were located here. The other is some 7 km by trail upstream (S) on Coronet Creek. Most ascents are made from these campsites, although Mounts Charlton and Unwin can be done directly form the NW end of the Lake by arranging for an early boat ride. Some climbs are facilitated by placing a high camp or bivouac on moraines above Warren Creek; no trail but only ½ day. A camp on Sandpiper Creek shortens the approach to Maligne Mountain. The Maligne Trail is the only other in the area which might possibly be of use to mountaineers. This runs from the outlet of the Lake along the W side (6 km), going up Maligne River to Maligne Pass (24 km more) and then descending Poligne Creek to the Poboktan Creek Trail (6 km).

Maps: 83C/11, 83C/12.

Caution should be exercised with respect to some of the older routes since snow and ice features have altered significantly. Many changes in nomenclature of peaks in this group have afflicted the literature. This text is definitive, but some of the references, particularly those prior to 1950, are at variance with each other and with this volume.

MOUNT UNWIN (3268m)
MOUNT CHARLTON (3217m)

These are the striking, snow-decked twin peaks seen from the N end of Maligne Lake, rising 5 km S of Samson Narrows. Mount Unwin is the W peak of the massif, Mount Charlton the E. Both peaks are frequently climbed on the same day (see Mount Charlton FA route). This combined ascent is one of the 2 or 3 finest tours in the area, easy but in a magnificent ambiance. Highly recommended.

FA Mount Unwin, July 1923, A. Carpé, W. D. Harris, H. Palmer. From a point some 6 km up Maligne River from the Lake, ascend a conspicuous slide and cross steep grass slopes to enter a hanging valley lying WNW of objective. Climb to a col (2780m) on the main **W ridge** which is taken (buttress and icy chimneys) to final snow slopes and summit. Ascent from Maligne River, 10¾ h; descent 5 h (AJ **36**-108).

FA Mount Charlton, July 1928, W. R. Hainsworth, M. M. Strumia. **N Glacier.** Take a boat to Samson Narrows and debark on the delta formed by the stream from Charlton–Unwin N Glacier. Go through timber, cross stream, and ascend E lateral moraine (true right). Cross bare ice of glacier tongue and work up toward W corner of basin to reach upper plateau of glacier (3 h from lake). Ascend crevassed glacier between walls of Mount Unwin and peculiar rock cleaver, over discomforting avalanche debris, to gain upper basin of glacier. Climb steep snow of headwall to Charlton–Unwin col (3 h). Follow a gentle ridge E to the summit of Mount Charlton; ½ h RT from col. Take a steep snow ridge W to the top of Mount Unwin; one h RT. Descent to Maligne Lake by same route, 3–4 h. Total

Mt Unwin

Mt Charlton

Mt Brazeau

Mt Paul

Samson Pk

H. Kruszyna

ACROSS MALIGNE LAKE FROM NORTH

time, including both summits, 11 h (AAJ **1**-49; AJ **41**-345; (CAJ **17**-22; **29**-186, winter ascent).

MOUNT MOFFAT (3090m)

Peak immediately W of Ultramaligne Lake, which lies at 2280m in the amphitheater formed by Mount Charlton to the N and Mount Moffat and Llysyfran Peak to the S. Ultramaligne Lake drains by the second major stream NW of Coronet Creek, which enters Maligne Lake 3.2 km from latter. The hike to this lake is worthwhile in its own right; 3 h from mouth of Coronet Creek.

FA August 1930, *H. Fuhrer, Hy Fuhrer*. **SE Ridge.** From Ultramaligne Lake, attack the steep wall to S which leads to broad saddle between objective and Llysyfran. One pitch of F4 with old piton. From saddle, scramble up SE ridge, simple except for two 30m cliffs with downshelving rock, best taken on ridge crest. Ascent 5 h. Descend N ridge to Moffat–Unwin col and then go down unpleasant scree, snow and glacier, regaining Ultramaligne Lake in 2 h. Total time from mouth of Coronet Creek, 12 h (CAJ **19**-153).

LLYSYFRAN PEAK (3141m)

4 km WSW of mouth of Coronet Creek.

FA September 1929, L. S. Amery, *E Feuz Jr*. From point on Maligne River about 10 km N of Maligne Pass, ascend into W glacial basin, working up to SE to gain a small peak on main ridge connecting objective to Mount Mary Vaux. Descend to N slightly and then climb S ridge to summit, ascent 8 h (CAJ **18**-10, photo; AJ **42**-45).

2. NW Ridge, August 1957, T. Messner, W. Pagle. From Ultramaligne Lake to saddle between objective and Mount Moffat as in FA route for latter peak. The NW ridge is then taken to the summit. Descent by Route 3; 16 h RT from camp at mouth of Coronet Creek (CAJ **41**-83; AAJ **11**-97).

3. SE Side, August 1930, C. G. Crawford, T. B. Moffat, D. R. Sharpe, H. F. Thompson. From Maligne Lake, ascend stream valley next W of Coronet Creek to piedmont glacier below objective and Mount Mary Vaux. The route initially follows the conspicuous snow couloir which leads to main crest. About halfway up take to the rocks of the SE face, which lead to the S ridge. Follow this to the top. It appears feasible to climb the couloir directly to the crest. Ascent 10 h (CAJ **19**-58; AJ **43**-259).

Note: The 1930 party found its intended descent route on the N ridge impracticable and was thus forced to descend W to a bivouac on Maligne River. The following day, they hiked the 25 km to the head of Maligne Lake. Taking a boat back down the lake to the ACC camp at the mouth of Coronet Creek, they arrived just in time to forestall the departure of a search party. The selfsame scenario was repeated 20 years later at the 1950 ACC camp (CAJ **34**-62).

MOUNT JULIAN (2760m)

Outlier NE of Mount Mary Vaux, 2.5 km S of mouth of Coronet Creek. A good viewpoint.

FA July 1930, ACC party of 8 led by J. A. Corry, C. G. Crawford. From mouth of Coronet Creek go through brush to high shelf at base of mountain. The route follows the prominent couloir in the NE face, a cave pitch near the top being turned on the left wall. Follow the **N ridge,** with some passages on the W side to the highest point. Ascent 6 h (CAJ **19**-57).

2. W Slope. From Maligne Lake, follow up stream draining piedmont glacier below Mount Mary Vaux, working around to W of objective. Ascend tiresome scree, angling S under cliffs to gain S ridge which leads quickly to top. Ascent 5 h, descent 3 h. From NW base of aforementioned cliffs, it is possible to descend rapidly NW to regain approach route.

MOUNT MARY VAUX (3201m)

Broad, massive peak with formidable NE escarpment, 4 km SSW of mouth of Coronet Creek; routes described **counter-clockwise.**

FA August 1923, M. Blakeslee, B. Herzberg, D. Sutherland, E. J. Widdecombe. **From SW** by the broad, gentle ridge sloping down to Maligne River.

2. S Face, August 1930, R. Baring, C. G. Crawford, K. Gardiner, S. B. Hendricks, W. Maclaren, P. Prescott. From campsite in upper Coronet Creek, ascend ledges and gullies to broad saddle between objective and Unnamed 2790m to S. Cross passes in NW direction and scramble rocky face, diagonally right at first and then back left. The final 200m is on snow, leading to the corniced summit. Ascent 7 h. This is the descent route of choice. After reaching the base of the mountain, it is possible to swing N through the pass between Mounts Mary Vaux and Julian and follow the glacier and then the stream which enters Maligne Lake 1.5 km W of the mouth of Coronet Creek; 5 h (CAJ **19**-60).

3. SE Ridge. July 1962, *H. Gmoser* and ACC party. Details uncertain, but is probable that the line lies well to the right of Route 2, along a rather indistinct crest leading to a forepeak (2880m). The summit is gained from the SE along a gentle but corniced snow ridge (CAJ **46**-157).

4. NW Ridge. August 1967, H. Carter, M. Marx, J. Wilkerson. From camp at Coronet Creek ascend next valley W to piedmont glacier below objective. Climb headwall to ridge connecting to Llysyfran Peak; scree on sloping ledges (F5). The exact line followed is unclear, but it seems not to have been the obvious snow couloir of Route 3 on Llysyfran. Once on the crest, take the easy snow of the NW ridge to the top (AAJ **16**-170).

UNNAMED (2790m)

Between Mount Mary Vaux and Coronet Mountain; the original Replica Peak because, viewed from the N, it is a smaller-scaled replica of Coronet Mountain; another excellent viewpoint.

FA July 1923, A. Carpé, W. D. Harris, H. Palmer. From

campsite in upper Coronet Creek, gain broad saddle between objective and Mount Mary Vaux. Contour S and ascend easy **SW slopes;** 3 h (AJ **36**-101).

REPLICA PEAK (2794m)

1.5 km E of Maligne Pass; name mistakenly, but now officially, shifted from Unnamed 2790m above. Of no interest.

CORONET MOUNTAIN (3152m)

Attractive glaciated peak at head of Coronet Creek.

FA August 1930, R. Baring, G. A. Gambs, K. Gardiner, S. B. Hendricks, W. MacLaren, P. Prescott, H. E. Sampson. **S Ridge.** From campsite in upper Coronet Creek via E tongue of Coronet Glacier. Passing close under E spur of Coronet Mountain, descend 200m or more into SE cirque (3½ h). Climb headwall to reach crest of S ridge, 250m with firm rock near top (2 h). Follow ridge to top. Near summit it becomes very narrow, 2 steep sections being bypassed by chimneys in the E wall (5 h). Ascent 10½ h. Because of glacial recession, this route, long and roundabout in any case, is no longer practical (CAJ **19**-48).

2. NW Ridge, August 1930, E. R. Clarke, W. H. Cleveland, M. Davis, J. M. Forkes, B. F. Jefferson, F. McCulloch, M. K. MacLeod, D. R. Sharpe. A complicated approach leads from upper Coronet Creek to the saddle between objective and unnamed 2790m. Circle around end of NW ridge onto W scree slopes. While it is possible to gain the NW ridge low down, that and the lower part of the ridge proper offer a sporting climb indeed. It is easier, however tiresome, to work diagonally up to a rib of reddish blocks which culminates on the upper part of the ridge, beyond the difficulties. Take the ridge (corniced snow) over a forepeak to the summit. Ascent from campsite, 6 h. This is the best descent route. 2½ h to Coronet Creek.

3. N Face, July 1962, P. Hodgkins, G. Neave, L. Norgren, W. Sharp, G. Stefanick, G. Strickholm, *W. Pfisterer*. An elegant route which ascends the hanging glacier on the N face. Approach as for Route 2. An obvious chimney just to right of terminus gives access to the glacier, which is ascended diagonally left to strike the NW ridge a bit N of the summit. 7 h up (CAJ **46**-157).

MOUNT HENRY MacLEOD (3288m)

2.2 km NE of Coronet Mountain across Coronet Glacier.

FA July 1923, A. Carpé, W. D. Harris, H. Palmer. From Coronet Creek campsite ascend E tongue of Coronet Glacier and rising névé close under objective. An easy gully, second from N, leads to the broad **SE ridge** over which the summit is reached in 6 h total (AJ **36**-103).

2. NW Glacier, July 1950, F. L. Cary, M. B. Howorth, D. L. Kerr, H. J. Kothe, L. Vladicka. From camp in upper Coronet Creek, ascend SE over moraine and grass slopes. Attack prominent buttress lying immediately S of terminus and lower icefall of NW glacier and forming its true left bank. Climb rock of buttress to gain upper section of glacier and subsequently MacLeod–Valad saddle; 5½ h. Ascend S to summit in ½ h more. Considerably more interesting than FA route.

Variant, party above. From grass slopes, work up to left to buttress forming N (true right) bank of terminus of NW glacier. Stay close to buttress left of icefall to reach snow above. The MacLeod–Valad saddle is gained in 4½ h from camp.

VALAD PEAK (3250m)

A minor snow eminence N of Mount Henry MacLeod, between it and Mount Brazeau.

FA July 1923, A Carpé, W. D. Harris, H. Palmer. Traversed from Mount Henry MacLeod (which see) en route to col below Mount Brazeau; 2 h (AJ **36**-103).

MOUNT BRAZEAU (3470m)

Culminating point of Maligne Lake group (Coleman-229).

FA July 1923, A. Carpé, W. D. Harris, H. Palmer, normal

route. From camp in upper Coronet Creek, ascend Mount Henry MacLeod by Route One and continue over Valad Peak to broad col below objective (8 h). Climb directly the scree and limited snow of the S face to the top in 2 h additional. Total time, returning by same route, 16 h (AJ **36**-105).

Variants. August 1930, large ACC party led by *H. Fuhrer*. A direct approach from the W to Brazeau–Valad col. From Coronet Creek campsite, follow dry creek bed to alplands. Work S and up snow slopes to couloirs, ascending the one to the left of that containing a waterfall. Higher, drop into couloir next S and climb easy slope to col, from which S face is ascended to summit. 7 h from camp (CAJ **19**-153). Recession of permanent snow in ensuing years has made this approach more problematical. In 1979, (a dry season), a capable party was unable to descend by this route.

It is also possible, and easy, to gain the Brazeau–Valad col from the Warren Creek drainage by circling S and then W on the glacier lying E of Mount Brazeau. In reverse, this is a quick escape route from the Brazeau massif, timber being reached in about 3 h.

2. NW Ridge, July 1950, three ACC parties. Gain Brazeau–Warren col from Coronet Creek as in Route 2 for Mount Warren. Take the steep snow/ice ridge to summit, bypassing rock towers to left (N). "Harder, but preferable to normal route."

3. N Face, August 1979, H. & R. Kruszyna, P. Vermeulen. A simple but elegant modern snow/ice route. From camp on moraines above Warren Creek, follow glacier tongue emanating from Brazeau–Warren col. Shortly before reaching col, turn left (S) and ascend snow slopes toward NW ridge. When angle steepens abruptly, work diagonally left (E) through a zone of bergschrunds and seracs out onto N face proper. Continue diagonally left or straight up as conditions warrant. The final bergschrund is most easily passed near its NE extremity. 6 h up (CAJ **63**-103).

Traverses. Mount Brazeau has been traversed in both directions, parties starting and finishing variously in the Coronet Creek or Warren Creek drainages. The most notable such exploit was accomplished by the 1950 Gibson party. Ascending Brazeau by the normal route from upper Coronet Creek, they descended the NW ridge and continued N over Mount Warren to make the FA of Monkhead (which see). After descending to Warren Creek, they returned at nightfall to the main ACC camp at the mouth of Coronet Creek.

MOUNT WARREN (3300m)

Halfway between Mount Brazeau and Monkhead.

FA July 1928, W. R. Hainsworth, M. M. Strumia. From camp on moraines above Warren Creek, ascend ice tongue heading toward Brazeau–Warren col. Gain the **SE ridge** of objective and follow it to the top. Approximately 5 h (CAJ **17**-25).

Note: The above is actually the descent route of FA party which, starting along Warren Creek from Maligne Lake, headed up too soon and became embroiled in many icefalls, etc. before reaching the SE ridge 200m below the summit. With the enormous ice retreat in recent decades, their original approach is even more emphatically not recommended now.

2. S Face, August 1930, C. Anderson, W. Boyd, J. A. Corry, S. B. Hendricks, D. M. Woods, T. W. Workman, *H. Fuhrer.* Follow trail along Coronet Creek about 5 km from end of Maligne Lake. Ascend along small stream to alplands below Mount Warren. Take prominent snow tongue to gully which leads to Brazeau–Warren col (6 h). Follow ridge around small subsidiary peak to base of steep S face of objective. Near the SW corner of face, climb a snow slope and then a snow couloir which leads onto summit plateau (4½ h). Ascent 10½ h; descent usually by FA route (CAJ **19**-154).

MONKHEAD (3211m)

At SE end of Maligne Lake; N peak of Brazeau massif. This name was previously applied to Mount Paul.

FA July 1950, E. & E. R. Gibson, D. LaChapelle, E. La-
Chapelle. On traverse N from Mount Warren in 2 h (CAJ **34**-
63).

2. W Face, July 1962, P. D. Baird, R. Brown, D. C. Morton.
1100m of rock climbing on 3 sections of cliff separated by
slopes of scree. Approach directly from camp near mouth of
Coronet Creek. Surmount the lowest cliff band via the first (N)
of two gullies splitting the W face (3½ h). Ascend scree slightly
right to base of second band (2600m) which is cleaved by 4
couloirs containing waterfalls visible from camp. Climb in the
northernmost of these couloirs, to the left of which is a narrow
rib. This crux section has 2 small overhangs, the second being
difficult. Zigzagging brings one to the upper scree slope (4 h).
Traverse far right (S) to the skyline ridge as seen from camp,
and climb it to summit plateau 100m S of cairn (4 h). Ascent
of this interesting route, 12 h (CAJ **46**-158).

3. N Face, August 1957, A. Auten, T. Messner, *H. Gmoser*.
Via the prominent, enormous couloir cleaving the lower part
of the face. Ascend a shaley band above this to a shelf and the
N glacier. Traverse glacier around to E side of objective, at-
taining the top by the SE snow slopes (AAJ **11**-96; CAJ **41**-83).

Descent from this peak has been problematical. FA party
apparently followed NE shoulder and then took a long gully
on N down to Warren Creek. Reportedly dangerous near bottom—falling rock and poor geological dip. Other groups, in
attempting to descend directly one or another of the more
northerly glacier tongues, encountered icefalls, etc. and were
often forced to retrace their steps. The optimum route, though
roundabout, seems to consist of working well S below Mount
Warren to intersect the more gradual tongue leading down
from the Brazeau–Warren col.

UNNAMED (3070)
Highest point on ridge line parallel to Brazeau massif and
forming NE wall of Warren Creek valley.
FA July 1950, ACC party; "dull."

UNNAMED (3090m)
  3 km E of Unnamed (3070m) above.

UNNAMED (3102m)
  4.5 km ESE of Maligne Mountain, at source of Southesk River.
  FA August 1930, J. A. Corry, G. Sanger, Mr. & Mrs. D. M. Woods. From Sandpiper Creek camp, follow creek to last draw on left. Ascend glacier (easternmost tongue) to "Sandpiper Pass" (apparently saddle between Maligne Mountain Peaks 3 and 5, which see). Cross glacier toward SE some 3.5 km and pass through shale gap W of objective. Swing around stream valley and strike up scree gully to **NW ridge** which leads easily to top. Ascent 7¾ h. At the time of FA, this peak was incorrectly thought to be Mount Southesk (CAJ **19**-154).

MOUNT PAUL *(Thumb)* **(2805m)**
  Striking castellated rock peak directly N across Maligne Lake from mouth of Coronet Creek.
  FA July 1928, W. R. Hainsworth, M. M. Strumia. From camp at mouth of Warren Creek, ascend a pronounced scree couloir leading to the **SE ridge** which is followed easily to the summit. Ascent 6 h, descent 2 h (AAJ **1**-55, CAJ **17**-26, **19**-57, photo).

MALIGNE MOUNTAIN (3913m)
  This is the most impressive mountain on NE side of Maligne Lake. It is a large massif with many high points, all of which have been ascended and none of which are separated by a col more than 100m deep. Two principal ridges project from the central and highest summit, Peak 5. One extends N for 1.5 km to Peak 3 (3130m) and to an unnamed point (3090m) 0.7 km farther N. A shorter SW ridge to Peak 2 (3110m) bifurcates thereafter, going W one km to Peak 1 (3060m) while the other fork goes SE for 0.7 km to Peak 4 (3060m). The several W outliers, which rise N of Mount Paul, are described after the

5 principal summits. North drainage is to Sandpiper Creek which enters Maligne Lake at Samson Narrows while S drainage is to Warren Creek. East glaciers drain to Rocky and Southesk Rivers.

Caution: As elsewhere in this region, there exists here also considerable confusion in the literature regarding nomenclature, elevations and routes, so references should be consulted with some skepticism.

Peak 4, FA 1929 (names of party unknown). From Warren Creek follow major NE tributary to S snowfield. Headwall below ice is passed more easily on W side. Once on glacier, approach peak from NE. 6 h up, 3 h down (AAJ **1**-310).

Peaks 1, 2, 5, FA July 1930, W. R. Hainsworth, J. F. Lehmann, M. M. Strumia, N. D. Waffl. From Warren Creek, follow tributaries leading NE and then N to gain glacial basin lying in SW quadrant of Maligne Mountain massif. Cross glacier to N, ascending a rock rib to reach ridge connecting Peak 1 with Unnamed (Hawley). Follow ridge to Peak 1; 6 h. Continue along gentle ridge to Peak 2 and then Peak 5, the highest point. Descent can be made from the saddle between Peaks 5 and 2 down to SE glacier which in turn can be followed to NE tributary of Warren Creek, thus rejoining the route of approach. Ascent 7½ h, descent 4 h (CAJ **19**-130, photo).

This traverse, also including Peak 3, can be done equally well from a camp on Sandpiper Creek by ascending one of the ice tongues coming from the NW glacier. It has been done in both directions, W to E and vice versa. Total time, 12 h (CAJ **19**-60).

Peak 5, SE Ridge. July 1962, R. Bruce, J. A. V. Cade, D. Morton. From Warren Creek, gain glacier to SE of mountain, as for Peak 4; 4 h. Cross glacier to SE ridge and ascend snow on its E side to within 150m of top. Then climb along crest, with traverses on S. Ridge is well broken and straightforward. 9 h from camp at Coronet Creek.

Peak 3, August 1930. C. G. Crawford, S. B. Hendricks, W.

R. MacLaren, P. Prescott, Mr. & Mrs. D. M. Woods. From
Sandpiper Creek in the course of the traverse described above.

UNNAMED *(Hawley)* (3000m)

Minor point 0.5 km SW of Maligne Mountain, Peak 1.

FA July 1928, W. R. Hainsworth. Via the S glacier, W. col
and SW slopes. 7 h RT from Warren Creek (AAJ **1**-56; CAJ
17-26).

UNNAMED *(Florence)* (2970m)

Rounded peak one km SW of Hawley.

FA July 1928, M. M. Strumia. As for Hawley to near col,
then by SE slope. 7 h RT from Warren Creek (AAJ **1**-56; CAJ
17-26).

UNNAMED (2820m)

Between Mount Paul and Florence.

FA August 1930, J. Alexander, R. Baring, C. G. Crawford.
From hanging valley N of Mount Paul, ascend an ill-defined
couloir toward gap in summit ridge. Couloir ends in friable
slabs some 15m below ridge. Thereafter take sharp crest to
top (AJ **43**-259; CAJ **19**-57).

UNNAMED *(The Wedge)* (3000m)

Sharp peak one km NW of Maligne Mountain, Peak 1.

FA August 1930, C. G. Crawford, S. B. Hendricks, W. R.
MacLaren. From Sandpiper Creek, gain glacier on NE slope
of Maligne Mountain and cross it to Peak 1 (3 h). Drop to col
between latter and Hawley. Descend 600m down couloir into
valley lying S of objective (3½ h). Ascend shaley slabs on **SW
flank** to sharp ridge leading to highest (E) point (2½ h). After
descending to valley, FA party followed it down to Maligne
Lake; this route would appear a less circuitous approach to the
climb (AJ **43**-261; CAJ **19**-60).

SAMSON PEAK (3081m)

Sharp, wedge-shaped peak on E shore of Maligne Lake; 3 km N of Samson Narrows.

FA July 1928, W. R. Hainsworth, M. M. Strumia. From lake shore 2 km W of objective, go up rock slides and talus slopes of **W face.** Ascend diagonally toward summit along scree-covered ledges, keeping below crest of NW ridge until easier summit slopes are gained. Ascent 5½ h; descent 3¼ h (AAJ **1**-51; CAJ **17**-24). Variations on this general line were made by ACC parties in 1950 and 1962.

LEAH PEAK (2801m)

5 km NW of Samson Peak on E shore of Maligne Lake; higher points 1.5 and 3 km to NE.

FA 1926, R. Ecaubert, *J. Weber.* From Maligne Lake, ascend through woods and up grass and scree to W face. Take it and **SW ridge** to top. Ascent 8 h; descent 4½ h.

Southesk Group

This group is bounded on the N and E by the plains and on the S and W by the line of Southesk River (W fork) and Rocky River. The area has received little attention from mountaineers, in part because the quality of the rock is generally poor and partly because few peaks are high enough to support glaciers and permanent snow. Although there is a network of established trails, the approaches along them are long, and then considerable bushwhacking is necessary in order to camp near enough the peaks to ascend them. On the other hand, this is an isolated, open-timbered region of considerable beauty, popular with hikers and fishermen. Its nomenclature is dominated by associates of the Earl of Southesk, whose party spent some time in the area and whose vicissitudes are well chronicled in his book.

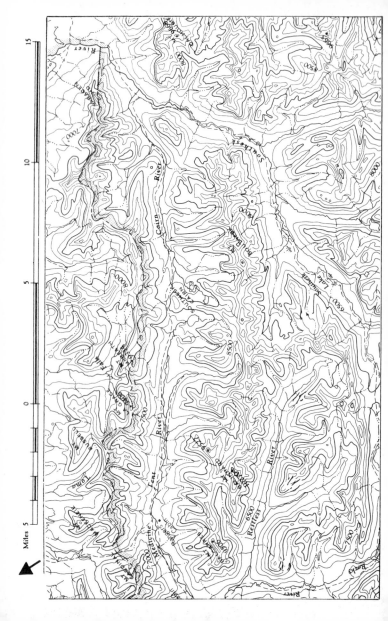

ACCESS

From Mountain Park. This route provides the most direct
access to the northern part of the Southesk Group and possibly
to the southern part as well. From the abandoned town site of
Mountain Park, drive about 7 km S on a good forestry road
to a picnic ground. Go E along the height of land about 3 km
(it is possible to drive part way) to a point from which a series
of clearings in the bush may be seen on the floor of the Cardinal
River valley below to the S. Descend into this valley through
these clearings to strike the river at a point slightly E of the
trail leading up into Rocky Pass on the other side. There is no
obvious trail on the N side of the valley, so time may be saved
and bushwhacking avoided by carefully plotting one's course
to the river before dropping down into the trees. The trail
markings shown on 83C/14 should not be taken too seriously
and the temptation to follow a straight outline on the valley
floor should be resisted, as it peters out in dense bush.

After crossing the Cardinal, find the trail which leads up
into Rocky Pass. It is hard to follow in the alpine meadows
between Mount Cardinal and Mount MacKenzie, but it reap-
pears on the S side of the pass. Drop down into the valley of
the Medicine Tent River and join the trail which runs from
Jacques Lake to Southesk Pass. This point can be reached from
the picnic ground in about 4 h. The Cardinal River may be
crossed without difficulty but the Medicine Tent requires wad-
ing and could be troublesome early in the season.

It is also possible to reach the same point by starting from
Medicine Lake and following Jacques Lake Trail and that along
Rocky River. This, however, is too long and indirect to be of
much interest to the climber.

Southesk River. A forestry road leading up Southesk River
is reported passable in good weather as far as Saracen Head.
From there, a trail runs W along Southesk River to Southesk
Lake and another branches NW along Cairn River to Southesk
Pass. The former is much used by horse packers taking fishing

parties in to Southesk Lake, but because of the problems which horse trails pose to foot travelers—frequent and often dangerous stream crossings—it is not recommended. Nor, for the same reason, is the latter.

A better way to reach the vicinity of Southesk Lake is to approach from Maligne Lake **via Warren Creek.** See under Unnamed (3240m) in Le Grand Brazeau. The route there described can be continued E to Southesk River and Lake. Estimated 2 days from Maligne Lake (CAJ **55**-90).

Maps: 83C/11, 83C/14. Peaks described from N to S.

BALCARRES MOUNTAIN

5 km NW of Mount Balinhard.

FA July 1974, P. Charkin, R. Kelly, J. Lamont, D. Pearson. Use approach from Mountain Park to Medicine Tent River, placing camp in horseshoe valley NE of peak. Ascend E face from R to L, gaining col between objective and unnamed peak to SE, from which summit is easily reached. F5; very loose.

MOUNT BALINHARD (3130m)

Most northeasterly peak in Rockies supporting a glacier; in SE angle of Rocky and Medicine Tent Rivers, 11 km SE of their junction.

FA August 1971, J. Carlson, R. Crampton, R. Hancock, who approached from Mountain Park over Rocky Pass to camp in the valley of the Medicine Tent. From river ascend stream to col (2570m) about 1.5 km N of objective, from which a splendid view of **N face** is obtained (3 h). Descend to glacier and ascend its center. Cross bergschrund and traverse 100m left (E) through a rockfall zone to reach rock rib to right of funnel of upper glacier. Climb directly upward, gaining the final rocks 100m below the summit, just above a large snow couloir which runs up diagonally right. Ascent from glacier, 8 h. Descend along E ridge to top of E buttress. Take steep (45°) N snow down to beginning of icefall, then traverse upper glacier W to regain route of ascent. Descent to Balinhard Creek, 6½ h (CAJ **55**-89). Approach via Balinhard Creek may be easier.

Along the ridge running SE from Mount Balinhard to Mount Southesk, there are several high points exceeding 2900m in elevation and two exceeding 3000m.

MOUNT SOUTHESK (3120m)
4 km NE of Southesk Lake; 6 km S of Southesk Pass.

FA August 1975, R. Haney, A. Lowen, *H. Fuhrer, W. Pfisterer*. From Southesk Lake, go up a dry creek bed to basin on SW side of peak (1½ h). Climb the direct corner line of the **SW face** to S summit (F3, 3 h). Follow ridge connecting to higher N summit, encountering a few exposed pitches, especially around a gendarme (1½ h). Ascent 6 h, total time 11 h (CAJ **59**-84).

UNNAMED *(Two Five Three)* (3150m)
At W head of Restless River (780368).

FA August 1975, *W. Pfisterer* and 5 Park Wardens. Via **SE ridge** (CAJ **59**-84).

UNNAMED ((3132m)
5 km ENE of Maligne Mountain across unnamed pass connecting heads of Southesk and Rocky Rivers (774363).

UNNAMED *(Chief Warden)* (3126m)
4.5 km WNW of Southesk Lake at head of Restless River.

FA August 1975, M. Miller, B. Wallace, *W. Pfisterer*. Via glacier on **N face** (CAJ **59**-84).

UNNAMED *(Warden Robinson)* (3000m)
One km NE of above (822355).

FA August 1975, B. McKinnon, J. Strachan, T. Davidson. Via **S face** (CAJ **59**-84).

The next morning we mounted again through strange, horrid and fearful crags and tracks, abounding in pine-trees, and only inhabited by bears, wolves and wild goats . . .

J. Evelyn

UP THE (WRONG) CREEK

FRYATT GROUP

The peaks of this important group cluster about the headwaters of Fryatt Creek and its major tributary, Lick Creek. Lying in the SW angle between the Whirlpool and Athabasca Rivers, the group is bounded on the S by Fortress Lake and by the line Alnus Creek–Divergence Creek to the W. Although several of the peaks exceed 3000m in elevation, glaciation is scanty and the small glaciers are unnamed. The dominant peaks are massive Mount Fryatt, which alone forms the divide between Fryatt Creek and the valley of Geraldine Lakes to the N, and Brussels Peak, an awesome limestone fang projecting some 300m above its pedestal. By Rockies standards, the rock is quite sound. Good limestone is encountered on Brussels Peak and the upper portions of both Mount Fryatt and Mount Lowell, while excellent quartzite is afforded by the peaks surrounding the head of Fryatt Creek—Mounts Belanger, Lapensee, Parnassus, Olympus, and Xerxes. As a result, the peaks of the Fryatt Group offer considerable climbing interest.

Historically, the Fryatt peaks had been approached, not by the direct route up Fryatt Creek, which penetrates to the center of the massif, but by circuitous and complicated routes from the NW and from the S. In 1926, Hickson and Palmer approached from the Whirlpool up the branches of Divergence Creek, ascending Mounts Fryatt, Lapensee, and Olympus. (At the time Hickson and Palmer were the respective presidents of the Canadian and American alpine clubs). A year later, the Ostheimer party, in the course of its monumental peak-bagging expedition, carried out a daring foray from Fortress Pass, climbing Catacombs Mountain and Mount Lowell, returning via Alnus Creek to the W end of Fortress lake. With the building of the Banff–Jasper Highway in the 1930s, the obvious E access route from Athabasca River up Fryatt Creek became also the easiest.

ACCESS

Leave Route 93A just N of Athabasca Falls, following a forest road marked "Geraldine Lakes." Approximately 3 km up this road, a blocked road branches left toward Athabasca River; park here. An excellent trail parallels the Athabasca for 7 km to a cable crossing, then follows up Fryatt Creek, crossing it twice before reaching the site of the 1936, 1960, and 1972 ACC camps just below a huge alluvial fan. Beyond the campsite, the trail crosses the fan to a lake, which is skirted on the right (N), then leads to the valley headwall featuring a splendid waterfall, and ends at the Sydney Vallance Hut, just beyond. Distance: about 22 km, with 670m elevation gain; average time with full pack: 8 h. This modern and comfortable hut, which accommodates 15, is equipped with cooking and eating utensils, a 2-burner Coleman stove, a cook stove plus a space heater, and foam mattresses. It is, however, a designated Park campsite, so it is likely to be full of backpackers. The hut serves as the most logical and convenient base for ascents of peaks surrounding Fryatt Creek—with the exceptions of Mount Christie and Brussels Peak—superseding earlier starting points (usually the ACC campsite). The route descriptions in this section reflect this fact. The upper Fryatt Creek valley, from the hut to the glacier at its head, offers considerable geologic interest, featuring natural bridges and disappearing underground streams.

An old but reportedly usable trail up Lick Creek branches left from the Fryatt trail about 10 km from the trailhead (sign). The Lick Valley is replete with muskeg, so travel is likely to be wet and tiresome. the valley of Geraldine Lakes may be reached by continuing up the aforementioned forest road. Although there is no trail beyond the lowest lake, it is a relatively easy bushwhack to the upper lakes. From the last lake the pass at the end of Mount Fryatt's ridge may be crossed to the Fryatt valley and the Vallance hut. This latter approach normally requires two days.

LITERATURE

Palmer. H. "Breaching the Barriers of Mt. Fryatt." App. **16**-421 (1926). Up the wrong creek, but the right mountain!

Garner, R. C. "The First Ascent of Brussels Peak." AAJ **7**-115 (1949). Movie cameras and sneakers, bolts and blasphemy.

Maps: 83C12, 83C5

FORTRESS MOUNTAIN (3020m)

N buttress of Fortress Pass.

FA August 1896, R. L. Barrett, *alone*. From Fortress Lake through heavy forest and up broken limestone cliffs of **S face** (Wilcox-174).

CATACOMBS MOUNTAIN (3330m)

NNW of Fortress Mountain; 6 km W of Athabasca–Chaba junction.

FA July 1927, W. R. Maclaurin, A. J. Ostheimer, *H. Fuhrer, J. Weber*. From camp beside small lake at head of Catacombs Creek, ascend easy but loose couloirs to crest of **W ridge,** which

is easily followed to the summit. Ascent, 4½ h, descent, 3½ h
(CAJ **16**-23.; Harvard **1**-51).

DRAGON PEAK (2940m)

4.5 km NE of Catacombs Mountain, directly W of Athabasca
River.

In the 15 km along the Divide from Fortress Mountain to
Lick Peak are several minor summits on the 2700m category.
FA of the one (2820m) next SE of Lick Peak, September 1979,
D. Waterman, *alone,* traverse via **NE ridge** (F4-5, overhangs)
and SE slopes.

LICK PEAK (2880m)

On Divide at head of Lick Creek.

FA September 1979, D. Waterman, *alone.* Approach from
Fryatt valley over Olympus–Parnassus col. Cross benches to
glacier N of objective and ascend it to **E ridge,** which is taken
to top. Class 3 on firm rock.

MOUNT CHRISTIE (3103m)

NE gable of massif between Fryatt and Lick Creeks.

FA July 1930, W. R. Hainsworth, J. F. Lehman, M. M. Strumia, N. D. Waffl. From Fryatt Creek, follow a tributary stream
toward Brussels Peak. Go N beneath the cliff band on scree
slopes until directly below the Christie–Brussels col, where a
weakness in the cliffs permits access to the col (5 h). Ascend
the easy **SW ridge** to the top in one h more (CAJ **19**-151; **44**-
147; AAJ **1**-302).

2. NE Face. July 1977, R. Berg, P. Ford. Details lacking, but
route follows the prominent rib on the face. Reportedly excellent rock to F6.

BRUSSELS PEAK (3161m)

A sheer rock tower; central and highest point of the massif
between Fryatt and Lick Creeks; an excellent climb.

Mt Christie   Brussels Pk   Mt Lowell   Xerxes

PEAKS ABOVE FRYATT CREEK

R. Kruszyna

FA July 1948, R. C. Garner, J. Lewis. From the Christie–Brussels col (see Mount Christie), the route generally follows the line of the **NE ridge.** From the col, cross E glacier to second broad chimney which leads up to large sloping shelf. Gain crest of NE ridge proper via a 12m chimney. Continue up vertical face, then a narrow chimney to top of a pinnacle. Straightforward climbing (loose rock) to left of crest leads to base of E buttress (Garner's "first step"). Contunue up the steep **NW face,** overhanging in places. A diagonal traverse right (12m) leads to an overhang which is turned to the right. A chimney is followed (12m) to a chockstone, then another chimney farther right is ascended to the platform at the top of the first step, 40m above its base. Climb left (E) into and up crack in bulging face ("Lewis crack"). Above, two short pitches lead to the first pinnacle on the summit ridge. The second pinnacle is ascended, the third traversed on the right, the fourth is easily surmounted, and the summit attained. Ascent from col, 9 h; descent 5 h; IV, F7 (AAJ **7**-115, marked photo; (CAJ **22**-21; **44**-53, marked photo; **55**-93; **56**-86).

Note: Numerous prior attempts to climb Brussels were undertaken, beginning in 1930 with a try by the Hainsworth–Strumia party which had just made the first ascent of Mount Christie. Subsequent attempts were made by parties including such notable climbers as: E. R. Gibson, S. B. Hendricks, R. C. Hind, F. Neave, F. S. Smythe, F. Beckey, and J. D. Mendenhall. Considerable controversy still surrounds the Garner–Lewis ascent, primarily because of the amount of hardware used. However, much of it had been placed by earlier, and unsuccessful parties, while the newly-developed expansion bolts were used only for protection, not for aid. Furthermore, the Garner party was trying to make a movie, did much of the ascent and all of the descent in thunderstorms and snow, and climbed in sneakers! More recent ascents have, quite naturally, utilized fewer pitons and taken much less time. Round-trip times from camp on Fryatt Creek now range from 11 to 13 h (AAJ **1**-304; (CAJ **24**-123; **44**-147).

2. W Face, August 1964, A. Gran, J. S. Hudson. From Christie–Brussels col (see Mount Christie), traverse S side of peak to Brussels–Lowell col and to the W buttress. Climb the prominent inside corner, which faces right, on the right side of the buttress, to its top. Traverse left around the buttress and ascend ledge system until a steep inside corner affords access to the huge scree-covered shelf which breaks the W face (bivouac). At the base of the final 100m wall, traverse 60m right and around the corner. Then ascend a steep chimney system to a gully which leads to the summit crest. Ascent 16 h V, F8, A3 (AAJ **14**-324; CAJ **48**-133, marked photo).

3. N Face, August 1979, G. Randall, D. Waterman. From Fryatt Creek approach through brush, over scree and up cliff band directly to base of face (4 h). Begin on left side of face directly beneath a large roof some 70m up. Zigzag up featureless rock, finally climbing a left-facing dihedral (F8). Pass the larger roof to the right (F9). Traverse back left and then go straight up to large ledge system below upper half of wall. Scramble left to last dihedral system on left margin of face, just before buttress separating N and NE faces. Climb two long, sustained pitches in these dihedrals (F10 and F9). Traverse right and ascend moderate rock to within 30m of the summit. Scramble to the top. A long day (bivouac on FA); IV, F10 (AAJ **53**-499; CAJ **63**-103).

MOUNT LOWELL (3150m)

1.5 km SW of Brussels Peak on ridge separating Fryatt and Lick Creeks.

FA July 1927, A. J. Ostheimer, *H. Fuhrer, J. Weber.* **S Ridge.** From Vallance Hut, cross Fryatt Creek and follow up stream valley toward easternmost of Three Blind Mice. Cross over ridge to col between E Mouse and objective (2460m). Climb steep, shaley cliffs and follow W buttress over scree and snow until it intersects main **S ridge.** Follow crenellated ridge (good rock) for about 1 km to summit. Ascent, 6 h; descent, 4 h. A good moderate route (CAJ **16**-24; **24**-122; Harvard **1**-51). Approach **variants.** 1. The 1927 FA party reached the Lowell–Mice col from a camp on the N side of Lick Creek in 2 hours. 2. From ACC campsite on Fryatt Creek, follow up stream toward Brussels Peak, then at timberline, traverse W around base of Lowell to gain W buttress. Ascent of peak via this approach, 7 h (CAJ **44**-148).

N PEAK (3120m)

One km N of main summit of Mount Lowell.

FA July 1936, E. R. Gibson, F. Neave, L. Tiefenthaler, W. Watson, A. T. Wiebrecht. Use approach variant 2 above. Ascend scree slopes to large **couloir** between main S summit and objective and climb it to ridge crest which is taken a short distance to summit; 7 h up, 4 h down (CAJ **24**-123; **44**-147).

2. N Ridge. July 1948, J. D. & R. D. Mendenhall. From Christie–Brussels col, contour around S side of Brussels Peak to Brussels-Lowell col. The route goes up the ridge over steep, shattered cliffs and gendarmes to the summit. Much loose rock (CAJ **32**-130).

UNNAMED *(Three Blind Mice)* (2720m)

Three small peaks 2 km SW of Mount Lowell.

FA July 1936, ACC party. These peaks may be climbed in various combinations, providing a pleasant, short day. Depart the hut, cross Fryatt Creek and ascend a draw leading to the **NW ridge** of the E Mouse. Ascend to this peak (Minnie Mouse), from which the second peak (Middle Mouse) is easily reached. Continue along the connecting ridge toward the W peak (Mickey Mouse), which is gained over a short stretch of interesting rock. Ascent, 4 h. Descent is easily made by the N ridge of the middle peak in 3 h (CAJ **44**-148).

UNNAMED *(Xerxes)* (2970m)

A dark, many-turreted peak 1.5 km E of Olympus, between heads of Fryatt and Lick Creeks.

FA July 1936, Mr. & Mrs. A. W. Kramer, A. McKay. From Vallance Hut, ascend along edge of glacier to prominent rib leading to the **N ridge,** which is then followed to summit. 8 h up (CAJ **24**-123).

2. W–E Traverse. July 1960, M. Taylor, *H. Kahl.* From hut, gain Xerxes–Olympus col (3½ h). The ridge running E toward the Three Blind Mice is generally followed, with many of the gendarmes being passed to N or S. Easy climbing on good quartzite to first tower SW of main summit (2 h). From this point, it is necessary to descend some 300m to S to pass a deep gap in crest. To follow crest throughout would involve several rappels and serious rock climbing (CAJ **44**-149).

UNNAMED *(Olympus)* (2940m)

At head of Fryatt Valley. The **E ridge,** from the Xerxes–Olympus col, is the preferred descent route on this peak as well as the easiest to ascend.

FA July 1926, J. W. A. Hickson, H. Palmer, *H. Fuhrer.* From camp at head of S terminal fork of Divergence Creek (the wrong creek), cross pass into Lick Creek drainage. The **S ridge,** which is gained by a large couloir on the W face, is followed simply to the summit. Ascent, 6 h; descent by same route, 6 h. To reach S ridge from Vallance Hut, go through the Olympus–Parnassus col (CAJ **16**-50).

2. NW Ridge. July 1936, R. P. Cross, J. Forbes, C. Gryte, R. C. Hind, F. Neave, M. Taylor, J. Thornton, A. T. Wiebrecht. From hut, cross glacier at head of valley to col between Olympus and Parnassus. Generally stay on the crest of the ridge, avoiding obstacles to the right (W); loose rock. When an imposing gendarme blocks the ridge, traverse W into an amphitheater, from which a steep couloir paralleling the ridge is climbed to the summit. Ascent, 5½ h (CAJ **24**-122).

Variant. July 1972, A. Abrahams, H. von Gaza. Follow the
NW ridge throughout. At the point where the large gendarme/
cleaver blocks the ridge, make an ascending traverse across the
W flank to regain the crest beyond (F6). Continue over rock
and then snow to the top. Done in this fashion, the NW ridge
offers a fine climb. It is also possible to pass through the notch
between gendarme and cleaver to the E flank, ascending
snow/ice in the NW couloir and then rock to regain the ridge
(F5); July 1974, J. K. Fox, D. McClintic (CAJ **56**-86; **59**-84).

3. NW Couloir. July 1960, ACC party. From just below the
Olympus–Parnassus col, ascend directly the prominent, steep,
snow/ice couloir which bifurcates the NW face. 6 h up. Done
preferably early in the season and early in the day (CAJ **44**-
151).

4. N Face. July 1936, S. B. Hendricks, A. W. Kramer, P.
Prescott, M. Sterling. From base of face, traverse right (W)
above lower cliffs, then climb prominent cliff band on W part
of face immediately above intermediate snow patch. Traverse
W and finish via NW couloir or ridge. Ascent, 10½ h (CAJ **24**-
122).

UNNAMED *(Parnassus)* (2910m)
   At head of Fryatt Creek immediately N of Olympus; a long,
wedge-shaped peak whose summit is at the N end.
   FA July 1936, E. Arneson, C. Compton, E. Lloyd, F. Neave.
NE Ridge. From Vallance Hut, gain glacier at head of Fryatt
Valley. Cross it and ascend snow to Belanger–Parnassus col.
Take the rocky ridge (excellent quartzite) to the summit, pass-
ing difficulties on the right (W). Ascent, 4½ h; descent, 3 h.
Recommended (CAJ **24**-123; **44**-151).

MOUNT BELANGER (3120m)
   Between heads of Fryatt and Divergence Creeks; 4.5 km S
of Mount Fryatt.
   FA July 1930, W. R. Hainsworth, J. F. Lehmann, M. M.

Strumia, N. D. Waffl. **N Face.** From hut, follow long valley
NW to pass between objective and 2900m bump to N (2 h).
Climb directly the steep snow/ice of the face to the N summit
(2½ h). Take the difficult intervening ridge (rock and snow)
to the main summit in 3 h more. 8½ h up (AAJ **1**-305; CAJ
19-152).

Variant. July 1936, O. Hay, S. B. Hendricks. G. McHattie,
P. Prescott. Climb the rock rib retaining the N glacier on the
left (E), rather than the ice itself. Ascent from hut, 9 h.

2. S Face. July 1936, E. Gale, R. C. Hind, M. Taylor. From
hut, gain glacier at head of valley and follow it N to S face of
objective. Ascend snow slopes and broken rock to reach large
couloir in face. Climb couloir a short distance, then work diagonally left (W) to W ridge which is followed to the top. Ascent,
5 h; descent, 3 h (CAJ **24**-123).

Variants. From lake near head of Fryatt Valley, traverse
meadows N under SE ridge of Mount Belanger until snow
slopes give easy access to the flat crest of **SE ridge.** From this
point, S face route above may be taken. Alternatively, ascend
the prominent couloir in its entirety (avalanche danger), or
cross the couloir to a steep gully leading to the crest of the SE
ridge which is then climbed to the summit. This last affords
the greatest interest (CAJ **44**-153).

MOUNT LAPENSEE (3106m)

One km WNW of Mount Belanger; in SE angle of terminal
forks of Divergence Creek.

FA July 1926, J. W. A. Hickson, H. Palmer *H. Fuhrer.* From
camp at head of S terminal fork of Divergence Creek, generally
by way of **S face.** Climb the large, prominent couloir over snow
and steep rock (falling stones) to col (2830m) between S tower
and main peak (5 h). Above, a short wall is succeeded by a
narrow, steep couloir which leads to the summit ridge (2 h)
midway between the two culminating points of almost equal
height, either of which can be reached in 20 minutes. Ascent

8 h; descent, 5½ h (CAJ **16**-48). The peak is not very accessible from the Fryatt Valley. Possibly the most reasonable approach involves reaching the Belanger–Parnassus col and traversing on an obvious horizontal shelf around to the 2830m col between Lapensee's S tower and the main peak.

MOUNT FRYATT (3361m)

The dominant peak in the SW angle between Athabasca and Whirlpool Rivers.

FA July 1926, J. W. A. Hickson, H. Palmer, *H. Fuhrer*. **SW Face.** Depart the Vallance Hut, go upstream along Fryatt Creek a few hundred meters, and then go NW up a watercourse to open meadows which are crossed N to the pass (2680m) at the end of the S ridge of objective (2 h). Follow the shaley ridge upward toward a series of crags which are bypassed on steep snow to the left (W). Scramble to a broad shaley shoulder immediately beneath the precipitous SE face. Traverse the **SW face** over mixed snow and rock diagonally upward to intersect the W ridge at the foot of the summit cliffs. A steep couloir (F4) penetrates the cliff band, above which the W ridge is followed until it abuts into the summit block. Make a short traverse right (E), ascend easy gullies, and follow a ridge leading back left to the top. Ascent, 8–10 h depending on approach route; descent, 5–6 h. A good climb (CAJ **16**-44; App. **16**-430).

Approach **Variants.**

1. The FA party camped at 1800m between two lakes in the E terminal fork of Divergence Creek, approaching by skirting the upper lake to S and then crossing a small glacier SW to the pass; 3 h.

2. From ACC campsite in Fryatt Creek, skirt SE ridge of objective to W and follow long valley to pass; 3 h (CAJ **24**-123).

3. From same camp, ascend cliff between outliers of Mount Fryatt to glacier lying SE of objective. Cross to broad shoulder on S ridge immediately beneath SE face; 4 h. This is the pre-

R. Kruszyna

MT. FRYATT FROM SOUTH

SW Face

W Ridge

ferred approach from the lower part of Fryatt Creek (CAJ **24**-123; **44**-149).

2. W Ridge. September 1972, A. D. Abrahams, H. von Gaza. From camp at head of valley of Geraldine Lakes at foot of W ridge (as in FA), or from Vallance Hut via Route One above to 2680m pass, descending glacier to base of ridge. The ridge is composed of a series of steps, the lowest being the most difficult. Surmount this 25m left (N) of the ridge crest (F6). The succeeding steps offer generally-sound rock and the standard rises to F5. The final section coincides with Route One. Ascent, 8 h from foot of ridge; recommended. FA party descended SW face directly to a small lake to regain camp; 5 h (CAJ **56**-86).

UNNAMED (2940m)

4 km N of Mount Fryatt; E of Geraldine Lakes.

UNNAMED (2910m)

In Whirlpool–Athabasca angle; W of valley of Geraldine Lakes.

FA 1935, Topographical Survey.

Then I was standing on the highest mountain of them all, and round about beneath me was the whole hoop of the world. And while I stood there I saw more that I saw; for I was seeing in a sacred manner the shapes of all things in the spirit, and the shape of all shapes as they must live together like one being. And I saw that the sacred hoop of my people was one of many hoops that made one circle, wide as daylight and as starlight, and in the center grew one mighty flowering tree to shelter all the children of one mother and father. And I saw that it was holy.

Black Elk

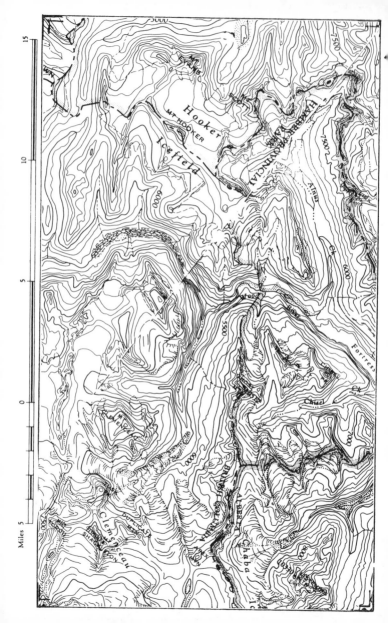

LAND OF LEGEND

WHIRLPOOL GROUP

The peaks of this scenic group lie chiefly about the head-waters of the Whirlpool River and its principal tributaries, Middle Whirlpool River and Simon Creek. The E boundary is the line Alnus Creek (Wood River)–Divergence Creek (Whirlpool River); while on the S it is bounded by Wood River. The W boundary is the watershed between the Fraser River sources and lateral branches of the Canoe River. The N extent is delimited by Simon Creek and its W source on the Divide.

The major peaks of the group—in particular Mount Scott and Mount Hooker—cluster about the rim of the Hooker Icefield, which contains more than 50 square km and discharges by the magnificent Scott Glacier to Whirlpool River. Due to ice retreat, a lake 1.5 km long now replaces much of the area formerly occupied by the Scott Glacier tongue. Immediately W of the historically important Athabasca Pass, the Brown Icefield containing some 35 square km, occupies the Canoe–Wood watershed.

Athabasca Pass is the historic passage from the Athabasca to the Columbia River drainage. Opened in 1811 by David Thompson, explorer and geographer for the Northwest Company, it served for several decades as the route of fur traders and travellers in traffic between the Plains and the Pacific. In early spring before high water, a fleet of boats would start from the Pacific and proceed up the Columbia to Boat Encampment on the Big Bend, near the entrance of the Canoe and Wood Rivers (now flooded behind Mica Dam). Concurrently, a party would leave Edmonton, and, by boat and pack train, make its way to the Pass from the E. The exchange of freight, letters, and passengers by the two parties was often attended by celebrations on the shores of the Committee's Punch Bowl, one of three small tarns located near the height of the land. After 1850, the Athabasca Pass route fell into disuse and obscurity, although it was examined in 1872 by Walter Moberly as a possible route for the Canadian Pacific Railroad.

One of the many travellers over the Pass to leave a written record was the Scots botanist David Douglas, who accompanied a trading party in 1827. While camped at the Pass, Douglas climbed the peak immediately W, naming it Mount Brown for his patron, the noted botanist Robert Brown. This ascent was the earliest above snowline in the Canadian Rockies. Upon his return to England, Douglas ascribed an elevation of 5200m to Mount Brown and 4900m to the peak flanking the Pass to the NE which he named Mount Hooker after Sir William Hooker, another well-known botanist. Although Douglas' elevations were greatly exaggerated, his report did serve to stimulate later mountaineering interest in the region. (A thorough discussion of this fascinating incident in mountaineering history may be found in Appendix G of Thorington's *The Glittering Mountains of Canada.*)

Lured by the legend of the highest peaks on the continent, A. P. Coleman and companions "rediscovered" Athabasca Pass in 1893, ascending Mount Brown. Important subsequent expeditions to the region include those of Palmer and Carpé in 1920, who made the first ascent of a major peak, Serenity Mountain; and the 1924 and 1928 Thorington parties, which ascended the remaining major peaks. In addition to the Athabasca, other important passes in the area are: Canoe, Whirlpool and Fraser, this last marking the divisional point between the W drainages to the Columbia and Fraser Rivers.

ACCESS

The peaks around Hooker Icefield and to Athabasca Pass can be reached by a horse trail following the N bank of Whirlpool River. From the old Banff–Jasper Highway (Route 93A), a fire road leaves just N of a bridge over the Whirlpool. Cars may be driven in approximately 7 km. The fire road is followed on foot another 6 km to a warden's cabin where the trail proper (yellow blazes) commences. There is a good bridge over Simon Creek; but ground is very swampy beyond second warden's cabin where Middle Whirlpool enters via multiple channels. Dryas flats are followed past entrance of Scott Creek to point where the Whirlpool narrows to one channel passing through a gorge.

To reach campsites below Scott Glacier, enter woods next to river where gorge begins. Follow marked trail (for 1953 and 1978 ACC camps) to a bridge over the gorge and thence to valley of Scott Creek where campsites are plentiful; 27 km from parking place.

From dryas flats opposite Scott Creek, the horse trail continues approximately 16 km to Athabasca Pass. It crosses the Whirlpool many times, forcing the foot traveller either to ford or bushwhack. The trail crosses to the S bank for the final time at the point where a major stream emanating from the valley between Mount Kane and McGillivray's Ridge joins the Whirlpool from the S. There are good campsites near the Committee Punch Bowl, but the mosquitoes are ferocious.

A rough trail up the Middle Whirlpool River is reported to

leave the main trail at warden's cabin at the confluence of Middle and main Whirlpool Rivers. However, no trace of it was found in 1972. As Simon Creek is trailless, access to the peaks at its head has been made from Wates–Gibson Hut in the Ramparts (which see) over Fraser Glacier to a camp in Simon Valley, or from Eremite Valley over Angle–Alcove col to Simon Creek.

Because of ice retreat and massive washouts of the left (E) lateral moraine of Scott Glacier, access to the Hooker Icefield has become increasingly difficult in recent years. The route of choice avoids the crest of the moraine, remaining in the valley until the icefall itself is reached. An unpleasant scramble over morainal material to the left of the steepest part of the icefall leads to easier going on the glacier itself. A bivouac camp above the icefall near Mount Scott facilitates ascents of peaks on the rim of the Icefield. (For ascents from Scott Creek, add about 8 h round trip to times from bivouac). Generally, routes in this group are on snow and broken rock, and are devoid of technical interest.

LITERATURE

A. P. Coleman's classic book, *The Canadian Rockies: New & Old Trails,* cited in the preface to this volume, is particularly pertinent to this region.

Hillhouse, J. G., & J. M. Thorington. "Climbs and Camps in the Whirlpool Mountains." AAJ **1**-60 (1929). Thorington and the "Philadelphia Connection" clean up!

Thorington, J. M. "A Mountaineering Journey through Jasper Park." CAJ **16**-86 (1928).

Thorington, J. M. "Trails of the Athabasca and Columbia, 1928." CAJ **17**-4 (1929).

Maps: 83D8, 83D9, 83C12, 83C5.

DIVERGENCE PEAK (2827m)

Between heads of Divergence Creek and Alnus Creek.

FA 1920, Boundary Commission, via **SW ridge** from camp in Alnus Creek (ABC 84, 103, 108).

ALNUS PEAK (2976m)

Head of Alnus Creek.

FA 1920, Boundary Commission. From camp in Alnus valley by way of S slopes and **SW ridge** (ABC 84, 103, 105). Between this peak and Mount Ross Cox lies an unnamed high point (2940m) at the E head of Ross Cox Creek.

MOUNT ROSS COX (3000m)

Between heads of Ross Cox and Alnus Creeks.

FA July 1972, H. G. & R. Kruszyna. **S Ridge/Traverse.** From camp on Scott Creek, ascend ridge separating valleys of Scott and Ross Cox Creeks. Descend to glacier at head of Ross Cox valley and cross it to col immediately W of objective. Ascend ridge of friable rock until it merges into steep face, then traverse S on horizontal ramp to S ridge. Climb good rock to summit (F5). Ascent 10 h. Descend N ridge to steep gully which leads down to N col, then via couloir to regain glacier and complete traverse. Descent route is easiest ascent route. Return to camp along Ross Cox Creek to its confluence with Whirlpool River. Descent, 7 h (CAJ **56**-87).

UNNAMED *(Terra Nova)* (3090m)

One km N of Mount Scott.

FA July 1953, R. C. Hind, S. G. Pearson. From Scott Creek camp via **N ridge** to a prominent notch. Avoid the first big step by a 12m traverse to right. A short vertical wall leads to easier going. Surmount a tower on ridge by an overhanging pitch on left, to gain summit rocks. Ascent 6 h. Descent by same route (2 rappels), 4 h (CAJ **37**-161).

Mt Scott

Mt Hooker

WHIRLPOOL PEAKS FROM EAST

MOUNT SCOTT (3300m)

At NE corner of Hooker Icefield.

FA June 1928, W. R. Hainsworth, M. M. Strumia. From bivouac on moraine S of Mount Scott, ascend scree and snow slopes to plateau between objective and Mount Oates. Make a tedious ascent over snow and shifting shale of **S slopes** to S summit (3 h). Continue N along corniced ridge to highest point in one h additional. Descent, 2 h. RT from Scott Creek camp, 14–15 h (CAJ **17**-15; AAJ **1**-63).

MOUNT OATES (3120m)

2 km SE of Mount Scott on E margin of Hooker Icefield.

FA July 1924, A. J. Ostheimer, M. M. Strumia, J. M. Thorington, C. Kain. **S. Ridge.** As for Mount Scott to plateau between latter and objective. Cross upper snowfield to prominent gully by which the **S ridge** may be reached. Follow ridge to top. 4 h up, 2 h down (CAJ **16**-92).

UNNAMED (*Bowers*) (3000m)

Between Mount Oates and Mount Ermatinger.

FA July 1953, J. F. Tarrant & ACC party. From Scott bivouac, gain upper plateau as above. Ascend icefall leading to saddle between objective and Mount Ermatinger. From here, a broad snow ramp on **S side** leads simply to top (CAJ **37**-155).

MOUNT ERMATINGER (3060m)

On E margin of Hooker Icefield, between latter and S Alnus Glacier.

FA June 1928, W. R. Hainsworth, J. G. Hillhouse, M. M. Strumia, J. M. Thorington. **S Buttress/Ridge.** From Scott bivouac, cross ascending snow slopes below W cliffs of objective to reach col (2770m) at head of S Alnus Glacier. Ascend a 30m chimney in S buttress to the long, flat ridge, after which the summit is attained over shale, snow and boulders. Ascent 4 h (CAJ **17**-15; AAJ **1**-64).

2. E Ridge. FA party on descent. As for Unnamed (Bowers) to saddle, then swing S to ridge which is taken to the top. 3 h up, 1½ h down.

3. N Face. August 1978, K. Hewitt, *E. Salzgeber*, and one other. Details lacking, but the face features a double bergschrund with very steep snow/ice slopes leading up to a series of parallel rock ribs. Avalanche and rockfall danger (CAJ **62**-92, 94, 95, photos).

SERENITY MOUNTAIN (3223m)

NW angle between Alnus Creek and Wood River; 5.5 km E of Mount Hooker, between S Alnus and Serenity Glaciers.

FA September 1920, A. Carpé, W. D. Harris, H. Palmer, by Route 2 below.

1. SW Slopes. August 1953, ACC parties. From Scott bivouac go through broad pass between objective and Mount Hooker and ascend SW snow slopes.

2. S Ridge. From camp below tongue of Serenity Glacier, ascend medial moraine and glacier to a pronounced col in ridge. Surmount a rock buttress by a steep couloir and follow the narrow, corniced ridge to the summit. Ascent 10½ h; descent 4½ h (App **19**-270).

Variant. July 1936, E. R. Gibson, S. B. Hendricks, B. McNeil, P. Prescott, M. Schnellbacher. Approach was made from Fryatt Creek (which see) via Olympus–Parnassus col and low snow pass to W on Divide to a camp on Alnus Creek. Cross creek and ascend through timber to reach S Alnus Glacier above icefall. Cross glacier to col E of objective and continue around S on Serenity Glacier. Ascend SE face to intersect S ridge. Ascent from camp, 7 h (AAJ **3**-44).

MOUNT HOOKER (3286m)

Massive and impressive mountain forming S rim of Hooker Icefield.

ra Nova

Mt Scott

Serenity Mtn

Mt Ermatinger

Hooker Icefield

Scott Glacier

Whirlpool River

WHIRLPOOL PEAKS FROM NORTH

R. Kruszyna

FA July 1924, A. J. Ostheimer, M. M. Strumia, J. M. Thorington, *C. Kain,* via Route 2 below.

1. SE Ridge. 1924 FA party, on descent. Gain Hooker Icefield from Scott Creek. Cross to the broad pass between objective and Serenity Mountain and swing S and W to ridge. Ascend rock of SE ridge to reach the great SE snow shoulder and follow the corniced ridge to the summit. Ascent from camp on Scott Creek, 8 h; descent 6 h (fast times!). A good route on an important peak (CAJ **37**-153).

2. W Ridge. From Scott Creek to Hooker Icefield, or start from Scott bivouac. Cross Icefield to col (2770m) at W end of objective (3 h from Scott bivouac). Avoid steep W buttress by traversing S and then ascend ledges along W margin of a broad couloir to gain ridge (2 h). Follow the ridge, passing a shaley tower on its S side, to the last rocks (3 h). Continue along corniced snow to top in one h additional. 9 h total from bivouac (CAJ **16**-94, marked photo).

3. NE Face. August 1968, F. Beckey, J. Rupley. From a camp 600m below summit, climb directly the snow/ice of the face, avoiding overhanging bulges. Descent by Route One; total time 14 h (AAJ **16**-410).

UNNAMED *(Sir Joseph)* (3030m)
   On Divide 3 km W of Mount Hooker, at SW corner of Hooker Icefield.
   FA July 1953, E. R. Gibson, C. Jones, W. March, H. Peckham. From Athabasca Pass via Kane Glacier and **SW ridge.** Descend E ridge to Hooker Icefield; this latter is the ascent route of choice from Scott bivouac.

MOUNT EVANS (3210m)
   NW margin of Hooker Icefield.
   FA July 1928, W. R. Hainsworth, J. G. Hillhouse, M. M. Strumia, J. M. Thorington. **SE Ridge.** From Scott bivouac,

circle S below Mount Ermatinger and then W below Mount Hooker, keeping well above the head of Scott Glacier. Reach the ridge at its lowest point and attain the summit over easy rock and snow. Ascent, 5 h; in descending, it is possible to glissade snow slopes immediately to the W (CAJ **17**-15; AAJ **1**-66).

The SE ridge has also been reached directly from camp on Scott Creek via the W retaining wall of Scott Glacier. An unpleasant approach requiring 6 h to reach the Hooker Icefield. Not recommended because no saving in time (CAJ **16**-94).

MOUNT KANE (3090m)

2 km SW of Mount Evans, between Kane Glacier and Whirlpool River.

FA June 1924, A. J. Ostheimer, M. M. Strumia, J. M. Thorington, *C. Kain*. **E Ridge.** From Athabasca Pass via tongue of Kane Glacier, S of McGillivray ridge, to upper névé (2 h). Follow snowfield to E col, reached over small schrund and short chimneys. Take ridge to top (5 h). Descent via W ridge to regain glacier. Total time, 13 h (CAJ **16**-91).

McGILLIVRAY RIDGE (2690m)

NE buttress of Athabasca Pass.

FA August 1893, L. Q. Coleman, L. B. Stewart. From the Pass via Kane Glacier and then scree (Coleman-207).

MOUNT BROWN (2799m)

W buttress of Athabasca Pass.

FA May 1827, David Douglas, route uncertain.

August 1893, L. Q. Coleman L. B. Stewart. From the Pass ascend to margin of Brown Icefield. Cross level névé to **SE base** of peak, then climb easy rock to summit. RT 6½ h (Coleman-206; CAJ **16**-92).

2. NE Ridge. July 1952, E. & E. R. Gibson, B. B. Gilman, H. S. Hall Jr., C. Jones, J. G. Kato, P. Prescott. From the little lakes 2 km N of peak by the Divide ridge. A short, easy rock scramble (CAJ **26**-126).

MALLARD PEAK (2844m)
3.5 km N of Canoe Pass; across Whirlpool River from Mount Kane.

FA 1920, Boundary Commission, via **SW ridge** (ABC 87, 99, 107).

The following peaks form the ridge which separates Middle Whirlpool River from Simon Creek. They are best approached from the Wates–Gibson Hut (see "Rock" chapter) via Fraser Glacier to Simon Creek, or from Eremite Valley via the Angle–Alcove col to Simon Creek.

NEEDLE PEAK (2970m)
W angle between Middle Whirlpool River and Simon Creek.

FA July 1934, C. Beattie, W. H. Cleveland, J. A. Corry, E. R. Gibson, R. Neave. From camp on Simon Creek tributary from Beacon Lake. Ascend the long **W ridge** to the snow patch at the NW corner of the final rock tower (2500m). Traverse to NE ridge and climb it; traverse left to E face as necessary. A slight overhang some 100m up presents the chief difficulty, although there are additional steep pitches and the rock is unstable. Ascent of tower, 3½ h; total time, 15 h (CAJ **22**-82).

BEACON PEAK (2986m)
1.5 km E of Beacon Lake.
FA 1921, Boundary Commission (ABC 125, 130).

WHITECROW MOUNTAIN (2831m)
2 km N of Beacon Lake.
FA 1921, Boundary Commission (ABC 126, 127, 130).

BLACKROCK MOUNTAIN (2910m)

NW of Whitecrow Mountain; head of W terminal fork of Simon Creek.

FA August 1933, E. R. Gibson, R. C. Hind, E. L. Woolf. From Simon valley, ascend steep ice of Blackrock Glacier and **E ridge.** Descent via NW ridge to valley between Blackrock and Elephas. Total time, 11 h (CAJ **22**-70).

Full many a glorious morning have I seen
Flatter the mountain tops with sovereign eye

W. Shakespeare

New grades of difficulty cannot be devised just for the purpose of satisfying an unjustifiable alpine ambition.

O. W. Steiner

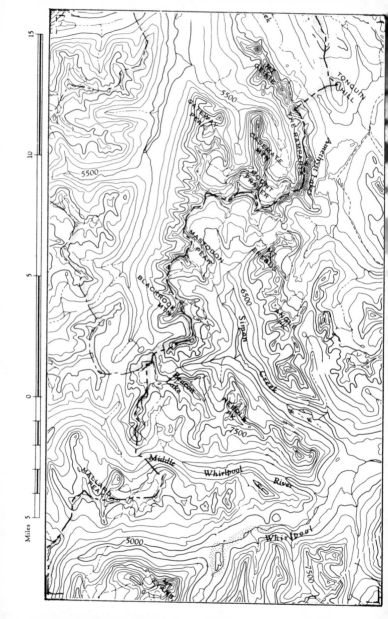

ROCK

FRASER–RAMPART GROUP

Between the headwaters of Whirlpool River and Yellowhead Pass, the principal peaks of the Divide are on the Rampart massif and center about its highest summit, Simon Peak. From this central point radiate five extensive ridges. The first, toward the S, carries the Divide toward Athabasca Pass, and forms the wall of rock peaks between the Fraser Valley and Simon Creek. The second is a prolongation of this and bears the peaks extending NW into the acute angle between Geikie Creek and Fraser River. The third ridge is short but boldly constructed, extending N into the cirque of Geikie Creek and bearing the peaks of Postern and Casemate which form the W wall of Bennington Glacier. The fourth ridge extends SE between Simon Creek and the sources of Astoria River, of which Mount Erebus is a prominent peak. The fifth is the most important, carrying the Ramparts in a great arc to the N and NW between Amethyst Lakes (Tonquin Valley) and Bennington Glacier. This portion of the range carries the Divide for 8 km to Tonquin Pass and the meadows adjacent to Moat Lake. Thence the Divide continues NW for 21 km direct to Yellowhead Pass.

The Rampart peaks are all spectacular; a precipitous escarpment rising above open meadows, crowned with jagged, turreted pinnacles reflected in the lakes below. Among them Mount Geikie, Redoubt Peak and Turret Mountain have attracted the special attention of climbers.

It should be noted that the earlier (and easier) routes were climbed from inside the Rampart arc (i.e., from the W and/or S), where the rock is broken but also down sloping. The more difficult modern routes lie on the precipitous E and N faces, where the rock is, however, generally firmer and more favorably tilted.

The ramifying glaciers, several of which exceed 3 km in length, deserve mention, those at the head of Simon Creek having an usually fine radial arrangement in an expansive basin. A glacial saddle (2160m) connects Tonquin Valley with the head of Simon Creek and occupies the depression between Mount Erebus and several peaks of Mount Fraser. The winding Bennington Glacier extending 5 km N from Simon Peak and forming the source of Geikie Creek (Fraser River), descends more than 1500m within 5 km into one of the deepest gorges of the region.

Amethyst Lakes, forming a linked body of water 5 km long, occupy the floor of Tonquin Valley immediately below and E of the Ramparts. The adjacent meadows form attractive camping places (much boggy soil, mosquito protection needed most of summer).

ACCESS

The major trail to Amethyst Lakes, a well-maintained horse trail, leaves the Edith Cavell road at Km 27, 150m above the second viewpoint (parking). The trail drops gradually to Astoria River and crosses it by bridge to the N (true left) bank just beyond Verdant Creek. The trail passes the Oldhorn warden's shelter, rises in switchbacks to timberline on the N valley wall, then descends to Brewster's Camp on the peninsula between the lakes. Distance: 19 km. National Park campgrounds here and below (E) Surprise Point. The latter is reached by trail crossing the outlet of the lower (S) Amethyst Lake. This trail continues S and connects with the Penstock Creek trail.

To reach the Wates–Gibson Hut, follow the main trail to Amethyst Lakes (above) as far as the Oldhorn warden's cabin. There cross the Astoria River (bridge) to its S bank. A trail, in places somewhat obscure, generally parallels the Astoria River up to the outlet stream from Chrome Lake. Although the bridge has been washed out, it is possible during low water to ford here and regain the trail. Better, though, and drier, circle S around Chrome Lake over bog and meadow, ford easily the inlet stream, pick up the faint trail from Eremite valley, and follow it back N until it intersects the obvious horse trail coming from Amethyst Lakes. Turn left (W) and follow this trail, which soon crosses Penstock Creek to its S bank on several log bridges, for approximately 1 km to Outpost Lake and the hut. The comfortable Wates–Gibson Hut, completely rebuilt in 1963, accommodates 30 (foam mattresses, Coleman and wood stoves, cooking and eating equipment). Distance 19 km; elevation gain; 200m.

The northern part of Tonquin Valley, Moat Lake and vicinity, is approached from Jasper most easily by the trail up Portal Creek and over Maccarib Pass. Drive up Marmot Basin Ski Area road 5 km to marked trailhead. Distance; about 18 km. The trail from Geikie Station, CNR, up Meadow Creek is no longer maintained, but is currently in good condition.

Several peaks in the northern Ramparts are best ascended from camps at the head of Geikie Creek, reached from Moat Lake over the W shoulder of Barbican Peak in 6–7 hours. A shorter, but more alpine route is to cross the Ramparts via Drawbridge Pass about 1 km east of Bastion Peak.

Mount Geikie was first noted by J. P. McEvoy during the

course of surveys in 1898 (Report G. S. C. Part D. 1900). Tonquin Valley was first visited by M. P. Bridgland in 1915, who occupied peaks E and N of the valley as survey stations.

LITERATURE

The best feeling for the early climbing in this region is conveyed in the series of articles by Cyril G. Wates (later written in collaboration with E. Rex Gibson):

"Mount Geikie." CAJ **13**-53 (1923)

"The Geikie Valley in 1923." CAJ **14**-53 (1924)

"The Ramparts in 1927." CAJ **16**-108 (1928)

"New Routes in the Tonquin." CAJ **18**-82 (1930)

"The Memorial Cabin in 1931." CAJ **20**-5 (1932)

"The Eremite and Beyond." CAJ **22**-63 (1934).

Fred Beckey's pioneering of modern high-angle routes is described, in his usual breezy fashion, in the following: CAJ **46**-81 (1963); AAJ **14**-203 (1964); AAJ **15**-159 (1966); AAJ **15**-369 (1967); AAJ **16**-168 (1968).

Also of interest is: Palmer, H. "An Early Visit to Tonquin Valley." AJ **38**-53 (1926).

Map: 83D/9

MOUNT ELEPHAS (2940m)

On Divide directly W of W head of Simon Creek.

FA August 1933, H. Burns, O. Haw, C. G. Wates, W. J. Watson. **E Ridge.** From camp near head of Simon Creek, reach small E glacier between objective and Mastodon. Ascend a broad, snow-filled gully to a notch on ridge and climb ridge and steep slabs to summit. On FA, descent was made to W, circling S and then E to recross Divide at low col, and so to camp. Total time 14 h (CAJ **22**-71).

MASTODON PEAK (2940m)

1.5 km N of Mount Elephas at SW corner of Mastodon Glacier.

FA August 1933, E. R. Gibson, R. C. Hind, W. J. Watson, E. L. Woolf. Take **S ridge** to top in 4½ h from camp on Simon Creek (CAJ **22**-68).

SCARP MOUNTAIN (3000m)

On Divide 4 km SW of Simon Peak; 3 km N of Mastodon Peak.

FA August 1933, E. R. Gibson, E. L. Woolf. **NE Ridge.** From Wates–Gibson Hut, cross Fraser and Simon Glaciers to reach col between objective and Simon Peak (Scarp Pass, 2700m) (7 h). Ascend crest of ridge, slabs at a steep angle (3 h). Descent on FA via Scarp Glacier to Icefall Lake and Geikie Creek (CAJ **20**-17; App **19**-49).

On the ridge extending NW from Scarp, in the angle of Fraser River and Geikie Creek, are several minor summits including **Rufus** (2759m), **Minotaur** (2780m), **Goodair** (2810m), and **Portcullis** (2630m) Peaks. At least one (Rufus) has been ascended by the Boundary Commission (1921).

CAMPUS PEAK (2810m)

S of Campus Creek.

FA July 1926, R. Cleveland, B. B. Gilman, B. F. Jefferson. From Campus valley by **NE face** (CAJ **16**-60).

ANGLE PEAK (2910m)

At S head of Eremite Valley.

FA July 1934, M. Aylward, J. A. Corry, R. P. Cross, A. W. Kramer, A. M. McKay, R. Neave, J. C. Southard, S. R. Vallance. **N Ridge.** From Wates–Gibson hut to Eremite Valley. Ascend moraines and snowfields to NW face of peak. Climb diagonally to rock rib at left (E) side of face, then follow ridge, first rock and then snow, to summit. 10 h RT (CAJ **22**-215).

ALCOVE MOUNTAIN (2810m)

1.5 km NW of Angle Peak.

FA August 1933, E. R. Gibson, O. Haw, R. C. Hind, W. J. Watson. From hut to Eremite Valley. Ascend N glacier and then steep snow above bergschrund of N slope to lower E summit, from which the highest point is attained. 6 h up, 4 h down (CAJ **22**-67).

Variant. 1934, L. Gest, A. W. Kramer, F. McCullough, *C. Häsler Jr.* Direct from N glacier to high point, descending above route.

ANCHORITE MOUNTAIN (2880m)

Between Alcove and Eremite Mountains.

FA July 1934, R. J. Cuthbertson, H. France, E. R. Gibson, P. Prescott, R. T. Zillmer. **SE Ridge.** From Eremite Valley, ascend snow couloir of E face to Alcove–Anchorite col, from which the ridge is followed throughout. Ascent 4 h, descent 3½ h (CAJ **22**-216).

2. Traverse. August 1975, H. G. & R. Kruszyna, D. Whitburn. From Eremite Mountain via **N ridge,** descending FA route above. 1½ h from Eremite.

EREMITE MOUNTAIN (2910m)

S buttress of Eremite Glacier; 1.5 km SE of Mount Erebus.

FA August 1931, E. R. Gibson, W. E. Streng, E. L. Woolf. **NE Face/NW ridge.** From Wates–Gibson Hut to Eremite valley. Ascend cliffs to hanging Eremite Glacier and cross to a shallow rib directly below Eremite–Erebus col. Ascend rib to col, 200m of good climbing on steep rock (F4). Thereafter follow NW ridge over broken rock to summit. Ascent 7 h (CAJ **20**-11; App. **19**-48).

2. E Face/SE Ridge. August 1974, R. B. Day, J. K. Fox. From hut to valley. Ascend S buttress near couloir from Eremite–Anchorite col to gain ridge, which is taken to top. 3 h from base; rockfall danger (CAJ **59**-89).

The simplest descent (and ascent) route on the peak goes down from the Eremite–Erebus col SW to the valley of Simon Creek. Then contour N to Fraser Glacier and so to the hut; 4–5 h. The reverse route (tedious) also gives access to Mount Erebus SE ridge (which see).

MOUNT EREBUS (3119m)

Highest peak on ridge between Eremite Valley and Simon Creek.

FA August 1924, L. Coolidge, G. Higginson, J.E. Johnson, A. *Streich*. Exact route uncertain, but could have been a variant of next described route or perhaps SSW Ridge (App **16**-244).

1. W Face. From hut, ascend Fraser Glacier and descend into valley of Simon Creek. Follow the prominent ramp which angles from S to N across the W face, immediately below the white band. Work back S toward crest of SSW ridge, which is gained about 50m below summit. Exposed slabs lead to top, 7 h.

2. SSW Ridge (normal route). August 1931, W.K. Voelter, *alone*. This route gives the easiest way to descend from the peak. From the summit, climb down slabs of Route 1 and descend ridge. When feasible, drop left (E) off ridge, descending snow and scree along W margin of the great slabs. Contour N to reach Fraser Glacier and hut. 3–4 h summit to hut; tedious as an ascent.

3. S Slabs. August 1945, D. P. & I. A. Richards. From camp at head of Simon Creek (or Wates–Gibson Hut), enter basin enclosed by SSW and S ridges. Ascend vast slabs (airy friction climbing) to skyline, finishing on **SE ridge.** Ascent 6 h (CAJ **29**-206).

4. SE Ridge. July 1934, C. Beattie, E. R. Gibson, M. McNeil, W. J. Watson. Gain Eremite–Erebus col as for Route 1 on latter, or from SW. Take enjoyable ridge to top (F3).

5. N Ridge. August 1965, G. Crocker, K. Hahn. From hut to Fraser Glacier and then S, ascending to ridge connecting

Memorial Peak to objective. Go easily along ridge, climbing a short step directly. Climb the first wall for approximately 4 pitches (F4), the line lying on the right (W) side of the wall. After a simple section, a second wall is encountered. Traverse diagonally left into a chimney, then back right and up (3 pitches, F4). The ensuing limestone band is taken just left of the crest (crux, F6), after which broken blocks lead to the peak. (Ascent 9 h; III. Recommended.

OUTPOST PEAK
Double summit above (S) Outpost Lake; between Fraser and Eremite Valleys.

SW PEAK *(Memorial)* (2880m)
FA August 1926, R. B. M. Bibby, J. M. Hoag, W. W. Maclaren, P. Prescott, G. Tollington, *H. Fuhrer, F. Rutis.* From hut to Fraser Glacier and then by slabby **NW slopes.** 3 h up (App. **16**-536).

2. E Ridge. An enjoyable scramble from NE Peak.

NE PEAK (2750m)
FA August 1930, B. Cautley, E. R. Gibson, W. E. Streng. From hut, ascend icefall and **glacier** between the two peaks. Ascent 3 h (CAJ **19**-127).

2. N Ridge. September 1956, E. & R. Reinhold, M. Weber. From hut to hanging N glacier directly above Outpost Lake. Cross to W to gain ridge. Climb ridge to gendarme, traversing E below overhang to wide loose chimney whose rock improves higher up. Gain top of W bastion from which an easy ridge leads to the summit. Ascent 7 h (CAJ **40**-85).

Variant. August 1965, L. Chalmers, G. Crocker. The N ridge is followed throughout. 6½ h up.

3. N Glacier. August 1931, H. F. Bulyea, H. Burns, W. E. Streng, C. G. Wates, W. J. Watson, E. L. Woolf. As above to hanging glacier. Ascend a steep snow couloir to **N ridge** and thus to top. Ascent 5 h. This route may be impractical now because of ice retreat (CAJ **20**-8; **22**-77, photo; App. **19**-47).

4. SE Ridge. July 1957, D. Morrison, W. Sparling, J. Tarrant. From Eremite Valley, head for cliff above triangular green patch on scree, immediately below where SE ridge appears to meet glacier. Ascend cliff, working left, and then take glacier back right to ridge, which is followed to summit over moderately difficult rock.

5. S Slopes. Gain Eremite Glacier, cross to N, and ascend easy scree to top. The easiest descent route, 3½ h to hut.

BENNINGTON PEAK (3265m)

On Divide W of head of Penstock Creek; between Fraser and Bennington Glaciers.

FA August 1926, R. B. M. Bibby, J. H. Hoag, N. W. Spadavecchia. **SW Ridge.** From Wates–Gibson Hut to Fraser Glacier. Head in direction of McDonnell Peak, then turn right and climb steep snow to McDonnell–Bennington saddle. Follow ridge E over snow to outslabbing rock. Turn difficulties to right (S), finishing in a narrow couloir. Ascent 9 h, descent 5 h (CAJ **16**-66; App. **20**-536).

2. E Ridge. Descent, August 1933, E. R. Gibson, R. C. Hind, E. L. Woolf. July 1945, R. C. Hind and ACC party. From hut to Fraser Glacier. Ascend into snow basin below ridge and exit to ridge proper along an obvious ramp. Follow ridge over numerous steps, generally taking difficulties head-on. The final step is climbed to the left (S) of the crest. A classic line, involving some 700m of rock climbing. II, F4; ascent 8 h, descent 6 h (CAJ **22**-73).

3. N Face. August 1963, F. Beckey, H. Mather. Initially the route goes up the center of the curving glacier in the NE basin, involving considerable ice climbing. Two bergschrunds must be passed to reach the pyramidal rock face, approximately

Parapet Mtn

E Ridge

Bennington Pk

McDonnell Pk

Simon Pk

Fraser Glacier

FRASER MASSIF FROM SOUTHEAST

500m high. Thereafter, climb highly exposed but excellent rock
to the top. A fine modern climb requiring a long day. IV (AAJ
14-203).

McDONNELL PEAK (3270m)

On Divide next W of Bennington Peak.

FA August 1919, A. Carpé, R. H. Chapman, H. Palmer. **S
Ridge.** To Fraser Glacier from hut. Cross dry glacier, then
névé, to rounded rock crest on S ridge. The summit is easily
reached over loose shale. Although doubtless the most frequently ascended route in the group, it is without intrinsic
interest. 8 h RT from hut (AJ **38**-56). Ski ascent, January 1931,
E. R. Gibson, J. Weiss (CAJ **19**-122).

2. NW Ridge. July 1924, A. J. Ostheimer, M. M. Strumia,
J.M. Thorington, *C. Kain.* On traverse from Simon Peak. Today
this route is usually done in reverse as the most direct route
to Simon Peak, returning the same way. One h in either direction (AJ **36**-341).

SIMON PEAK (3322m)

Highest peak in group and highest Divide peak between
Fortress Lake and Yellowhead Pass; together with Bennington
and McDonnell Peaks constitutes massif of Mount Fraser.

FA July 1924, A. J. Ostheimer, M. M. Strumia, J. M. Thorington, *C. Kain.* **S Glacier/SE Ridge.** From hut, ascend Fraser
Glacier to snow saddle at end of McDonnell S ridge and cross
to Simon Glacier. Ascend glacier, passing icefalls on E, to Simon–McDonnell col, from which SE ridge is taken to summit.
This roundabout route has been completely discarded in favor
of the traverse from McDonnell Peak (which see). Ascent 8 h;
6 h on traverse over McDonnell Peak (AJ **36**-323, **38**-56). **Ski
ascent,** April 1936, E. R. Gibson, R. C. Hind (CAJ **24**-68).

2. W Glacier/SW Ridge. August 1929, H. A. Burns, E. R.
Gibson, C. G. Wates. From Geikie Meadows via Icefall Lake to
tongue of Scarp Glacier (3½ h). Ascend glacier for some 2 h,

then climb icefall on left into snow cirque bounded by the
Simon–Scarp ridge, which is attained over steep slopes. Follow
long ridge to summit. Ascent 10 h. FA party completed traverse
over McDonnell to hut (App **17**-385; CAJ **18**-83; **41**-106).

CASEMATE MOUNTAIN (3090m)

3 km NW of Simon Peak, between Bennington Glacier and
Icefall Lake.

FA August 1928, D. L. Busk, J. E. Johnson, *H. Fuhrer*. **N
Ridge.** From Icefall Lake, ascend prominent couloir in W face,
working left on ledges higher up to reach NW ridge just above
Casemate–Postern col (2 h). Climb this ridge for some 600m
until steep cliffs are encountered. Traverse left to N ridge and
climb same over steep, loose and icy rock to summit. 6–8 h up,
5–6 h down (CAJ **17**-54; AJ **40**-385).

POSTERN MOUNTAIN (2490m)

2 km NW of Casemate Mountain on same ridge.

FA August 1927, E. R. Gibson, *E. Niederer*. **SE Ridge.** From
Geikie Meadows cross to slopes above Icefall Lake and ascend
gullies of S face to gain ridge at a point somewhat above Casemate–Postern col. Follow easy ridge to summit, an abrupt 30m
pitch being met halfway to the top, and a 6m notch beyond in
the narrowest part of the ridge. Ascent from Icefall Lake, 5½
h; total time from Geikie Meadows, 17 h (CAJ **16**-116).

Para Pass, between Parapet Mountain and Paragon Peak,
provides access to routes on those peaks, as well as to Oubliette
and Dungeon. From the Wates–Gibson Hut, follow the valley
of Penstock Creek to the obvious snow couloir leading to the
Pass. Because of recession, the ascent takes longer than formerly, now about 3 h. Sometimes danger from crevasses and/
or cornices. From Para Pass, an easy ramp contours around
the W side of the Ramparts, making accessible from the hut
peaks as distant as Dungeon. The Pass is also important as an

"inside passage" from the hut to Geikie Meadows, although again, glacial recession has made the route more difficult. Para Pass was first crossed in 1926 by C. Nicol, F. N. Waterman, C. G. Wates, who descended Bennington Glacier to Geikie Meadows (CAJ **6**-246). In 1945, the Pass was crossed by B. Cork, E. R. Gibson, W. R. Latady, who then traversed the conspicuous snow band on Parapet to the Bennington Névé, the Bennington–MacDonnell col and Fraser Glacier (CAJ **29**-229). This traverse has greatly increased in difficulty in recent years.

PARAPET MOUNTAIN (3090m)

On Divide between Bennington Peak and Para Pass.

FA August 1924, L. Coolidge, G. Higginson, J. E. Johnson, *A. Streich*. **N Ridge.** From Para Pass ascend cliffs by any of several possible lines (easiest to left) to crest of ridge, which is taken over two short steps to the summit. Ascent from hut, 6 h; descent 4 h (CAJ **20**-13).

PARAGON PEAK (3030m)

On Divide immediately N of Para Pass, between Surprise Point and Bennington glacier.

FA August 1919, A. Carpé, H. Palmer. **E Ridge.** From Wates–Gibson Hut, ascend to crest of ridge extending W from Surprise Point. Follow ridge W to base of peak. Then proceed over boulders and a snowslope to foot of E ridge, which is climbed to the summit. One pitch of F4; 5 h up, 4 h down. An enjoyable introduction to the Ramparts (AJ **38**-57; CAJ **22**-66).

2. W Face/S Ridge. August 1949, J. Bishop, D. Greenwell, J. Hutton, E. LaChapelle. From Hut to Para Pass. Traverse ledge on W face to almost below Paragon–Oubliette col. Climb couloirs up and to the right across W face to gain S ridge about 100m below summit. Follow ridge to peak; ascent 9 h.

3. NE Face. July 1971, P. Armstrong, N. Savage, O. Swartling. From camp at Surprise Point, ascend steep snow couloir to Paragon–Oubliette col, then climb rock of NE face to summit.

OUBLIETTE MOUNTAIN (3090m)

On Divide next N of Paragon Peak.

FA July 1932, W. R. Hainsworth, M. M. Strumia, *H. Fuhrer.*

W Face. From hut over Para Pass and along W side ramp to Oubliette–Dungeon col (5 h). Retrace a short distance and ascend two rock steps, then an overhang, and, following a zigzag, a vertical 8m wall. Gain the **N ridge** near the lower N summit (3 h). Rappel a 3m gap in ridge to a horizontal ledge by which the W face is recrossed to the S. When within sight of S ridge, turn directly up toward summit, which is reached without further difficulty. Ascent 10–11 h. This convoluted route has been superseded by Route 2 below (CAJ 21-72, marked photo; AAJ 1-534; AJ 45-341, route diagram).

2. W Face. August 1933, E. R. Gibson, O. Haw, R. C. Hind, E. L. Woolf. This line lies considerably to S of FA route above and is accordingly more direct. From hut to Para Pass and then along W side of ramp. After crossing Paragon–Oubliette couloir, turn the next ridge into an amphitheater. Climb chimneys and short walls directly to N ridge beyond (S) the 3m gap of Route 1; much variation possible in this section. Ascend a spectacular 20m pitch overlooking Amethyst Lakes (excellent rock, F4) to the final, almost level ridge leading to the top. 8 h up (CAJ 22-75).

3. S Ridge. August 1951, R. Irvin, G. Mowat, J. Mowat. Reach the Paragon–Oubliette col either from Para Pass via the Paragon ramp or from the E ridge of Paragon by traversing a horizontal ledge (as in FA). Scramble up down-sloping ledges encumbered with loose rock. Climb a 7m overhang, and, after more scree ledges, reach a second, more severe overhanging pitch of 20m. Pass this 30m right (E) by a difficult open chimney and crack, after which the summit is easily attained. One h

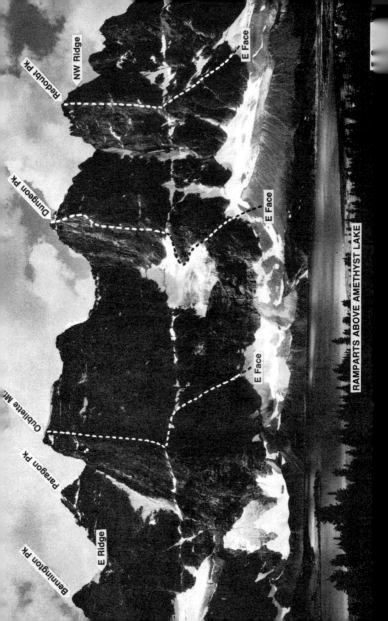

RAMPARTS ABOVE AMETHYST LAKE

Redoubt Pk

NW Ridge

E Face

Dungeon Pk

E Face

Oubliette Mt

E Face

Paragon Pk

Bennington Pk

E Ridge

from col. This is the quickest descent route, involving a free rappel over the 20m overhang (CAJ **35**-96).

4. E Face. July 1962, F. Beckey, D. Gordon, B. Greenwood. Approach from the S side of Amethyst Lakes over scree and snow to foot of great E wall. Keeping about 200m N of the E nose, ascend steep quartzite toward the conspicuous ledge some 300m up. (An easier alternative: ascend snow and couloirs to S of nose to reach the ledge). A short, class 5 pitch is climbed below the ledge, which is then traversed for several exposed pitches to the nose. A succession of textbook pitches is ascended left of the nose (occasional running protection) until a gendarme is encountered. Climb two class 5 pitches to the gap behind the gendarme and then a steep, muscular wall pitch. Thereafter, easier climbing to the top. A long day, at minimum, should be allowed. A major wall problem with considerable danger of falling rock, but nevertheless a first-rate modern route (CAJ **46**-81, marked photo).

DUNGEON PEAK (3130m)

On Divide one km NW of Oubliette Peak.

FA August 1933, E. R. Gibson, R. C. Hind, E. L. Woolf. **W Face.** From hut over Para Pass and along W side ramp to Oubliette–Dungeon col (5 h). Descend to second ledge below col and traverse it until about midway across W face of objective. Climb up to broad, debris-covered ledge beneath summit mass. Continue up a diagonal chimney followed by a series of short, steep snow slopes to the summit (9½ h from hut). The original party completed the traverse by descending the NW ridge, Dungeon–Redoubt couloir, W slope of Redoubt to Drawbridge Pass (which see), and then the couloir down to Amethyst Lakes. A messy route, 8 h down (CAJ **22**-76, marked photo).

2. E Face. August 1967, F. Beckey, D. Eberl. From opposite peninsula on Amethyst Lakes ascend moraine slopes to the right base of the great central buttress. A deep left-slanting chimney veers some 150m steeply to the right edge of the hanging ice patch of the first band. Thereafter, work up snow and rock near ice edge, then rock to the band on its corner directly beneath the summit. The route goes directly upward, following a slight spur on the face. Some 120m below the summit, traverse right to more broken rock. Difficulties are generally in the F4–F5 range but the hardest pitch is F7. A very long day on a good route (AAJ **16**-168, marked photo plate 82).

REDOUBT PEAK (3120m)

Next N of Dungeon Peak on Divide ridge, just before it begins to arc NW and then W.

FA August 1927, F. H. Slark, *F. Rutishauser,* presumably via the **W face** or **N ridge.** The climbers met with a fatal accident on the descent and their bodies were never found. Their summit record was discovered by the party of the following year and a rucksack was found some distance down the W slope (AJ **40**-385; CAJ **16**-117, 241; **17**-54).

2. W Face. August 1928, D. L. Busk, J. E. Johnson, *H. Fuhrer.* Gain Lookout Pass (see below) from a camp near Moat Lake (2 h). Traverse W slopes for about 1.5 km, ascending slightly to triangular snow patch below and just W of objective in 2 h more. Above this, three broad scree ledges run horizontally across the face, separated by belts of cliff. Gain the first ledge without difficulty. Ascend a chimney with a peculiar chockstonelike formation to reach the second ledge. Traverse right (S) to easier rock and ascend alongside a vertical depression, finally working back left to reach the third ledge. Traverse left and climb up to a shoulder on the N ridge. Turn the final buttress by an easy chimney on the NE. Ascent from triangular patch, 3 h; descent 2 h. Total time 13 h (AAJ **1**-16, marked photo; CAJ **17**-53).

3. N Ridge. July 1957, D. LaChapelle, R. Jones, D. K. Morrison. Approach as for Route 2 toward triangular snow patch. Skirt ridge of N outlier and ascend a narrow snow couloir to a small col at base of ridge proper. Follow it to the top. Ascent, 6 h from Moat Lake (CAJ **41**-106).

4. E Face. August 1965, F. Beckey, J. Fuller. From Amethyst Lakes, ascend snow toward lower part of central buttress of face. Considerable difficulty in crossing bergschrund to rock of buttress. After reaching ledge ⅓ of way up, climb directly up vertical crest of buttress (the two most difficult pitches). Keep in midface and always watch for rockfall. An intricate pattern of traverses, ledges and steps leads to easier going near the top. A long, exposed route with a high level of danger from rockfall; V (AAJ **15**-159).

Beyond Redoubt Peak, the ridge carrying the Divide drops in elevation as it swings NW to Bastion Peak. In this 4 km section are two low passes, Lookout (SE, 2520m), and Drawbridge (NW 2460m), separated by **Drawbridge Peak** (2720m), a minor eminence. Lookout Pass provides access from the Tonquin Valley to Redoubt Peak and possibly Dungeon Peak also (which see, FA route and traverse). From Moat Lake ascend boulder slope between two snow-filled couloirs. Just below Pass climb the right (W) of two chimneys, even though it appears more difficult (2 h). Drawbridge Pass gives access to Bastion Peak and is sometimes used as an "inside passage" connecting Moat Lake with Geikie Meadows. A straightforward ascent on talus and snow (2 h). To reach Lookout Pass, traverse below (S) Drawbridge Peak.

BASTION PEAK (2970m)

On Divide where it abruptly swings N; S buttress of Tonquin Pass.

FA August 1925, J. W. A. Hickson, H. Palmer, *H. Kohler.*
SW Ridge. From Moat Lake to Drawbridge Pass (2 h). Traverse W to SSW ridge and gain shoulder at 2650m in 1½ h more. Traverse W to well-marked couloir, above which three chim-

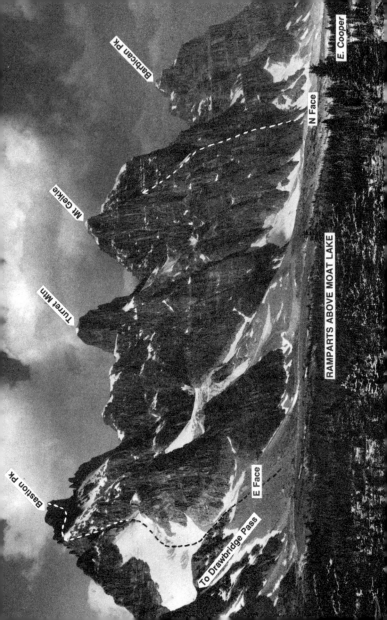

Barbican Pk

E. Cooper

N Face

Mt Geikie

Turret Mtn

RAMPARTS ABOVE MOAT LAKE

Bastion Pk

E Face

To Drawbridge Pass

neys lead to summit (3½ h). Ascent 7 h; descent 6½ h (AJ **38**-63; App **16**-246).

2. SE Ridge. August 1927, E. R. Gibson, *E. Niederer.* To Drawbridge Pass from camp at Moat Lake. Traverse W over shale slopes to gain the pronounced SE ridge. Climb ridge, circumventing steep buttress higher up by a wide 15m chimney. A final slab leads to the top. 7 h up (CAJ **16**-110).

3. E Face. August 1965, F. Beckey, J. Fuller. From Moat Lake ascend to the snow slopes on the NE side of the peak, then climb the ice to left (S) of several prominent rock buttresses. Climb right to gain a little saddle behind the frontal buttresses and then ascend two pitches of steep ice to the rock wall of the upper E face. Climb a rock pitch and then traverse up and to right, mainly on rock. Keep as high as possible but do not continue along the knife-edged ridge. Always work to right (N). Arrive finally at a notch where the summit tower is 80m directly above. Traverse left for 30m and then climb directly upward in a system of cracks and chimneys. This last 60m section appears to require aid but free climbing is possible, although considerable protection may be desired. Excellent rock (AAJ **15**-161).

Ramrod, the pinnacle at the foot of Bastion Peak, was first ascended in July 1957, D. LaChapelle, T. Church, D. K. Morrison. **NE Face.** Start at E corner and move out to middle of face. There follows a traverse, slab walls, and a wide chimney requiring a rolling turn to gain an overhang at its top. Walls and ledges lead back to the E corner, after which a final 25m pitch on the E face leads to the top. 3 h up, 2 h down on rappel (CAJ **41**-67).

TURRET MOUNTAIN (3120m)

1.5 km W of Bastion Peak.

FA August 1926, A. W. Drinnan, *L. Grassi.* From camp on Geikie Meadows, contour E to second of two small lakes (Black Inkwell) below Geikie–Turret col. The line of the ascent is the couloir of the **SW face,** between the summit mass and the great W tower. As there are overhangs in the couloir, it is necessary to start considerably to the left (W), ascending steep rocks and a narrow chimney to a notch behind a prominent sphinxlike gendarme. Descend slightly and traverse a narrow ledge to a broad one which permits rounding a buttress into the couloir, above the overhangs. Ascend the couloir nearly to the top, then bear right to the W face of the summit tower, which is climbed over loose blocks held together by ice and snow. Ascent from Black Inkwell, 4½ h; descent 2½ h (CAJ **16**-55, marked photo).

2. N Face. August 1979, C. Jones, B. Wagstaff. The route begins on the left (E) side of the prominent N buttress and ascends to the prow of the buttress (F8, A1). Above, the climbing is easier but requires ingenious route finding. Mixed climbing, with ice to 60° is encountered in turning the final headwall to the right to gain the notch between the summit and the W tower, from which the top is readily attained. Two days up on FA; V, F8, A1 (AAJ **53**-563).

MOUNT GEIKIE (3270m)

Major peak in NW part of Rampart massif (AJ **33**-147; CAJ **4**-11; **13**-53; **14**-53).

FA July 1924, V. A. Fynn, M. D. Geddes, C. G. Wates, via Route 2 below.

SE Face. August 1926, A. W. Drinnan, *L. Grassi.* This route is preferable to that of the FA and is now generally followed. From camp on Geikie Meadows contour E to first small lake (Blue Inkwell) where the ascent proper begins. Initially, the route follows the great couloir in the face, which rises to the E ridge one km E of the summit. Ascend snow in the couloir until approximately halfway up to the ridge. Here the couloir presents a slight fork to the left (W). Exit and climb diagonally across the face, bearing W and reaching the main crest just E of the summit (App **19**-51; CAJ **20**-20, marked photo; **22**-80; AAJ **1**-8).

2. E Ridge. The route coincides with the above up to the left fork. Continue up the great couloir, climbing the loose rocks on its W side to gain the crest of the E ridge (5 h from Blue Inkwell). A step in the ridge now forces a traverse on its N side, the ridge being regained by a steep, narrow crack and snowslopes. Circumvent a second step (black rock) by traversing to S along a ledge which is partly obstructed by a red-yellow colored rock. Regain the ridge, cross a depression, and reach the summit. Ascent, 12 h; descent 12 h (AJ **36**-344; CAJ **14**-62, marked photos; **20**-18; App **16**-244).

3. W Ridge. August 1967, A. DeMaria, J. Hudson, J. Kelsey. From near Moat Lake to Geikie–Barbican col (Paugak Pass). Scramble scree and traverse along N side of ridge. Cross snow and gain ridge proper, following it to a tower. Pass this and two more towers on the S, then ascend a steep pitch and follow a stream bed to 300m buttress split by an icy gully. Ascend easy rock to left of gully, then three harder pitches, and, after crossing gully, go right and around corner of buttress. Cross several scree gullies and climb to flat area below final section of buttress (bivouac on FA). Descend slightly right and work to easier terrain, over which the top of the buttress and finally the summit are gained. III, F6, A1 (AAJ **16**-169).

4. N Face (L). August 1972, J. Hudson, R. Robbins. The route follows the prominent buttress which forms the left (E) side of the face. Ascend a small hanging glacier and a couloir-chimney system between a spur on the left and the main N face. From a small notch at top of spur, climb over broken rock and occasional patches of snow/ice to large blocks at base of steep headwall. Class 3 and 4 to this point. Technical difficulties are concentrated in ensuing 250m wall; 8 pitches up to F9 and A3. Easier climbing up broken rock on left leads to the top. 2 bivouacs on FA; V, F9 A3 (AAJ **16**-60, marked diagram).

5. N Face (Center). August 1979, D. Hannibal, G. Lowe. Details lacking, but the line goes up the thin rib in the middle of the face. 4 days up on FA; VI, F9, A3 (AAJ **53**-565, marked photo plate 81).

SE PEAK (2940m)

Minor eminence on E ridge, E of col at head of great couloir of Routes 1 and 2 above.

FA July 1927, H. A. Burns, E. R. Gibson, G. B. Pickford, C. G. Wates, *E. Niederer*. Via **S slopes** (inadvertently) en route (abortively) to main summit (CAJ **16**-114).

BARBICAN PEAK (3120m)

Final Rampart peak, 2 km WNW of Mount Geikie.

FA July 1924, V. A. Fynn, M. D. Geddes, F. H. Slark, C. G. Wates. **SW Ridge.** From camp on Geikie Meadows immediately S of objective. Ascend shale slopes of S face from E to W under cliffs to well-marked col on SW ridge (5 h). Follow ridge until summit buttress is reached, then traverse diagonally E across S face to prominent couloir from which summit ridge is gained. Ascent 8½ h; descent 6 h (AJ **36**-342; CAJ **14**-60).

Variant/S Face. July 1927, H. A. Burns, E. R. Gibson, G. B. Pickford, C. G. Wates, *E. Niederer*. By the prominent couloir of the S face until it becomes vertical at its intersection with the upper SW ridge, from which the latter is continued. This is to be preferred to the original route and is also the best descent route (CAJ **16**-112).

2. NE Face. July 1966, F. Beckey, J. Fuller. Initially ascend the Geikie–Barbican couloir (snow/ice), then veer right onto faces and ledges. About 150m below summit, traverse right up ramp to wet, vertical section. Then follow a difficult chimney, a left traverse on unstable blocks, and a vertical wall leading to an airy ridge crest and the peak (AAJ **15**-369; CAJ **50**-66).

3. N Ridge. July 1966, J. Hudson, D. Jensen, F. Sarnquist. From Tonquin Creek attain ridge via snow gully. Follow ridge throughout except for occasional detours on E face. One difficult pitch near top (AAJ **15**-369).

There is nothing Nature more shapeless or ill-figured than an old Rock or Mountain.

T. Burnet

Such uncouth rocks and such uncomely inhabitants!

H. Walpole

Neither indeed is there any hill or hillocke, which doth not containe in it the most sweete memory of worthy matters.

H. Kirchner

AROUND JASPER

In this section we describe routes on a variety of selected peaks which can be readily approached with Jasper as a base. In many instances, the climbs can be done in one day from the town. For others, one approaches on the preceding day, camps or bivouacs, makes the climb and returns to the fleshpots the second evening. An automobile is essential, and, for the Colin Range (which see), a boat is useful if not necessary.

SOUTHWEST OF JASPER

Here we group diverse peaks which rise in the angle formed by Athabasca River on the E and Miette River on the N. The outstanding summit is Mount Edith Cavell, a conspicuous landmark in the view S from Jasper. Other than the Cavell massif, the peaks are located N of Astoria River and E and N of the Ramparts. In this latter area, there are few peaks of interest to today's mountaineers, so several peaks described in previous editions have been here deleted.

ACCESS

The more southerly peaks are reached from the Edith Cavell Road, which leaves Route 93A 12 km S of Jasper and terminates at the base of Mount Edith Cavell. The Astoria River trail leaves the auto road above the second viewpoint (see Chapter 12 for details). Some 5 km along this trail, a side trail leading to Verdant Pass diverges left (S), giving access to the W ridge route on Edith Cavell and to Throne and Chevron Mountains. The Portal Creek trail (see "Rock" chapter) is used to reach peaks between Portal Creek and Astoria River, as well as peaks of the Trident Range immediately N.

Maps: 83D9, 83D16.

Cavell Group

CHEVRON MOUNTAIN (2880m)

Between Verdant and Campus Passes.

Probable FA, August 1915, A. J. Gilmour, E. W. D. Holway (CAJ **7**-64).

July 1953, J. G. Kato, M. & T. V. Wilshire. Via Astoria River trail and Verdant Pass to base of peak. Ascend E slope and, turning N, follow corniced SE ridge to bare rock. Climb **S ridge** to within 60m of summit, finally crossing steep snow patch to top. 13 h RT from Cavell Road (CAJ **37**-99).

NE PEAK (2780m)

FA July 1963, W. Angus, P. Dowling. Take **E ridge** from Verdant Creek; 6½ h up (CAJ **47**-164).

BLACKHORN PEAK (3000m)

SE angle between Campus Creek and Astoria River.

FA July 1926, R. Cleveland, B. B. Gilman, B. G. Jefferson. From Campus valley by way of **SW face.** A chimney leads up to a prominent buttress, at the right edge of which there is a deep, narrow chimney leading high up through the belt of black rock. Each chimney is about 12m high, with firm rock and no falling stones. From the top of the second chimney a ledge is gained by a short traverse and followed toward the W ridge, the latter being attained through a short, broad couloir. The arête cannot be followed throughout, but the summit is reached by a short detour on the SW face. Ascent 6 h; descent 4 h (CAJ **16**-59; Harvard **1**-72; **20**-536).

2. N Face. August 1965, F. Beckey, G. Fuller. Climb steep snow slopes to the entrance of a prominent couloir that divides the N face. It may be difficult to gain the rock at this point. Class 4 and 5 climbing of 400m to E summit. Keep out of the couloir because of falling rocks. It is possible to descend to a notch and climb the W peak if desired (CAJ **49**-122).

THRONE MOUNTAIN (3120m)

SW angle between Astoria River and Verdant Creek.

FA July 1926, J. W. A. Hickson, H. Palmer, *J. Weber.* From Astoria River trail (branch on S bank), gain the cirque between objective and Blackhorn Peak. A couloir penetrating the summit cap and some steep slabs lead to the top. 9 h up; 7 h down (CAJ **16**-51).

2. NE Ridge (N Armrest). August 1966, H. F. Microys, *alone.* From Astoria River trail shortly before it crosses river to base of ridge. Easy climbing to two notches in ridge. Descend into the first (20m) via a chimney. Descend by SE side, then climb steep wall with good holds into second (30m). Take ridge to top. Descent by same route. Round trip from Cavell Road, 8 h (CAJ **50**-67).

3. NE Face. August 1964, *H. Schwarz,* alone. Via the Verdant Pass trail until directly in front of mountain. The route goes up the 800m face, inclined at 55°, slightly to right (N) of center. Ascend small glacier at foot of face, then climb sloping ledges and steep pitches of solid rock to upper snowfield. Ascend this on a snow rib, exiting on the summit ridge some 60m NW of the top. Mostly class 4, approximately 4 h on face proper (CAJ **48**-131, marked photo).

MOUNT EDITH CAVELL (3363m)

Highest and most impressive of peaks in vicinity of Jasper.

FA August 1915, A. J. Gilmour, E. W. D. Holway. From Verdant Pass, ascend broken cliffs to subsidiary W peak. From the depression beyond take the narrow W ridge to the corniced summit. Ascent 6½ h; descent 4½ h (CAJ **7**-63; **23**-59, winter ascent).

2. E Ridge. July 1924, variant, L. Coolidge, G. Higginson, J. E. Johnson, *A. Streich.* August 1924, integral, J. W. A. Hickson, *C. Kain.* This justly popular route may now be regarded as **the normal route,** the FA route being used only for descent. From end of Cavell Road, take a path along E moraine, then cross glacier to prominent col at foot of E ridge (3 h). Above col ascend easy rock ledges, with occasional snow, to shoulder conspicuous in views from N. Continue along ridge to base of buttress formed by band of black rock (one h above shoulder). Climb buttress directly, which offers interesting climbing on sound rock. (The original party avoided the buttress by traversing a ledge S to a couloir by which the crest was regained). Follow ridge to summit. Ascent 10 h (App **19**-244).

N Face. There are to date four routes on this magnificent wall. They are described from E to W rather than in chronological order. Rockfall danger is high on these routes.

E. Cooper

N Face Direct

MT. EDITH CAVELL NORTH FACE

E Summit, N Face

E Ridge

3. E Summit. July 1967, Y. Chouinard, J. Faint, C. Jones. This route on the left (E) side of the face ascends more or less directly to the E summit. Start to right of conspicuous snow patch in lower face and work up to a ledge system 400m up, on a level with upper part of Angel Glacier. Continue over broken rock and snow to a buttress leading directly to E summit. Stay mostly on rib to summit. Excellent mixed climbing; can be done in one day with early start. V, F8 (AAJ **16**-58, Plate 63).

4. July 1978, M. Hesse, J. Krakauer, J. Hladock. Few details, but this line lies to right of above, presumably on the rib rising just left of the left (E) corner of upper Angel Glacier. Approach as for direct route (see below). The climbing is mostly on ice with some steep mixed sections; V (AAJ **53**-209; CAJ **62**-98).

5. N Face Direct. July 1961, F. Beckey, Y. Chouinard, D. Doody. This route follows the central buttress leading directly to the summit. Ascend to ice slope left of Angel Glacier, then climb some 250m of steep quartzite left of cascading ice (danger of falling ice). Ascend the ice face to get on the upper Angel Glacier. Climb glacier to the rounded buttress in center of upper face. It may be difficult to gain the rock. Climb upward on increasingly difficult rock; rockfall can be expected. Belay from protected corners and attempt to stay on crest of buttress. Eventually make a difficult traverse right; 1½ pitches on ice-covered rock. Then climb upward again on right side of ice gullies. The buttress becomes narrower and the rockfall danger lessens. Follow crest to where it merges into final ice face 150m high and 55–60°. Climb final 70m of extremely dangerous shale to summit. Nearly 1200m of climbing, requiring two days with bivouac on FA. Speed is the primary safety factor, so it is better to go unroped as much as possible. V, F7 (AAJ **13**-53, Plate 37).

6. McKeith Spur. July 1978, L. Bruce, H. Kent. To the right (W) of above, using same approach to upper Angel Glacier.

Details lacking, but route follows an obvious spur halfway up the face. 40% rock, 60% ice; V, F7 (AAJ **53**-209; CAJ **52**-98).

North of Astoria River rises a group of minor summits of little interest to climbers, the Portal–Maccarib Group. **Mount Clitheroe** (2747m), at the W end above Amethyst Lakes, and **Oldhorn Mountain** (3000m), N of Throne Mountain across Astoria River, offer excellent views of the Ramparts and are occasionally ascended for that reason. North of the valley of Portal and Maccarib Creeks rises the compact Trident Range, which supports some permanent snow. Again there is little mountaineering interest save perhaps for the highest peak, **Majestic Mountain** (3086m), which is ascended over its SW ridge. Farther W, N of Moat Lake and Tonquin Creek and W of Meadow Creek, is another group of uninteresting peaks, the Meadow–Clairvaux Group. The magnificent view of the Ramparts from **Vista Peak** (2795m), however, makes an ascent rewarding (CAJ **12**-158, panorama).

The information you have is not what you want. The information you want is not what you need. The information you need is not what you can obtain.

O.L. Bear

NORTHWEST OF JASPER

Most of the summits in this area offer no real challenge to the alpinist, although practically all have been visited. The absence of severe, sustained ridges and faces, the indifferent quality of the rock, and the minimal permanent snow combine to render the region rather bland compared to the greater part of the Rockies.

Hunters and trappers, operating for the most part from Jasper House, frequented these ranges over a century ago, mostly during winter for food and furs. Parties of railroad surveyors and explorers traversed the Snaring and Snake Indian drainages as routes across the Divide. The original winter traverse in January 1875 by E. W. Jarvis and C. F. Hanington was particularly noteworthy and is chillingly well described in the CPR Report of 1877, p. 145.

In recent years, few mountaineering parties have cared to frequent these ranges; hence the area is not discussed in detail here. Rising directly NW of Jasper is the attractive group called the Victoria Cross Ranges, enclosed within the Miette and Snaring Rivers. North of the Snaring, but S of the Snake Indian River, lies another seldom visited region much like the Victoria Cross Ranges, the De Smet Range. Still farther to the N and W, lying principally along the northern boundary of Jasper National Park, are several more significant ranges, among them the Starlight Range, The Ancient Wall and the Persimmon Range.

Although of scant interest to mountaineers, this is good hiking country. Local inquiry from Park officials in Jasper will provide recent details on trails. The data given in the **Trail Guide** also is accurate and reasonably current.

Maps: 83D16; 83E1; 83E7; 83D/15E.

MOUNT BRIDGLAND (2930m)

A bold rock tower 10 km NNW of Yellowhead Pass, E of upper part of Miette River.

FA September 1946, E. R. Gibson, F. S. Smythe, D. Wessel.
SW Ridge/S Face. Approach from Yellowhead Pass up Miette River (old trail) to small lake (1760m) S of objective. Ascend through forest and up scree to crest of SW ridge. Follow this to small peak separated from main tower by a sharp col. Contour on NW side to gain col at base of final steep face, which is riven by an enormous cleft. Climb to left (W) of cleft, working left, and make an exposed traverse left under overhangs to reach easier rock over which the summit is gained. One hour from col; 8½ h from camp at lake (CAJ **30**-80).

2. E Face. August 1973, F. Beckey, B. Leo, C. McCarty. Details lacking, but a tortuous, sometimes interesting route on steep rock of the E buttress. The final headwall involves 2 pitches of nearly vertical rock culminating in a dramatic overhang (AAJ **48**-164).

Anyone who thinks there's safety in numbers hasn't looked at the stock market pages.

I. Peter

NORTHEAST OF JASPER

In the large area bounded on the W by Athabasca River and on the S by Maligne River are located several ridges of minor summits, in particular, the Colin Range, the Jacques Range, and the Miette Range. Although not of high elevation, many of these predominantly limestone peaks offer excellent rock climbing. Local climbers have, in recent years, put up a multitude of routes of varying length and difficulty, details of most of which cannot be given here, in a mountaineering guide. With some specific exceptions, notably the Colin Range, we merely try to point out those places where good climbing can be found. Local inquiry in Jasper, or of the Edmonton Section of the ACC, may prove helpful.

Maps: 83C13, 85D/16E, 83E/1E, 83F/4W.

North of Medicine Lake rises a ridge of slabby peaks, the "Rainy Day Slabs," offering a variety of rock routes (CAJ **64**-90). Above the valley of Beaver Lake next NE are three connected peaks ranged parallel to the valley, as follows:

UNNAMED (2570m)
FA 1958, T. Meisner and party. Ascend **NW ridge** to NW summit (2450m) and continue traverse to central peak (2560m). Main summit, FA August 1960, E. Hopkins, T. Meisner, P. Payne via **SW face.** Leave Jacques Lake trail 1.5 km N of Beaver Lake and ascend directly up the steep frontal slabs. Some protection used on FA. Ascent 10 h (CAJ **44**-93, marked photo).

Colin Range

Visible from Jasper, this group of striking limestone peaks lies immediately across Athabasca River from Highway 16, some 15 km NE of the townsite. The Centennial Hut, completed in 1967, is on the right (N) side of Garonne Creek at an elevation of about 2050m. While the hut was constructed and is maintained by the ACC, it is under Parks administration as a designated campsite, thus a camping permit is required. The hut sleeps 8; ostensibly a stove, pots, etc. are provided, but it is wise to come equipped.

Parties approaching the Centennial Hut usually drive to the S end of the Jasper airfield and cross Athabasca River by boat. Look for the trail about 0.5 km N of the mouth of Garonne Creek. The hut trail may also be reached by hiking along the good trail on the E side of Athabasca River from the bridge on Highway 16 (shortest way). Alternately, hike N after crossing the footbridge at either the fish hatchery or the fifth bridge at the bottom of Maligne Canyon. This is part of the famous Athabasca Trail used by the fur traders to cross the mountains.

Because many peaks in the Colin Range are not named, a number and letter system is used here in an attempt to simplify descriptions. The unnamed peaks are prefixed with the letters CR for Colin Range and numbered between the named peaks of Grisette and Colin from 1 to 6. Subsidiary peaks have letters attached to the numbered peaks which they adjoin, starting with A for the most westerly.

CR1 (2570m)

One km NE of Roche Bonhomme, with 3 subsidiary peaks (1A, 1B, 1C) to the NE toward Nashan Creek.

CR2 (2600m)

1.5 km N of Roche Bonhomme, with its spectacular NW ridge visible from Highway 16.

FA June 1957, D. G. Linke & 3 members of ACC. From footbridge over Maligne River at fish hatchery, hike N along Athabasca River for about 5 km to a canyon with hoodoos. Negotiate the canyon (difficult with high water) and follow the creek around the NW ridge of objective and ascend scree and rock to col between peaks 2 and 3. An easy ridge of broken rock leads to the top (CAJ **42**-42).

2. NW (Meisner) **Ridge.** Follow Route One to top of the canyon and take the first wide avalanche slope leading to the ridge. The ridge provides good rock climbing; there is one place where a rope sling is necessary to rappel from a sharp tower back onto the ridge.

CR3 (2630m)
CR4 (2540m)
 2.5 and 3 km N of Roche Bonhomme, respectively.

CR5 (2570m)
 4.5 km N of Roche Bonhomme, with connecting peaks to W and S.
 FA August 1964, R. G. Harlow, *H. Schwarz.* On traverse from CR6 (which see) along sharp intervening ridge. On descent, party followed W ridge to col between CR5 and CR5C (next W) and descended steep scree to Garonne Creek. The peak is now more frequently climbed directly from the Centennial Hut over CR5C, with return as above (CAJ **48**-129).

CR5A (2030m)
 Farthest W of peaks subsidiary to CR5. This small peak has been popular as a practice climb. It may be recognized from Highway 16 by its smooth W slabs and double summit.
 1. To top of Hoodoo Canyon as for CR2. Then climb N up tree-covered slopes to first summit and cross a gully to the foot of a knife-edged ridge which is taken to the top.

2. Climb directly from the bottom of Hoodoo Canyon up S ridge and slabs to final ridge (CAJ **44**-91).

3. Climb the smooth W slabs (F5). 1979, R. Pors, C. Shokoples (CAJ **64**-90).

CR6 *(Garonne)* (2630m)

At head of Garonne Creek, 1.5 km S of Mount Colin.

FA August 1964, R. G. Harlow, *H. Schwarz.* **NW Ridge/ Traverse.** From hut to Colin–CR6 col. Scramble easy rock and pass a face on its W side. The ridge becomes very sharp. Some 70m from the top avoid a sheer step by a ledge on the E face, leading to a spur which forms a narrow chimney with the face. Ascend the chimney to the top of the spur, which is here separated from the face by approximately one meter. Make a difficult move to regain face (aid piton on FA) and follow ridge to summit without further complications. Continue traverse by descending SW ridge toward CR5 (which see) (CAJ **48**-128).

2. W Face. July 1975, D. & U. Mager. Start 50m left of gully splitting face and climb to a large ledge (F5). Reach the smooth main face and climb it up to and along a large obvious crack (F6). As the crack turns right, make a delicate traverse (F7) to another crack leading directly to summit (CAJ **59**-89).

MOUNT COLIN (2687m)

The highest point of the Colin Range, offering a variety of good rock routes. The ascent by the SE ridge is often compared to that of the normal route on its Banff counterpart, Mount Louis; the latter is, however, rather more demanding. It was on this SE ridge that the famous British climber, Frank Smythe, used his first piton in 30 years of climbing. His contempt of hardware was well known but first ascents have a way of warping one's philosophy.

FA August 1947, N. E. Odell, J. Ross, F. S. Smythe. **SE Ridge/ Traverse.** From Centennial Hut to Colin–CR6 col. Scramble easily up to a 20m overhanging step, which is climbed up down-

SE Ridge

Centennial

SW Face

NW Ridge

"MT. COLIN FROM WEST"

sloping rock on the right (E) of the crest. Continue to the top over straightforward rock. Ascent, 4–5 h; descent 2½–3 h. FA party completed traverse by descending NW ridge (see below), with one rappel (CAJ **31**-77).

2. NE Ridge. July 1958, E. Hopkins, D. G. Linke, P. Payne. Approach via trail on Jacques Creek to camp near where stream from Colin–Hawk col joins (approximately 8 km). Ascend to saddle at foot of ridge and then to shoulder above. Avoid yellow band of poor rock by a traverse left and then ascend shallow couloir for several pitches to regain crest. At a 10m overhanging slab, move left to second of two shallow grooves and climb it, finally angling left to summit. Not recommended because of loose rock. Descent via Route One to col and then NE down into Jacques Creek drainage (CAJ **42**-42).

3. NW Ridge. August 1951, R. K. Irvin, G. Mowat. J. Mowat. From hut gain Colin–Hawk col. Ascend ridge until a rounded buttress 20m high blocks the ridge. Move out 3m on a ledge on the 70° W slabs and climb a crack which decreases in size and increases in difficulty (piton on FA). In the last 5m, the holds are small and very far apart. Continue straightforwardly to the summit. 2½ h col to summit (CAJ **35**-98).

There are now four routes on the spectacular SW face, which are described from N to S rather than in chronological order.

4. W Summit. June 1976, C. Greyell, D. Jay. The route follows the buttress which rises left of the second major couloir left (N) of the main summit and finishes on a minor eminence ("W summit") on NW ridge. Start on left side of detached pillar and gain its top. Move right and climb to ledge at top of first large buttress (F5 maximum). Continue upward for 6 pitches to reach top of the buttress which defines the major couloir; loose rock and inadequate protection. Traverse left to small pedestal on left side of final buttress. Ascend rotten rock to an alcove. Climb a jamcrack with overhang at top (F8). The final pitch goes straight up, then right to corner of buttress (F6–F7). 12½ h on face; III, F8 (CAJ **60**-84).

5. SW Face, Direct. Prior to 1962, *W. Pfisterer.* This classic route follows generally the left edge of the great central pillar, consisting of a series of slabs, chimneys and dihedrals. Considerable variation is possible in lower sections, but it is important gradually to work right so as to top the pillar 100m directly below the summit. To this point, difficulties are in the F3–F4 range. From the top of the pillar, climb the smooth slab right and then left, using very thin cracks (F6). Ascend broken, but loose, stacked blocks to top. About 18 pitches, requiring 5–8 h from base of face, III, F6; highly recommended (CAJ **35**-98).

6. SW Face, Central. July 1975, R. Bandfield, B. Hagen. Directly below the summit at the foot of the face is a wet cave, the "Black Hole." Start at fourth dihedral to right of hole and climb up to intersect first dihedral coming up from hole. Continue up dihedral for 2 pitches to "Sickle Blade," a prominent groove curving down and right from the "handle," a similar chimney starting 70m above the hole. Ascend Blade to junction with handle, then up to a ridge. Follow this to a zone of interlocking dihedrals and continue up to the crux slab of Route 5. 10½ h on face; III, F7 (CAJ **59**-89, marked photo, page opposite).

7. Centennial. This route starts on a detached pillar and goes up generally the right side of the great central buttress. It joins the direct route just below the crux slab. III, F6.

Winter Ascent. January 1970, P. Ford, P. Gibb, R. Howell. From hut with skis and then on foot to Colin–CR6 col. SE ridge ascended, several pitons used (CAJ **54**-89).

HAWK MOUNTAIN (2553m)

3 km NW of Mount Colin.

FA J. Weiss, prior to 1947.

1. Traverse from N to S, 1951, R. K. Irvin, G. Mowat, J. Mowat. A pleasant walk-up.

2. Direct via SW face, 1964, D. Kronstedt, *H. Schwarz*. A rock climb on steep and often loose rock (CAJ **48**-131).

3. From hut via Colin–Hawk col and the easy SE ridge.

MORRO PEAK (1678m)

At NW end of Colin Range and 1.5 km SE of Highway 16 bridge over Athabasca River. Often used for rock-climbing schools and practice climbs. The **W face** provides good climbing and may be easily reached via the Athabasca Trail. The farther you go along the face, the better the climbing (CAJ **44**-91).

Farther N and E as one goes toward the Jasper Park East Gate, there are a number of crags within easy reach of Highway 16 on which routes have been reported. There is at least one route on **Disaster Point** (CAJ **64**-90) and also on **Roche Ronde** (2138m) dirctly N across Athabasca River from the former. On **Roche à Perdrix** (2134m), opposite the Park Gate, are several routes (CAJ **44**-89). Perhaps the most spectacular crag in this area is Roche Miette, described below.

ROCHE MIETTE (2316m)

4 km S of Highway 16 in vicinity of Disaster Point. Its awesome N and E aspects are well seen from the highway.

N Face. May 1980, P. Charkiw, P. Paul. From the pedestal at the base of the face proper, the route angles diagonally up from lower right to upper left. Difficulties are continuous and rarely less than F5; one pitch involves aid. Rock surprisingly good. Good bivouac sites 100m and approximately 2/3 of way up face. Elevation of route, 400m; 9 pitches and 18 h on FA. Descend down the back (trail). III, F8, A3 (CAJ **64**-97, route diagram and photo).

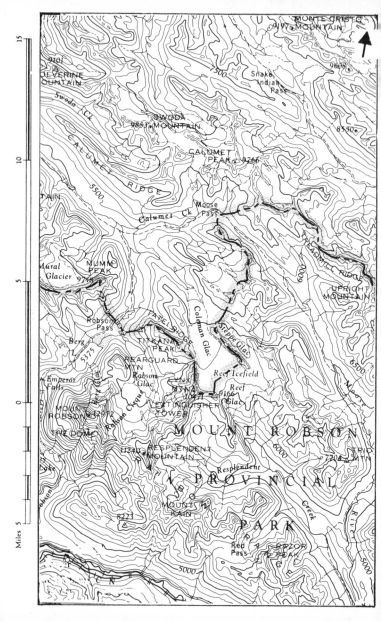

THE KING

ROBSON GROUP

In no area of the northern Canadian Rockies is a group of mountains so dominated by one peak as is the Robson Group. Indeed, if one stops at the Mount Robson viewpoint on Highway 16, the words of Milton and Cheadle are as apt today as in 1865: "On every side the snowy heads of mighty hills crowded round, whilst, immediately behind us, a giant amongst giants, and immeasurably supreme, rose Robson's Peak."

The first climbers to approach the peak were the Coleman brothers and G. B. Kinney, who in 1907, after more than a month's journey from Lake Louise (Laggan) made a tentative probe to timberline on the S. The following year, after a month's journey from Edmonton, they twice attacked the E side, on both occasions climbing the Dome. In 1909 the determined Kinney was back once more, this time with the young packer, Donald (Curly) Phillips, and made several attempts on the face lying between the Emperor and Wishbone Ridges on the W side. Their high point has never been determined, but it is plausible that on their last attempt they reached the upper section of the Emperor Ridge, though how far from the summit is not certain. Phillips later said they stopped 50 or 60 feet from the top. Kinney's bold attacks and his burning ambition to climb the peak have a permanent place in the history of Mount Robson, and even though he failed to reach the top, he is the first great protagonist of the mountain.

The group covered lies N of the Fraser River and E of the Robson River and S of Robson Pass. The N boundary is Moose Pass, on the Alberta–British Columbia Divide, and the E boundary is those peaks E of the Moose River on the Divide. These latter peaks (Treadmill Peaks) are no longer covered because they offer no interest to mountaineers.

It is well to remember that this is one of the most popular climbing areas in the Canadian Rockies. Thus it is not uncommon to find a half dozen parties, some numbering 10–15 members, attempting Mount Robson on any suitable day. There is, however, hardly any traffic on any of the other peaks.

APPROACHES & FACILITIES

Berg Lake–Robson Pass. This approach gives access to most of the climbing routes in the area, with the exception of a few on the S and W sides of Mount Robson. Start from the Robson viewpoint and service station on Highway 16 (Provincial Park campground nearby). Follow a road toward Mount Robson for 2 km to a bridge (car parking). Take the trail some 4 km to Kinney Lake and continue via switchbacks along the NE shore to reach the gorge of Robson River. Now ascend 600m up the spectacular Valley of a Thousand Falls to Berg Lake. Follow the trail along the N shore past the chalets and on to Robson Pass. There is now a manned ranger station (radio) at the Pass, but climbing registration is not (yet) mandatory. A very long day's backpack.

Along the Berg Lake trail, there are several designated campsites, with outhouses, as follows:

1. S end of Kinney Lake,
2. NE corner of Kinney Lake,
3. Just before steep ascent of Valley of a Thousand Falls,
4. On flats below (W) of Berg Lake outlet,
5. On N shore of Berg Lake near inlet, and
6. Robson Pass.

Most climbers will find the chalets at the N end of Berg Lake too expensive. Inquiries about accommodations there should be made at the Mount Robson Ranch, located some 3 km S on a dirt road (sign) opposite the Mount Robson filling station. At the ranch, pack horses can be hired to carry gear up to Berg Lake; they are probably well worth taking for any extended climbing from the Robson Pass area. In 1980, it cost about $40 to take one load (70 kg) to Robson Pass. Since pack trains leave only when a party is going in to the chalets, a couple of days delay is not uncommon.

Ralph Forster Hut. This hut is situated at 2550m on the SSW ridge of Mount Robson. It is the overnight stop before climbing the normal route on the mountain, as well as the sought-after haven of those parties traversing the peak after climbing one of the more difficult routes. Mattresses, cooking utensils and dishes for 12, Coleman stove, and lantern. Water may be found by traversing into gully on left (NW) of ridge. The hut is invariably filled to overflowing in good weather, so climbers should consider bringing their own tents, etc.

As for Berg Lake to SE side of Kinney Lake. After reaching a gravel beach continue for some 5 minutes, then leave trail and work up on the right of a large couloir/avalanche chute to catch the trail to the hut (hard to find at start). The trail stays in trees, with one short rock band to be negotiated, until well onto the scree slopes above. Work into the amphitheater, pass a hand cable, and trend left to gain the lowest notch in the SSW ridge (2350m). Follow ridge to hut (short chimney, not easy with heavy frame pack). Allow a full day from the parking lot for this grueling hut grind. If warm weather is anticipated it is advisable to start at first light, as these slopes have no water and can be excruciatingly hot. A popular plan is to hike to the footbridge below Kinney Lake the evening before the approach. Nearly 1700m elevation gain to hut.

LITERATURE

Foster, W. W. "Mount Robson." CAJ **6**-11 (1914). In this and subsequent articles, the first ascent and two further bold tries are chronicled.

Kinney, G. B. & D. Phillips. "To the Top of Mount Robson." CAJ **2**-2 (1910). The original account of Kinney and Phillips' enigmatic 1909 climb to near Robson's summit.

Wheeler, A. O. "The Alpine Club of Canada's Expedition to Jasper Park, Yellowhead Pass and Mt. Robson Region, 1911." CAJ **4**-1 (1912). The historic first circuit and description of the Robson area.

Map: 83E3.

UNNAMED (2750m)

Triple summit 2 km N of Red Pass.

FA July 1933, M. M. Strumia, J. M. Thorington. **SE Face.** From Yellowhead Highway gain Red Pass. Good climbing on good rock. 8 h from highway (CAJ **22**-216).

MOUNT KAIN (2880m)

10 km SE of Mount Robson.

FA July 1934, M. M. Strumia, *alone.* **W Ridge.** Follow W bank of stream that issues from S cirque of peak, then round objective to W and NW (col) where a short but steep climb leads to summit plateau (CAJ **22**-217).

RESPLENDENT MOUNTAIN (3426m)

A fine summit, though dwarfed by Mount Robson. Well worth climbing from high camp placed for the Kain route on Robson, or as an objective in its own right (CAJ **6**-65).

N Ridge

N Glacier

Ice Arête

E. Cooper

E Spur

MT. RESPLENDENT FROM NORTH

FA August 1911, B. Harmon, *C. Kain*. **NW Slopes** (normal route). Follow the Kain Face approach up Robson Glacier (which see), but instead of heading up the icefall to pass over the Dome, climb to the col (2920m) 1.5 km NW of objective. From the col take the straightforward NW snow slopes to the top. 8 h from camp at Robson Pass; descent 4 h.

2. N Ridge. July 1920, P. B. & W. A. D. Munday. As for NW slopes until the base of the mountain is reached. Instead of climbing to the col, take a short ice slope leading to the foot (2680m) of the rock ridge which descends NNW from the upper snow slopes. The ridge gives good climbing on firm rock; thereafter take the upper snow slopes. 8 h from Robson Pass (AJ **37**-53, 396).

3. N Glacier (alternate to normal route). This glacier, between the N ridge and Ice Arête, is taken to the summit plateau, where it trends right to join the normal route. 8 h from Robson Pass.

4. Ice Arête. July 1913, C. H. Mitchell, H. H. Prouty, J. Watt, *W. Schauffelberger*. This fine route lies on the ridge that descends NNE, then N, and finally NNW from the summit. As for the normal route, then, when one km beyond the Extinguisher, work left (SE) to gain the NNW rock ridge which descends from the Ice Arête. Climb the rock ridge, passing pinnacles on the right, and descend slightly to the saddle at the base of the Ice Arête proper. Climb the ridge to the final 300m snow dome, the steep summital slopes generally being turned on the right (W) where the normal route is joined (CAJ **6**-70).

5. E Spur. July 1973, J. Lowe, M. Weiss. This spur rises from the E glacier some 1000m to the S forepeak (3270m). Approach from Robson Pass via Snowbird Pass and the Reef Icefield to the head of Resplendent Valley (one day). The spur offers both snow and rock, with the difficulties coming near the top, the lower section being class 3 and 4. IV, F7; 7–10 h up.

UNNAMED (2970m)

The culminating point in the ridge above the Extinguisher.

FA 1955, A Fabergé and ACC party. After passing Extinguisher on the Robson Glacier, head up **NW slopes** between Extinguisher ridge and rocky N ridge of Mount Resplendent. 6 h from Robson Pass.

UNNAMED (3000m)

One km SW of Lynx Mountain.

FA August 1955, ACC party. **NW Ridge.** As for Lynx, SW ridge, to base of ridge and so to top. 7 h. The NE ridge is also climbed, often as part of a traverse including Lynx.

2. S Ridge. The glacier running NW from objective is ascended to its head from where the 2860m col to S of peak is attained. Take ridge to top.

LYNX MOUNTAIN (3180m)

7 km SE of Robson Pass.

FA July 1913, ACC party led by *W. Schauffelberger*. **SW Ridge.** Ascend Robson Glacier and cross moraine to SE, then make for glacier which descends between Lynx and Unnamed 3000m. Climb to col at head and then up rock of SW ridge. 6 h from Robson Pass.

2. W Ridge. August 1955, ACC party. Approach as for SW ridge, but gain W ridge at its base. Pleasant scrambling to summit. 7 h from Robson Pass.

3. N (Chushina) Ridge. August 1974, L. Camp, J. Casey, R. Fletcher, *O. Setzer*. This ridge rises from Snowbird Pass. From Robson Pass, cross E moraine of Robson Glacier and traverse meadows toward objective. Gain ridge crest via steep snow mixed with rock halfway between summit and Snowbird Pass (as in FA) or start from Pass proper. The rock crest becomes a broad snow/ice ridge leading steeply to the top. "Pleasurable." (CAJ **59**-89).

TITKANA PEAK (SE 2820m, NW 2780m)

The summits are 1.5 km apart on the ridge NW from Lynx Mountain.

FA August 1908, L. Q. Coleman *alone*. Simply by the **W slopes.**

MOUNT ROBSON (3954m)

The Monarch of the Canadian Rockies, aptly known to the Indians as "The Mountain of the Spiral Road" (Yuh-hai-has-kun) on account of its distinctive horizontal banding. Mount Robson has captured the imagination of generations of climbers. By reason of its position, its challenge and its history, it is not only one of the great peaks of North America, but one of the great peaks of the world.

FA July 1913, W. W. Foster, A. H. MacCarthy, *C. Kain*. **Kain (NE) Face/SE Ridge.** One of the classic routes of North America and a fitting memorial to the Austrian guide, Conrad Kain. The initial slopes are subject to avalanche. Follow the Robson Glacier from Robson Pass, passing the Extinguisher to gain the part of the glacier where it steepens toward the col (2920m) at its head. From here make a rising traverse right (W) (some icefall danger) to pass over the snow slopes above the Dome (incorrectly marked on 83E3). Most parties make a high camp here; one day from Robson Pass. Access to the SE ridge proper is by the predominantly icy NE slope (Kain Face) that rises above and to the right of the Dome. Climb up between the ice bulges on the right and the exposed rock on the left, working left to avoid danger from the ice bulges (conditions often make this section treacherous to descend late in the day). Once on the ridge, it is worth studying the route up the final ice slopes ("The Roof"), as the ice formations vary from year to year. The line taken is usually straight up the SE ridge. A final difficulty is posed by the summit "mushroom." 7–10 h from Dome, 5–7 h on descent; IV, F5 (CAJ **6**-11, 19).

MT. ROBSON FROM EAST

E. Cooper

Mt Warn

Emperor Ri...

Helmet

N Face

Fuhrer Ridge

SE Ridge

Extinguisher

Robson Glacier

Kain Face

Dome

Variant. Parties have passed right (NW) underneath the ice bulges to gain the SE ridge near the shoulder (CAJ **48**-109).

Winter Ascent. March 1965, A. Bertulis, F. Beckey, L. Patterson, T. Stewart.

2. SSW Ridge (normal route). The rock ridge on which the Robson Hut sits bounds the lower of the two icefalls which descend S from the summit area. July 1924, M. D. Geddes, T. B. Moffat, M. Pollard, *C. Kain.* From the hut make for the top of the rock ridge ("Little Robson") where the final section of the route may be studied. Ascend the connecting ridge from Little Robson to the area under the ice cliffs of the upper icefall (danger from falling ice). From here work left above the right branch of the "Great Couloir" and up on the "Schwarz Ledges" to outflank the ice cliffs on the left (W). Once above the ice cliffs, one must negotiate the seracs of the "Roof," the best line varying from year to year. On occasion, it is best to traverse right (E) completely across the Roof to finish by the Kain Route. III, 5–9 h, hut to summit, 4 h down (CAJ **19**-6, **45**-111).

Variant A. The cliffs of the upper icefall were first climbed on the right (E) by the "Hourglass," where the ice cliffs butt against the rock walls which funnel the upper icefall on the right (E). From the hut gain the lower glacier and cross in a rising traverse to right (avalanche danger) under the upper icefall in order to reach the Hourglass, a snow/ice chute to the left of the rock wall. Climb the Hourglass and join the Kain Route at the Shoulder. This variant may be preferred if the Schwarz Ledges are snow covered. It was by this route that the 1913 FA pary descended (CAJ **37**-72).

Variant B. August 1936, H. S. Hall, Jr., *H. Fuhrer.* The rock walls to the right (E) have also been climbed. Take Variant A and pass the Hourglass in favor of the rocks. This variant is suitable only when the rocks are free of snow, but in those conditions it is probably the safest way to go (AAJ **2**-418; CAJ **24**-123).

3. Wishbone Arête. This W ridge is well seen from the Robson viewpoint on the Yellowhead Highway, the two branches joining some 500m below the summit. The right-hand branch, which gives the climbing route, lies to the left of the "Great Couloir" descending from the summit. August 1958, D. Claunch, H. Firestone, M. Sherrick. Continue on the Berg Lake Trail past the turnoff to the normal route, then strike directly up the rocky buttress that forms the lower continuation of the ridge. Alternatively, traverse (W) from the Robson Hut at the 2400m level on the "Yellow Bands." The lower section of the ridge is straightforward and parties usually bivouac near 2700m on the first day, after hiking up from Kinney Lake. In dry years there is seldom water on the arête or the direct approach to it. The principal rock climbing difficulties occur below the prominent notch, just before the junction of the Wishbone, while after the junction the angle eases. Should this upper section be icy, it constitutes the crux, otherwise rock scrambling. Underneath the summit the distinctive ice gargoyles are encountered; the ice cap is generally gained by a leftward diagonal traverse. 1–1½ days from high bivouac to top, with descent to Robson Hut; V, F6 (AAJ **10**-1, CAJ **39**-92).

This notable climb was the scene of several attempts, the boldest that in 1913 by B. S. Darling, H. H. Prouty, *W. Schauffelberger,* who turned back in storm some 100m from the summit (CAJ **6**-29).

4. Emperor Ridge. This magnificent NW ridge rises above Emperor Falls on Robson River and was attempted many times before being climbed. The strongest early attempt was that in 1930 by L. O'Brien and R. L. M. Underhill, who turned back some 150m short of the summit (CAJ **19**-73). The hard part of the ridge begins near 3700m where the pyramidal lower section (which has a right-leaning couloir roughly at its center) converges on the lower-angled summital ridge.

July 1961, R. Perla, T. M. Spencer. Robson River must be crossed, most easily in the flats just below Berg Lake, and then a choice of routes presents itself: up either the left (N) bounding

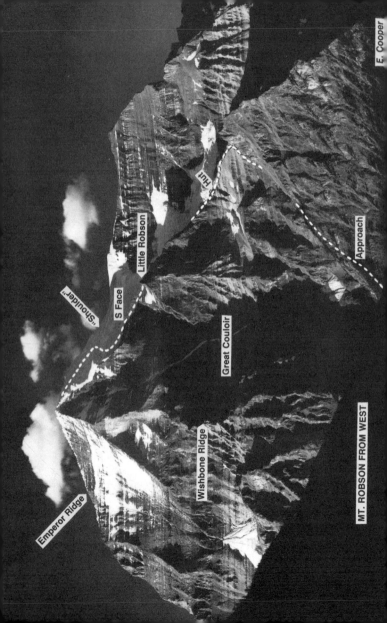

E. Cooper

Approach

Hut

Little Robson

S Face

"Shoulder"

Emperor Ridge

Great Couloir

Wishbone Ridge

MT. ROBSON FROM WEST

the ridge of the pyramidal face (as in the FA), the face itself, or the right (W) bounding ridge (as in 1930, probably the easiest). In any case, a bivouac should be placed as high as possible (above 3000m) on the day of approach in order to have time for the difficulties to come. Once one reaches the point of convergence, the climbing involves going over, around and through the ice gargoyles of the long final ridge. The usual technique is to thread the rope between the formations to effect a running belay. Oddly, this upper section may be more reasonable under cloudy or even stormy conditions than on a warm, sunny day. V; a very long day from bivouac to Robson Hut (FA party bivouacked on summit) (CAJ 45-106).

5. N Face. With its purity of line and directness of purpose, this elegant face may fairly claim to offer one of the finest ice routes in the Canadian Rockies. August 1963, P. Callis, D. Davis. The initial problem is to reach the Robson–Helmet col (3250m), in former times gained over the Dome from Robson Glacier. Nowadays there are two popular alternatives. 1) From NE end of Berg Lake work up scree slopes on the W side of Rearguard to gain the easy-angled N tongue of Berg Glacier between Rearguard and Waffl at about 2100m (this point can also be reached via Rearguard–Waffl col from Robson Glacier). Then pass under the N faces of Waffl and Helmet along the bench of Berg Glacier and gain the col. 2) Leave Berg Lake Trail at SE end of Lake, ford river, and round lake to S shore. Then go up scree slopes to meet the rocky buttress which lies to the right (W) of Berg Glacier and descends toward the lake. Climb the rock to the high glacier plateau and so to the col. It is advisable to camp on the W side of the col because of the usual wind at the col. The route goes up the ice slopes above, the line taken varying according to the conditions, and needs no further elaboration. In the early season, loose snow (avalanche danger) may overlay the ice; in late season blue ice is common. Approximately 800m of ice climbing at an average angle of 52°. IV, one long day, with usual descent down Kain route to camp at col (AAJ **14**-64).

6. Fuhrer Ridge. The ridge rises above Helmet Col and gives a classic route relatively free of objective danger. Recommended. July 1938, J. W. Carlson, W. R. Hainsworth, *H. Fuhrer.* Reach the Robson–Helmet col as for N face and place a high camp. The intial ⅓ of the route is up snow/ice while in the upper section ice and snow covered rocks are encountered. The upper route lies in depressions between rock ribs and finally emerges into steep snow/ice on the N face just below the summit ridge. IV, F5; 10 h from Helmet col, 8 h in descent (some rappels) (CAJ **26**-8; AAJ **3**-287).

Variant. July 1970, *M. Bleuer* party. Should the upper rocks be ice covered, a long right traverse can be made along a snow "bench" ⅓ of the way up and then the extreme left side of the N face ascended, thus joining the original route just below the summit ridge.

THE DOME (3090m)

A rounded snow bump in the Robson cirque, 1.5 km SE of Mount Robson, incorrectly marked on 83E3/E. It is not a separate summit.

FA August 1908, A. P. Coleman, L. Q. Coleman, G. B. Kinney, J. Yates. By snow and rock of **E side** (en route to attempt Robson). The N face has also been done as a training climb. In the early attempts on Robson from the E, the route lay up the Dome, which appears in some of the accounts as the "Helmet" but must be distinguished from today's Helmet (Coleman 323; CAJ **2**-1).

THE HELMET (3420m)

The minor peak under the NE buttress of Mount Robson.

FA July 1928, G. Engelhard, *H. Fuhrer.* Approach as for N face of Mount Robson to the Robson–Helmet col and climb the snow/ice of the **S ridge.**

2. N Ridge. A fine climb which may be combined in a traverse that includes Waffl and, optionally, Rearguard for a full day. Gain the Helmet–Waffl col (2800m) from Berg Glacier or by traversing Waffl, N–S. The ridge has two rock steps separated by a sharp snow ridge. III, F5; 4 h from col.

3. SE Ridge. July 1934, W. R. Hainsworth, M. M. Strumia. Approach as for the Kain Face on Mount Robson, then pass over the Dome to the base of this elegant snow ridge, which rises from the glacier plateau between the Dome and the Helmet. Take the ridge to junction with S ridge, and so to top.

MOUNT WAFFL (2890m)

Named in memory of N. D. Waffl, who in 1930 perished in an avalanche while attempting Mount Robson alone; incorrectly named Waffi on 83E3/E.

FA July 1934, W. R. Hainsworth, M. M. Strumia. **E Ridge.** Follow Robson Glacier to E shale slopes and thus to rock step which constitutes the lower part of the ridge.

2. S Ridge. Most usually descended while traversing Waffl and Helmet, N–S. Also climbed from Helmet–Waffl col.

3. N Ridge. The most popular route, simply gained from Robson Pass by the NW scree slopes of Rearguard to the Rearguard–Waffl col.

REARGUARD MOUNTAIN (2720m)

Just (S) above snout of Robson Glacier.

FA August 1913, ACC party. Simply reached over S scree slopes from Robson Glacier or from Rearguard–Waffl col approached over W slopes from Robson Pass.

2. N Face. August 1955, E. Blade, D. Claunch, J. Crosby, M. Shor. An intricate rock climb with many traverses. Route lies to right of N face couloir, difficult bands being overcome by traversing, usually right, to lines of weakness. 700m of rock climbing; F4, 8 h (AAJ **10**-124).

3. N Face Couloir. August 1924, ACC parties. Via the conspicuous couloir, subject to stonefall. Not recommended.

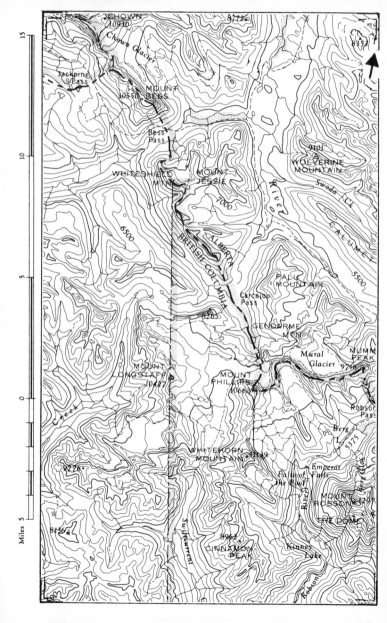

PACKTRAIN PEAKS

Here we describe two groups of glaciated summits, the Whitehorn and Resthaven Groups, which rise on or near the Divide N of the Robson Group. From Robson Pass NW to Resthaven Mountain is an airline distance of some 40 km. The watershed itself goes generally W for about 9 km from the Pass to Mount Phillips, then turns abruptly N for 6 km to Carcajou Pass. It then continues 13 km farther NW over minor summits to Bess Pass. After passing over Mount Bess, the Divide again swings W to Jackpine Pass and trends W some distance beyond. Historically, access to these groups has been gained by using a packtrain, and that method should not be ruled out even today, especially for the Resthaven Group. Specific access information is given under the separate groups below.

WHITEHORN GROUP

Facing Mount Robson and its satellites across the valley of Robson River, the principal peaks of this group rise in an irregular curve from Robson Pass to and beyond Whitehorn Mountain, the dominating peak. The Longstaff massif forms a linked extension to the W, rising across the basin of Swiftcurrent Glacier and comprising a line of glaciated summits about 15 km in length, of which Mount Longstaff is the chief. The main Swiftcurrent Glacier, which receives a sizeable tributary from the E slopes of Mount Longstaff, has an extreme length of nearly 10 km and an area of 30 km². The valley of Small Creek bounds the group on the W. For a good account of early exploration in this area see CAJ **4**-1. A high-level route from Jackpine Pass to Robson Pass is described in CAJ **16**-198.

ACCESS

The most common approach to the higher summits is that for Berg Lake (see Chapter 14). For the Longstaff massif, the best approach is up Swiftcurrent Creek. The trail leaves Highway 16 approximately 6 km W of the Robson viewpoint and extends 6 km up the valley to gravel flats and the amphitheater below the glacier tongue. It is also possible, but long, to reach Swiftcurrent Glacier from Berg Lake over the high pass N of Whitehorn Mountain (which see). A logging road extends 13 km up Small Creek, giving access to a minor group some 13 km W of Mount Longstaff. There is also a logging road on Horsey Creek next W (16 km) which gives access to a further subgroup around the NW head of this stream.

Maps: 83E3; 83E/4E; 83E/5E.

MUMM PEAK (2962m)

N buttress of Robson Pass (CAJ **34**-71, winter ascent).
FA August 1910, J. N. Collie, A. L. Mumm, *M. Inderbinen.*

From Robson Pass via scree of **S face.** Snow slopes and a short chimney just below top. Ascent, 4 h (AJ **25**-467; App **12**-34).

UNNAMED *(Saurian)* (2880m)

1.5 km W of Mumm Peak on Divide.

FA August 1913, W. E. Stone, *W. Schauffelberger* and four others. Via snow & rock of **W ridge.** Last 30m consists of short rock faces and chimneys. Descent to S through two chimneys. W ridge has been reached from E col by a traverse on ledges of N face (CAJ **6**-238; **39**-118).

UNNAMED (3000m)

Central and highest point between Mumm Peak and Mount Phillips.

FA August 1913, F. W. Godsal, A. L. Mumm, P. Pearce, *M. Inderbinen.* From Robson Pass over scree and **S glacier** (AJ **28**-356).

GENDARME MOUNTAIN (2922m)

4.5 km NW of Mumm Peak; N rim of Mural Glacier.

FA August 1911, A. O. Wheeler, *C. Kain.* Gain Mural Glacier over col between *Saurian* and Unnamed (3000m) and ascend easy **S slopes** (AJ **26**-396; CAJ **4**-34).

MOUNT PHILLIPS *(Resolution)* (3249m)

On Divide at point where it makes 90° turn from E to N; N of Whitehorn Mountain.

FA August 1910, J. N. Collie, A. L. Mumm, J. Yates, *M. Inderbinen.* **E Slope.** From Berg Lake, head NW and ascend over **SE glacier** (App **12**-341; CAJ **3**-173).

2. E Ridge. August 1955, G. D. Boddy, A. Bruce-Robertson, W. Sparling, D. M. Woods. Approach from Berg Lake over glacier to NW of lake to col (2590m) (511937); 7 h. Cross névé to E ridge which is followed to summit; 7½ h (CAJ **39**-119).

3. W Slope. August 1916, A. J. Gilmour, E. W. D. Holway,

H. Palmer. From camp near tongue of Swiftcurrent Glacier, ascend main glacier to a small pocket glacier on SW slope of objective. Ascend its icefall and, higher, a steep snowslope to the domed summit. Ascent, 8 h; descent 3 h (App **15**-9).

WHITEHORN MOUNTAIN (3395m)

Major peak 8 km WNW of Mount Robson across Valley of a Thousand Falls (AJ **26**-403). Probably the best place to start is a camp on the flats above the Valley of a Thousand Falls.

FA August 1911, *C. Kain, alone*. **W Ridge.** From camp as above, go up steeply through underbrush and over boulders to the E glacier. Cross the glacier and take a glacial ramp to a high pass (2710m) N of subsidiary peak (2840m). Descend on W side and circle to W ridge (7 h). Ascend the ridge, staying mostly on its S flank. Near the top, traverse S and ascend a couloir to final snowcap. Ascent, 11–12 h; descent by same route, 8–10 h (CAJ **6**-49, 52; App **17**-338).

2. NW Face. 1973, J. Lowe, M. Weiss. As above to base of face. Climb directly up middle of 500m snow/ice face, ice cliffs presenting the major difficulty. 3–4 h on face; III.

3. N Ridge. 1973, J. C. Glidden, D. Hamre. As for Route One to base of NW face (5 h). Start up E side of NW face over 3 pitches on rock, then climb ice faces and snow ribs. The final pitch involves a traverse on vertical ice beneath the "white horn" to gain the summit. 4½ h on climb, 15 h RT from camp. 11 pitches; III, F4 (AAJ **19**-163).

4. SE Ridge. July 1938, J. H. Carlson, W. R. Hainsworth, *H. Fuhrer*. From camp above Emperor Falls, gain and ascend SE glacier. Climb S flank of ridge to reach the crest above the big notch visible from Berg Lake. Thereafter, a series of short, steep rock pitches and traverses leads to the summit. 12 h up; descent by Route One (AAJ **3**-290; App **22**-248).

5. Traverse. August 1913, *C. Kain* with large ACC party. Ascent by Route One. Two descent routes were followed, one directly down steep snow of SE face to SE glacier. The other

W Ridge

NW Face

N Ridge

SE Ridge

E. Cooper

WHITEHORN MOUNTAIN FROM NORTHEAST

went down the narrow S ridge (poor rock, several rappels) to reach the SE glacier; not recommended. It is not possible to descend directly to the Robson trail from the terrace above the Valley of a Thousand Falls, but rather one must traverse N over many moraines to regain the approach route (CAJ 6-55).

MOUNT LONGSTAFF (3180m)

5.5 km W of Mount Phillips across Swiftcurrent Glacier; NW of Whitehorn Mountain (AJ 26-396).

FA July 1916, A. J. Gilmour, E. W. D. Holway, H. Palmer. From camp near tongue of Swiftcurrent Glacier, ascend ice and take **E ridge** to top without difficulty. 12 h RT (App 15-7; CAJ 8-133).

UNNAMED (3055m)

S summit of Longstaff massif, 2 km S of main summit.

Across glacier (7 km²) to SW are three unnamed minor peaks. Point 2827m was ascended in 1915 by A. J. Gilmour and E. W. D. Holway from Small Creek. Point 2820m was ascended in 1916 by above with H. Palmer (App 15-11).

Do nothing in haste, look well to each step, and from the beginning, think what may be the end.

E. Whymper

RESTHAVEN GROUP

This compact group rises mostly N of the Divide, N from a short section of the watershed running some 8 km from Bess Pass to Jackpine Pass. All of its major peaks, with the exception of Mount Bess, lie on the Alberta slope, with Mount Chown in the center being the highest. The Resthaven Icefield and Chown Glacier, which together comprise some 50 km² of glaciation, discharge to Smoky River to the E.

ACCESS

The most reasonable overland approach involves going to Robson Pass (one day, see "The King" chapter) and then following the well-maintained (1981) trail up Smoky River to Chown Creek (2 days more, minimum). To reach Short Creek and the Resthaven Icefield takes perhaps 2 additional days. Using pack horses should be investigated. Another overland possibility is Holmes River. There is a logging road, extending from Highway 16 SE of McBride for 20 km (1973). From the end of the road it is still nearly 30 km of bush to Bess Pass. The 1981 party reached the vicinity of Bess Pass by helicopter.

Maps: 83E5; 83E6.

MOUNT BESS (3216m)

The most northerly peak of the Alberta-British Columbia boundary to exceed 3000m. N buttress of Bess Pass and E buttress of Jackpine Pass.

FA August 1911, J. N. Collie, A. L. Mumm, J. Yates, *M. Inderbinen*. **SW Ridge.** From Bess Pass, ascend W to top of a spur, then go up limestone and steep snow slopes to gain ridge higher up. Several cliff bands and icy gullies. Follow ridge to flat summit (AJ **26**-14; App **12**-347; CAJ **4**-137; **16**-201).

2. S Face. August 1915, J. Arnold, C. Hinman, M. Jobe, D. Tyler, *D. Phillips*. Up easy slopes from Bess Pass. Sole difficulty is 15m cliff not far from top (CAJ **7**-98).

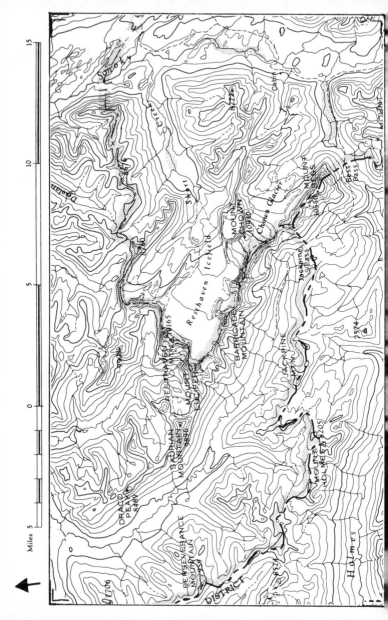

Note: Subsidiary NW summit (2917m), 3 km N of main peak, traversed via W slopes and **N ridge** en route to Mount Chown, August 1929, H. I. Buck, A. J. Gilmour, N. D. Waffl (CAJ **18**-27).

UNNAMED *(Lauserhue)* (2940m)

4.5 km E of Mount Chown on E margin of Chown Glacier.

FA July 1981, C. Gmoser, S. Goodhue, R. Laurilla. A straightforward ascent via **S ridge** (AAJ **56**-165).

MOUNT CHOWN (3381m)

Central and highest of group.

FA 1924, G. Hargreaves, W. B. Putnam. By way of Chown Glacier and **SE snow slopes.**

BARRICADE MOUNTAIN (SE, 3180m; NW, 3120m)

NW of Mount Chown; S rim of Resthaven Icefield. A 3.5 km long ridge with several high points between the extremities.

SE Peak. FA August 1929, H. I. Buck, A. J. Gilmour, N. D. Waffl. From camp on Jackpine River, approach via small glacier on SW side of objective. Gain the **S ridge** by a long snow tongue and continue over easy but loose rocks to summit. 3 h from glacier (CAJ **18**-27).

NW Peak. FA August 1911, J. N. Collie, A. L. Mumm, J. Yates, *M. Inderbinen.* Approach from E up Resthaven Glacier's N margin (two icefalls). Cross the Icefield to base of peak (7 km from tongue) and ascend **SE ridge** (AJ **26**-13; CAJ **4**-137; App **12**-345).

MOUNT LUCIFER (3060m)

W corner of Resthaven Icefield.

RESTHAVEN MOUNTAIN (NE, 3120m; SW, 3098m)

N margin of Resthaven Icefield.

FA 1923, Topographical Survey.

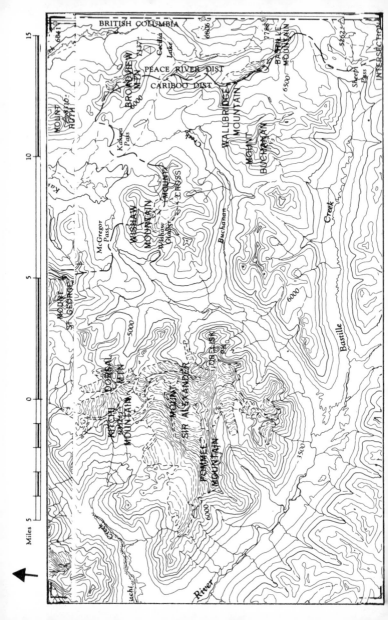

END OF THE LINE

SIR ALEXANDER GROUP

From Jackpine Pass, immediately W of Mount Bess in the Resthaven Group, the Divide swings W and then N through less alpine terrain where no peak exceeds 2700m. In its irregular NW-trending course, it eventually reaches Intersection Mountain (2452m), an airline distance of approximately 65 km from Jackpine Pass. Here the 120th Meridian intersects the watershed, the point at which the Alberta/British Columbia boundary no longer follows the summit of the Rocky Mountains but instead the 120th Meridian. The Divide continues generally NW, reaching Jarvis Pass in some 35 km airline from Intersection Mountain. The pass summit contains several small lakes.

The first recorded crossing of this section of the watershed was made during the winter of 1874–75 by E. W. Jarvis and C. F. Hanington, surveyors for the Canadian Pacific Railroad. The party, consisting of eight men and six dog trains, left Fort George on the Fraser and reached the Divide on February 25. From this point they were obliged to proceed on foot and reached Jasper House on March 5, to find it unoccupied. They continued their journey and reached St. Anne in 12 days (CPR Report, 1877–145).

The peaks of the Sir Alexander Group rise some 15–25 km S and W of Jarvis Pass, well W of the Divide and entirely on the Fraser slope. This isolated group is dominated by two great peaks, Mount Sir Alexander and Mount Ida. Although neither surpasses the magic mark of 3300m, the facts that the valleys are lower than elsewhere in the Rockies and that treeline and snowline are 300–400m lower as well, combine to make them as singular as other great peaks. The area of ice and snow around Mount Sir Alexander is approximately 90 km^2 while that around Mount Ida is about 20 km^2. Around the flanks of Mounts Ida and Sir Alexander are about 20 small peaks, 2400–2900m, several of them spectacular towers. Climbing is, however, generally on ice and snow. This group, together with the Hart Range to the N, at the headwaters of the N branch of Porcupine River, constitutes the northern termination of the continuously alpine portion of the Canadian Rocky Mountains.

The history of the early exploration of the region and the initial attempts to climb Mount Sir Alexander take on the character of a saga. The routes of overland approach were complicated and tedious, either by Snake Indian River from Jasper or from Robson Pass to Smoky River. Ten days of steady travel was the minimum required from Jasper, but more often 12 or 14 days were needed. In July 1914, C. P. Fay and party, on a scientific expedition, reached Jarvis Pass, passing within 10 km of Sir Alexander and obtaining photographs of it and Mount Ida (App 13-238; CAJ 6-170). Later that same summer first appeared the mountain's persistent protagonists, Mary Jobe and Donald (Curly) Phillips, of Mount Robson fame. On their attempt from the SE, they reached approximately 2400m on the N glacier (CAJ 6-188). Jobe and Phillips returned in 1915 with a stronger party, Phillips and two others climbing the NE ridge to within perhaps 100m of the top before being blocked by cornices (CAJ **7**-82). In 1916, F. K. Vreeland approached from the W by canoe, reaching the glacier at the base of the W face; his photographs provided the key to the FA 13 years later (AAJ **1**-114). M. Jobe and D. Phillips made a winter approach in 1917 (App **14**-223; CAJ **9**-79). Finally, in 1929, Phillips again was involved with Mount Sir Alexander, this time as the outfitter for the successful FA party.

ACCESS

The days of the pack train are over and no one is going to backpack 10 or 12 days just to reach the area. The only sensible approach is by air. The 1954 party used a seaplane from Prince George, B. C., landing on the largest lake W of Jarvis Pass. Although they made the FA of Mount Ida, the heavy bush makes Jarvis Pass an impractical base for Sir Alexander and its satellites. Trails shown on maps are ethereal. The 1967 party also used a float plane, to Dimsdale Lake in the Hart Range, N of the Sir Alexander Group proper. In 1978, a Calgary party helicoptered from McBride to a camp by the lake (1670m) above and S of the large lake at the head of Edgegrain Creek. A high camp at 2400m between Sir Alexander and Mount Kitchi facilitates ascents.

LITERATURE

Boles, G. "The Sir Alexander Range." CAJ **62**-4 (1974). A modern approach.

Jobe, M. L. "Mt. Alexander Mackenzie." CAJ **7**-82 (1916). As on Robson, unlucky Curly is stopped just short.

Waffl, N.D. "Mount Sir Alexander." AAJ **1**-106 (1929). Vreeland's photos do the trick.

Maps: 93H16, 93I1, 93I2.

OBELISK PEAK (2510m)

4.5 km SE of Sir Alexander. A striking rock tower E of icefields with smaller tower (2270m) one km farther E (CAJ **6**-194, **62**-6, photos).

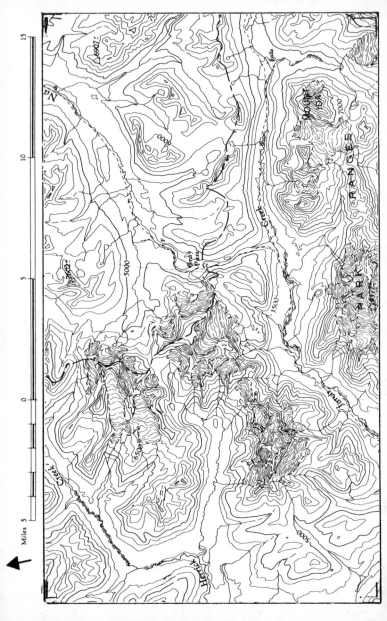

POMMEL MOUNTAIN (2750m)

5 km WSW of Sir Alexander.

FA July 1978, G. Boles, L. Kubbernus, G. Scruggs, M. Simpson. From high camp at 2400m between Mount Kitchi and Mount Sir Alexander, cross glacier to SW and turn **W ridge** of objective to W snow slopes. Ascend these to rejoin W ridge higher up and so to top. 7½ h up (CAJ **62**-4).

NILAH PEAK (2970m)

1.5 km S of Mount Sir Alexander.

FA July 1978, G. Boles, L. Kubbernus, G. Scruggs, M. Simpson. From high camp as above, traverse glacier E of Mount Sir Alexander to col between it and objective. Spectacular pinnacle at col *(Nilah's Toe)*. Ascend **N ridge** and snow slopes to W to summit. Ascent, 8 h (CAJ **62**-4).

MOUNT SIR ALEXANDER *(Kitchi)* (3270m)

Originally named Kitchi (Cree for "mighty"), but that name has been transferred, inaptly, to the much smaller peak to the N.

FA July 1929, H. I. Buck, A. J. Gilmour, N. D. Waffl. **W Face.** From high camp N of objective cross glacier and climb icefall between rock cliffs to gain upper part of W glacier. Cross glacier to S, below great NW snow/ice face, and round W buttress to rocky W face. Toward the SW end of the face, a rock rib comes down. Ascend snow just right (S) of this rib and continue upward over a series of ledges to a cliff. Traverse right until the band can be passed and then ascend to snow of the SW ridge which is taken to summit. This is the descent route of FA party. They climbed the face much farther to the left (N), ascending ledges to a steep ice couloir (25m) which penetrates the cliff band and gives access to the upper snows. Not recommended. 12 h up on FA (much step cutting in couloir), but following route as first described should reduce time considerably (AAJ **1**-106; CAJ **18**-14; marked photos in both).

Pommel Mtn

Mt Kitchi

Mt Sir Alexander

Dorsal Mtn

Obelisk Pk

SIR ALEXANDER MASSIF FROM NORTH

Edegrain Creek Valley

Variant. July 1978, L. Kubbernus, G. Scruggs, M. Simpson. Gain Sir Alexander–Nilah col as for latter (which see). Traverse left (W) to middle of SW face and ascend series of rock bands and ledges, working right (S) to gain snow of S ridge. This line is right (S) of FA descent route (CAJ **62**-4).

MOUNT KITCHI (2850m)
4 km N of Mount Sir Alexander, to which the name was originally applied. References should be consulted with this in mind.

FA July 1978, G. Boles, L. Kubbernus, G. Scruggs, M. Simpson. **SE Ridge.** A vertical band is passed by descending and then reascending snow slopes on SW side (CAJ **62**-4).

DORSAL MOUNTAIN (2660m)
4.5 km NNE of Sir Alexander, E of Mount Kitchi.

MOUNT ST. GEORGE (2780m)
On Divide 11 km NE of Mount Sir Alexander; 6 km W of Kakwa Lake.

MOUNT ST. PATRICK (2910m)
1.5 km WNW of Mount St. George (see in literature as St. George).

FA July 1929, A. J. Gilmour and 3 others. An easy scramble by **S ridge** (CAJ **18**-19).

2. N Ridge. July 1954, Bernays party (see Mount Ida). From camp on Edgegrain Creek, ascend glacier NE of objective and then climb a near-hanging glacier to gain a dip in N ridge. Ascend rock and corniced snow to summit (AAJ **9**, 2-97; CAJ **28**-25).

MOUNT IDA (3180m)
14 km N of Mount Sir Alexander (App **13**-251; CAJ **6**-177, 196).

MT. IDA FROM SOUTH

G. Bole

FA July 1954, D. J. Bernays, A. R. & F. L. Dunn, J. M. Newell. From high camp at lake (1830m) immediately S of objective, ascend SE buttress, staying mostly on E side, to gain crest of **SW ridge,** which is followed to summit cliffs. Surmount these via an obvious ice-filled cleft and attain the summit over a final corniced ridge. Ascent, 6 h; from camp at lake above (S) head of Edgegrain Creek, 8 h (AAJ **9**, 2-97, sketch map and photos; CAJ **38**-24, marked photo; **62**-4).

THREE SISTERS
Three peaks in E–W line to W of Mount Ida, overlooking Jarvis Creek. **Koona Mountain** (2690m) and **Awasie Mountain** (2690m) are unclimbed.

WALRUS MOUNTAIN (2780m)
Westernmost of Three Sisters.

FA July 1967, Wallerstein party (see Petrie). From camp in Jarvis Creek tributary to W of objective, ascend to and follow **S ridge** to top. F2–3 rock; 6 h up (AAJ **16**-171; CAJ **51**-176).

KISANO MOUNTAIN (2858m)
Massif 14 km W of Mount Ida, in forks of Jarvis and Kitchi Creeks. Two principal summits with extensive glaciers on NW slopes. SW summit is **Mount Dimsdale** (2810m).

MOUNT PETRIE (2880m)
4.5 km directly W of Dimsdale Lake; easternmost of Hart Range.

FA August 1967, T. Grefall, D. Morton, C. O'Dell, L. Spitzer, G. & M. Wallerstein. From Dimsdale Lake via easy **E ridge** in 8 h (AAJ **16**-171; CAJ **51**-176).

MOUNT PLASKETT (2910m)
Southern peak of double summit 1.5 km W of Mount Petrie; higher N peak is **Mount Ovington** (2940m).

FA August 1967, Wallerstein party (see Petrie). From Dimsdale Lake ascend gully to 1800m pass in S ridge of Mount
Petrie and gain glacial basin beyond (high camp on FA). Climb
snow to **S ridge,** swinging around onto W side to upward-
sloping ledge. Follow this and ascend loose gully to notch in
ridge, which is taken to the top. Ascent from high camp, 6½
h (AAJ **16**-171; CAJ **51**-176).

*On neither side let foot slip over/Invading Always, exploring Never, For this
is hate and this is fear.*

W. H. Auden

NORTHERNMOST ROCKIES

PINE CREEK PASS TO
THE LIARD RIVER

The Rockies near Pine Creek Pass (once considered for the CPR) do not provide interesting mountaineering, but starting at latitude 57°20′ and extending NW for 150 km are a series of peaks just under 3000m with sizeable glaciers and sharp rocky summits. These groups are drained on the W by the headwaters of Gataga and Kadach Rivers, and on the E by those of the Racing and Muskwa Rivers. The peaks were first seen by the early explorers who travelled up the Finlay River, which, along with the Parsnip, Fox, and Kechika, occupies the Rocky Mountain Trench and defines the W border of the Northern Rockies. These early explorations are described in P. L. Haworth's *On the Headwaters of Peace River* and in R. M. Patterson's *Finlay's River*. Much of the Finlay and Parsnip river valleys are now flooded by the Peace River Dam.

To date there have been only 6 mountaineering expeditions in the entire area. The Gibson–Smythe party visited the Lloyd

George Group in 1947. In 1960 the NW peaks of the Roosevelt–Churchill Group were climbed by a group led by Captain Jones of the Royal Fusiliers. The area around Big Snow Mountain was explored by the West party in 1961. A California–Washington group led by G. Wallerstein climbed Mounts Roosevelt and Churchill, and peaks between, during the 1966 season. In 1973, T. W. Swaddle and companions climbed Churchill Peak and several of its outliers. The most recent expedition, in 1974 by a group from the University of Newcastle, ascended several peaks in the country between Churchill Peak and Mount Stalin.

ACCESS

The many lakes and few strips in the Northern Rockies are attainable almost entirely by air. The best departure point is Fort Nelson where either land or float plane can be chartered. In 1973 a bush pilot named Anderson operated out of Sikanni Chief strip on the Alaska Highway. Some of the pilots know of small strips and open ridges that are used for landings and do not appear on maps, so local inquiries can be very productive.

The winters in these regions are exceptionally cold and frequently there is little snow until the spring storms of March, April, and May. Summers are cool and often rainy. The rivers are high in June and July, so August and even September are the best months for travelling. Some of the glaciers appear stagnant, probably due to low accumulation in the cold winters and small ablation during the cool summers.

LITERATURE

Smythe, F.S. "An Expedition to the Lloyd George Mountains of north-east British Columbia." In *Climbs in the Canadian Rockies,* Hodder and Stoughton, London, 1950. To the back of beyond.

Great Snow Mountain Area

This region lies between 57°20′ N and 57°30′ N and 124°10′ W. Best access is by float plane to Redfern Lake. From there it is a two-day bushwhack with packs up the N side of Besa River to a camp from which both **Great Snow Mountain** and **Great Rock Peak** (both about 2900m) can be climbed via Class 3–4 rock and snow. **Mount Circe** and additional peaks to the W appear to be unclimbed.

From a second camp beside the Achaean Glacier five more peaks were climbed, usually on Class 4 rock, snow and ice. These included **Mount Ulysses,** about 3000m, the highest peak in the area. Maps indicate that there are additional unclimbed peaks beyond **Mount Calypso,** the westernmost peak of the group climbed by the 1961 party. Ascents were made by S. Arighi, A. Maki, M. Petrilak, R. C. West (CAJ **45**-1).

Lloyd George Group

The region contains the largest snowfields in the Northern Rockies. The main group lies just N of 57°50′ and between 124°50′ and 125° W. The rock is very poor (friable sediments) and the bush is very dense. Access to **Mount Lloyd George** is best from Haworth Lake, while the S peaks of the group and a few peaks of about 2750m S and SE of Lloyd George can probably be reached most easily from Chesterfield Lake or Fern Lake. These peaks can also be approached from the head of Tuchodi Lake by following a reported trail up the Tuchodi River.

From camp near the NE end of Haworth Lake, the 1947 access to the main peaks was via Stagnant Glacier and either climbing a 750m couloir to the ridge N of the glacier or by passing around Survey Peak to the upper glacier and snow-fields. **Mounts Crosby,** and **Glendower, The Cloudmakers, Survey Peak, Criccienth Mountain, Columbine Peak** and Bardsey and Lupin Ridges near Haworth Lake were also climbed. Several peaks on the E side of the Lloyd George Icefall such as **Mount Smythe** and the detached peak 6 km SE, **Mount Walsh,** may be unclimbed. Ascents were made by E. R. Gibson,

H. S. Hall, Jr., N. E. Odell, J. Ross, F. S. & N. Smythe, D. Wessel (CAJ **31**-38).

Roosevelt–Churchill–Stalin Group

This is the largest of the three groups and extends 60 km NW from Tuchodi Lakes (850m). Access by float plane is limited to Tuchodi Lake and Wokkpash Lake, 15 km N of Mount Stalin. A good airstrip capable of handling a light twin was built in 1966 on the W side of Racing River, 13 km E of Mount Roosevelt, to serve a copper mine. More recently, a road (45 km) from Mile 401 on the Alaska Highway, passable to private cars, has been constructed to the mine, whose operation is intermittent because of fluctuations in the world price of copper. Contact the plant manager for permission before using the road. From a base camp near the Churchill mine, all the peaks from Roosevelt to Churchill can be climbed from subsidiary camps in the adjacent valleys. Foot travel in this region is not onerous since the brush is not too dense, but stream crossings can cause considerable delay. The climbs themselves are not difficult, consisting usually of snow and F2–F3 rock.

Map: 94K, Tuchodi Lakes.

From Wokkpash Lake (1258m) the 1960 expedition climbed **Mount Stalin** (2900m) and 10 other summits, one over 2750m and six more over 2600m. Ascents were made by J. Bignell, P. Hassett, B. Holmes, R. Jones, R. Lemon (CAJ **44**-58, map).

A group of peaks in the 2700m class are accessible from Tuchodi Lakes via valleys in which foot travel is reasonably rapid. The 1966 party moved from the high pass W of Churchill Peak via the Gataga River valley and Gataga Pass to Tuchodi Lakes in 4 days travelling time. There are some interesting looking peaks near the source of Racing River which can probably be reached most easily from Tuchodi Lake and the pass 8 km SW of Mount Stalin that leads into the Racing River drainage. Ascents were made by R. Gnagy, B. Lilley, A. McDermott, M. McNicholas, G. & M. Wallerstein (AAJ **15**-370).

In 1973, an ACC party drove into the copper mine and subsequently placed a camp on Churchill Creek. Ascents of three 2600m peaks *(Clementine, Howe, Darien)* were made by M. H. Benn, C. Jablonski, T. S. Sorensen, T. W. Swaddle (CAJ **58**-51).

The 1974 expedition of the University of Newcastle-upon-Tyne Exploration Society climbed 4 peaks (2600–2700m) in the S angle between Racing River and Churchill Creek. Personnel: P. D. Brettell, T. Jacks, R. G. Pearce, P. G. Rogers, G. D. Withers (CAJ **58**-51).

Our age today of doing things of which antiquity did not dream.

J. Fernell, 1530

"Come wander with me," she said,
"Into regions yet untrod
And read what is still unread
In the Manuscripts of God . . ."

H. W. Longfellow

APPENDIX OF PASSES
(Elevations in Meters)

ASTORIA (Ar)
2315

Portal Creek—Astoria Creek
Chak Peak—2590

ATHABASCA (Ar-P)
1750

Whirlpool River—Pacific Creek
Mt. Brown—Mt. Hooker (trail)

AVALANCHE (Ar-P)
1580

Beaverdam Creek—Morkill River
Interpass Ridge—Big Shale Mtn.

AZURE LAKE (Ar)
1965

Blue Creek—Rockslide Creek
Sunset Peak—Saghali Mtn.

BEAVERDAM (Ar-P)
1485

Beaverdam Creek—Renshaw Creek
Mt. Pauline—Interpass Ridge (trail)

BEDAUX (Ar)
1480

Fern Lake—N Kwadacha River
Mt. Bedaux—Lambard Peak

BESS (Ar-P)
1620

Holmes River—Smoky River
Mt. Bess—Whiteshield Mtn.

BUSH (A-P)
2395

Valenciennes River—Forbes Creek
Mt. Niverville—Valenciennes Mtn.

BYNG

(Snake Indian)

CAMPUS (Ar)
2240

Simon Creek—Campus
Campus Mt.—Chevron Mtn.

CANOE (Ar-P)
2050

Canoe River—Whirlpool River
Mt. Brown—Mallard Peak

318

CARCAJOU (Ar-P) 1570	Holmes River—Smoky River Palu Mtn.—2520 (trail)
CARDINAL (Ar) 1905	Medicine Tent River—Cardinal River Mt. Cardinal—Mt. MacKenzie (trail)
CASKET (Ar-P) 1640	Casket Creek—Forgetmenot Creek Intersection Mtn.—2135 (trail)
CATARACT (A) 2515	Brazeau River—Cataract Creek 2990—3135
CLINE (A) 2760	McDonald Creek—Brazeau River Mt. Stewart—3205
COLONEL (Ar-P) 1870	Colonel Creek—Snaring River Mt. Machray—The Colonel (trail)
DRAWBRIDGE (Ar-P) 2575	Amethyst Lakes—Giekie Creek Drawbridge Peak—Redoubt Peak
EAGLE'S NEST (Ar) 1905	Eagle's Nest Creek—Rock Creek through Persimmon Range
ELYSIUM (Ar) 2025	Minaga Creek—Snaring River (trib) Emigrants Mtn.—Elysium Mtn.
FETHERSTONHAUGH (Ar-P) 1805	Morkill River—Fetherstonhaugh Creek Mt. Sprague—Mt. Fetherstonhaugh (trail)
FORGETMENOT (Ar-P) 1770	Fetherstonhaugh Cr.—Forgetmenot Cr. Mt. Fetherstonhaugh—2135 (trail)
FORTRESS (Ar-P) 1335	Chaba River—Fortress Lake Fortress Mtn.—2885 (trail)
FRASER (P) 2010	Fraser River—Baker Creek 2430—2670
GATAGA (Ar) 1630	2745—2745 Gataga River—Tuchodi River (N fork)
GLACIER (Ar) 2090	Sulfur River—Mowitch Creek Vega Peak—Noonday Peak

GRANT (Ar-P)   Grant Brook—Snaring River
1935   Mt. Machray—Salient Mtn. (trail)

GRAY (Ar-P)   Dimsdale Lake—Barbara Creek
1356   Mt. Petrie—Ochakwin Mtn.

HOWSE (A-P)   Conway Creek—Blaeberry River
1530   Howse Peak—Mt. Conway

INDIAN (P)   Muhigan Creek—Whistlers Creek
2730   Fortalice Mtn.—Indian Ridge

JACKPINE (Ar-P)   Holmes River—Jackpine River
2040   Jackpine Mtn.—Mt. Chown

JACQUES (Ar)   Jacques Creek—Nashan Creek
1775   Emir Mtn.—Mt. Colin (trail)

JARVIS (Ar-P)   Jarvis River—Kakwa River
2955   Mt. Hanington—Mt. Jarvis (trail)

JOB (A)   Job Creek—Coral Creek
4900   Coral Mtn.—6065

JONES (Ar)   Pauline Creek—Meadowland Creek
1875   2390—2240

JONAS (A-Ar)   Jonas Creek—Brazeau River
2270   Sunwapta Peak—2835

KAKWA (Ar-P)   Buchanan Creek—Kakwa River
1880   Mt. Campbell—Francis Peak

LOOKOUT (Ar-P)   Amethyst Lakes—Geikie Creek
2530   Redoubt Peak—Drawbridge Peak

LOREN (Ar-P)   Meadowland Creek—Chalco Creek
1540   Mt. Pauline—2348

MACCARIB (Ar)   Portal Creek—Maccarib Creek
2180   Maccarib Mtn.—Vertex Peak (trail)

MALIGNE (Ar)   Maligne River—Poboktan Creek
2235   Replica Mtn.—Endless Chain (trail)

MARMOT (Ar)   Portal Creek—Whistlers Creek
2245   Marmot Mtn.—Terminal Peak

MCGREGOR (Ar-P)   Kakwa River—McGregor River
1535   Wishaw Mtn.—Mt. St. George

MERLIN (Ar)   Nashan Creek—Rocky River (trib)
1925   Mt. Merlin—Mt. Dvomove (trail)

MIETTE (A-P)   Miette River—Grant Brook
S-2120 M-1965 N-2185   Mt. McCord—Razorback Mtn. (trail)

MOAT (Ar-P)   (S portion of Tonquin Pass)

MOOSE (Ar-P)   Calumet Creek—Moose River
2000   Calumet Peak—2485

MORKILL (Ar-P)   Muddywater River—Morkill River
1655   Mt. Forget—Mt. Sprague (trail)

NIGEL (A)   Brazeau River—Nigel Creek
2105   3035—2850 (trail)

PARA (Ar-P)   Amethyst Lakes—Giekie Creek
2675   Parapet Mtn.—Paragon Peak

PAUGAK (P)   Tonquin Creek—Giekie Creek
2545   Barbican Peak—Mt. Giekie

POBOKTAN (A-Ar)   Poboktan Creek—Brazeau Lake
2270   Mt. Poboktan—Flat Ridge (trail)

PROVIDENCE (Ar-P)   Buchanan Creek—Cecilia Lake
1705   Wapiti Mtn.—Broadview Mtn.

RED (P)   Moose Lake—Moose River
1765   Razor Peak—Mt. Kain

ROBSON (Ar-P)   Berg Lake—Smoky River
1650   Mumm Peak—Titkana Peak (trail, hut)

ROCKY (Ar)   Muskeg River—Phroso Creek
1965   2485—Persimmon Range (trail)

SANDPIPER (Ar)   Rocky River—Sandpiper Creek
2635   Maligne Mtn.—2950

SHALE (Ar-P)   Morkill River—Pauline Creek
1900   Big Shale Hill—Mt. Talbot (trail)

SHEEP (Ar-P)   Bastille Creek—Sheep Creek
1635   Intersection Mtn.—Bastille Mtn.

SHOVEL (Ar)   Maligne River—Athabasca River
2300   Curator Mtn.—2575 (trail)

SIFTON (Ar)   Kechica River—Fox River
1020   Scarcity Mtn.—Flat Top Mtn.

SNAKE INDIAN (Ar)   Snake Indian River—Twintree Creek
2025   Monte Cristo Mtn.—2850 (trail)

SNOWBIRD (Ar-P)   Reef Icefield—Robson Glacier
2425   Lynx Mtn.—Titkana Peak

SOUTHESK (A-Ar)   Cairn River—Medicine Tent River
2240   Mt. McBeath—Southesk Cairn (trail)

SUNSET (A)   Cline River—Norman Creek
2065   Mt. Coleman—3065 (trail)

SUNWAPTA (A-Ar)   Nigel Creek—Sunwapta River
2030   Mt. Athabasca—Nigel Peak (road)

SWIFTCURRENT (P)   Swiftcurrent—Small Creek
1950   2825—2480

THOMPSON (A-P)   Rice Brook (Bush)—Watchman Creek
1985   Mt. Bryce—Watchman Peak

THOREAU (Ar)   Thoreau Creek—Popes Creek
2035   2235—Minny Ridge

TONQUIN (Ar-P)   Moat Lake—Tonquin Creek
1950   Bastion Peak—Tonquin Hill (trail)

TRIDENT (A-P)   2865—Spring Rice

UPRIGHT (Ar-P) 1980	Upright Creek—Snaring River Upright Mtn.—2545
VERDANT (Ar) 2105	Astoria River—Whirlpool River Mt. Edith Cavell—Chevron Mtn.
VISTA (Ar-P) 2085	Meadow Creek—Tonquin Creek Caniche Peak—Tonquin Hill (trail)
WHIRLPOOL (Ar-P) 1810	Whirlpool River—Baker Creek Mallard Peak—2540 (trail)
WHISTLERS (Ar) 2425	Crescent Creek—Whistlers Creek Fortalice Mtn.—Muhigan Mtn.
WILCOX (A) 2425	Tangle Creek—N Saskatchewan River Mt. Wilcox—Nigel Peak
YELLOWHEAD (Ar-P) 1145	Miette River—Yellowhead Lake Tete Roche—Miette Hill (road)

It is certainly terrible what a poor devil has to contend with in this country in order to make an honest living.

G.C.L. Preuss, 1843

INDEX

He who waits long at the ferry will get across sometime.

Gentility will never boil the pot.

Even a pig will keep its ain sty clean.

There's meat and music here, as the fox said when he stole the bagpipes.

The highest mountain in the land is oftenest covered with mist.